HOW TO REST
WOODEN
RUNABOUT

DON DANENBERG

MOTORBOOKS
INTERNATIONAL

Motorbooks International titles are also available at discounts in bulk quantity for industrial or sales-promotional use. For details write to Special Sales Manager at Motorbooks International Wholesalers & Distributors, Galtier Plaza, Suite 200, 380 Jackson Street, St. Paul, MN 55101-3885 USA.

Library of Congress Cataloging-in-Publication Data Available

ISBN 0-7603-1100-5

Front cover, top left: Although a "gray boat" that has weathered the elements for years may appear ready for the kindling pile, it probably requires no more attention than a boat that looks good but has been marginally maintained with an emphasis on varnish and chrome. *Photo by* Classic Boating Magazine. *Top center:* Electrical, mechanical, and interior components must, of course, be removed from the boat before a proper restoration can begin in earnest. *Photo by* Classic Boating Magazine. *Top right:* The work, however, is well worth the effort, as illustrated by this detail of a beautifully restored dashboard and rear deck. *Bottom left:* Author Don Danenberg uses the router method of fitting planks. *Bottom right:* Several runabout hulls undergo restoration at Danenberg Boatworks in Manistee, Michigan.

Title page: Photo by Classic Boating Magazine

Back cover, main: A 1955 Chris-Craft Capri. *Photo by* Classic Boating Magazine. *Top left:* Author Don Danenberg hand-carves a plank seam into the covering boards.
Top center: A hull is carefully leveled and blocked prior to reconstruction at the Danenberg Boatworks. *Top right:* Good taping and masking procedures produce tight, crisp color lines.

"Clear Penetrating Epoxy Sealer" in Chapter 5 © 2002 Steve Smith, all rights reserved, used by permission.

Edited by Jack Savage & Dennis Pernu
Designed by Koechel Peterson & Associates

Printed in China

Disclaimer:
Whereas steam by its very nature is extremely hot; the inhalation of noxious fumes emitted by stains and varnishes is debilitating to most human nervous systems; sawdust is known to cause irreversible damage to respiratory organs; and power tools tend to feature quickly spinning and/or reciprocating cutting implements, **great caution** must be exercised and safety equipment utilized when performing any of the procedures described and/or illustrated on these pages. The reader's purchase or appropriation of this book by other means constitutes his or her agreement to absolve both MBI Publishing Company and the author of all responsibility for any physical injury or loss of mental capacities that arise from the reader's disregard for steam's intrinsic heat-conducting properties, the misuse of power tools, or the failure to otherwise observe proper safety procedures.

CONTENTS

DEDICATION

This book is dedicated first to all of those people whose love for these antique and classic boats led them to invest in their reconstruction. Second, to all of the experts and boatwrights who taught me what I needed to know.

I would like to thank Norm and Jim Wangard of *Classic Boating* magazine for bravely publishing articles that I have written on this subject for more than five years. I must also thank my father, James R. Danenberg, for teaching me a great work ethic and the common sense necessary to apply it.

FOREWORD

We first met Don a decade ago in Mt. Dora, Florida, where he was exhibiting his customer's large runabout that has since gone on to become one of the most award-winning classic boats in North America. Don rebuilt the big 24-footer using his enhanced traditional restoration technique, which he describes in this book, the first ever to cover vintage runabout restoration.

We knew Don was on to something because his restoration retained the boat's original scantlings, yet didn't leak, even after 10 years. The original boat was only watertight for the first couple of years.

We also knew that Don had to become a contributing editor to the magazine. Before Don popularized his enhanced traditional restoration technique there were no uniform restoration standards. Everybody, whether amateur or professional, pretty much did things according to the convenience of their timeframe and capability. There evolved a lot of shortcut methods that only worked in the immediate short term.

Without any concise guidance, the do-it-yourselfers tended to gloss over the structural integrity of their boats and became "mop-and-glow" specialists, concerned with what they could control: varnish and chrome. The boats looked pretty and did well with show judges; the owners just had to hope that the batteries kept the bilge pumps running.

Don's restoration articles, which evolved into this book, empowered the amateur and even the professional with a unified common sense approach to runabout restoration, a technique that works on any make of plank-on-seam batten hull form. No longer were boat owners fiberglassing tired old bottoms or epoxying planks of wood together to keep out leaks. Don's enhanced traditional method retains the boat's original scantlings while incorporating modern *flexible* sealants and adhesive compounds. Now, restorations can last the life of the restorer, which has never happened before.

We often say the vintage runabout represents an era of lost craftsmanship. Yet, seasonal unemployed farmers and high school kids built most of these brand-name boats on production lines. Through repetition, they became very good at what they did, but they were not craftsmen, nor could they actually build a boat. It might be better stated that the vintage boat represents a lost "production technique."

Few of the current practicing runabout restorers have had the benefit of learning their craft from serving under shipwrights as Don has. Now in *How to Restore Your Wooden Runabout,* Don passes on his insights and experience to the rest of us. By following Don's examples and allowing yourself the time to learn and do good work, your classic can embody craftsmanship that it never had, or, in the least, be returned to its original construction.

—Jim Wangard
Classic Boating Magazine

INTRODUCTION

When anyone takes on the challenge of bringing an antique boat back to its former glory, it's worth asking an important question: What is restoration?

If, for example, you were to start with a dilapidated "gray boat" otherwise destined for the burn pile and replace nearly all the unsound old wood with new wood but use the original engine, running gear, and hardware, would this be a "restored" boat, or would it be one that's been completely rebuilt? Or, if you were to start with an antique boat, its frames and planks weakened to a mere one-quarter of their original strength and its original brass fasteners dezincified to one-quarter of their original strength, and then proceed to strip, bleach, stain, and varnish the original hull, would *it* be a "restored" boat, given the fact that it's no longer seaworthy?

The Antique and Classic Boat Society (ACBS) recently changed some of its judging guidelines, placing an emphasis on preservation of the original components, specifically the wood. ACBS-sanctioned show judges are instructed to be far more lenient with scars and repairs of original wood. This begs the questions: Are we interested in restoration or preservation? Are we preserving all of the original components in order to claim that this is the original, with the actual wood that our forebears rode in when this boat was a sound, seaworthy, speedy, and nimble craft? Or, should we restore the whole vessel to seaworthy condition?

Antique and classic wooden powerboats were built extremely light to achieve their advertised speeds. Today, three to six decades after leaving the factory—often including years spent in derelict condition—it is nearly impossible to consider the wood "restorable." The best you can hope for is to restore it to the strength you would expect in a 50- to 60-year-old boat. While penetrating sealers can stop future rot by cutting off moisture and oxygen, they will not return the weakened wood to its original fracture- or fastener-holding strength.

The most important consideration in any restoration of these craft is the framework, which must first be made sound with at least some new wood. After more than 100 restorations, from smaller runabouts to a 117-footer, I have never yet seen a wooden boat that did not need at least some frames replaced. Original steel and brass fasteners should all be replaced with silicon bronze. Topside frames and deck beams should also be exposed, repaired, and refastened. Every hour and dollar you spend on planking and finishes will depend on whether or not the framework is sound and free from flexing at its joints. Any hidden rot spots should be addressed.

Imagine if you could go back in time and ask Chris C. Smith, Gar Wood, or John Hacker how long you should expect your wooden boat to last if it had been in marine use for 50 years? Would you take an unrestored 40- to 80-year-old automobile or airplane out of the barn and invite your family for a ride merely because it had fresh paint and upholstery?

To simply perform a "cosmetic" restoration to these boats is analogous to a person with advanced lung cancer getting a tan, a new suit, and a haircut. With this book, I hope to lay out a roadmap for a successful and proper seaworthy restoration, so that early mistakes won't undo the many hours and dollars you've invested in your project.

Specifically, *How to Restore Your Wooden Runabout* covers the woodworking aspects and procedures for the reconstruction and restoration of "antique" and "classic" batten-seamed, carvel-planked, inboard-powered runabouts. The ACBS has designated the following classifications for these types of gasoline-powered boats:

Historic: A boat built before 1919
Antique: A boat built between 1919 and
   1942 inclusive
Classic: A boat built between 1943 and
   1968 inclusive
Production Contemporary:
   A production wooden boat built 1969 to present

Custom Contemporary: A modified or one-off wooden boat built 1969 to present

Replica: A boat built in a non-production manner, intended to be one of a kind and usually a copy or duplicate of a boat previously built or manufactured.

These category designations coincide with World War I, World War II, and 1968, generally the end of mass-production of wooden speedboats. These dates are important mostly because the demands of war spurred technological leaps in boat construction and gasoline engines. These developments were then incorporated in pleasure boats when peacetime pleasure-boat production resumed.

In the early 1970s, when nearly all production pleasure boats were built of fiberglass, these venerable wooden boats were deemed too expensive and time-consuming to maintain; many having outlived their single-decade expected life spans. Far too many examples of these boats were stripped of their hardware and engines, bulldozed into piles, and burned. Most often they were just left in—or behind—the barn, to suffer the ravages of time and the elements. A few individuals with foresight kept some of the glamour of the wooden boats alive by collecting those that had been well maintained. With the necessary skills, some retired wooden boat builders maintained their livelihoods by restoring and maintaining these boats for customers who wished to keep alive the beloved memories of their youth. Today, because of their rarity, these antique and classic wooden boats can be valued in the tens to hundreds of thousands of dollars. Properly restored, these boats can hold and improve their investment values along the same lines as antique automobiles. Plus, woodworking skills are an enjoyable hobby and such restoration crafts provide entertainment, fun, and pride in a "job well done."

SURVEYING TRADITIONAL CONSTRUCTION

Before purchasing the first antique or classic boat that you find available, I recommend that you attend some boat shows. This will give you an opportunity to decide exactly what you want and speak to the owners about the merits of different styles of boats. You will be much more informed when the time arrives to purchase your own.

Once you set out to acquire your own vintage boat, you'll find that prices vary widely depending on condition, rarity, originality, and other factors. Any time you consider plunking down thousands, or tens of thousands, of dollars for an antique boat, it makes sense to get the opinion of a professional surveyor.

The Myth and Problems of Swelling

Keep in mind that there are many wooden boats in use that have been marginally maintained with an emphasis on varnish and chrome, but whose

---

GAR WOOD, INC.

MARYSVILLE, MICHIGAN

March 4, 1931

SERVICE DEPARTMENT: BULLETIN NO. 13

RECONDITIONING USED GAR WOOD BOATS

The time for preparing all boats which are to be used this coming season is close at hand and this bulletin is intended for the distributors and dealers who have placed their demonstrators in storage during the winter and/or have owners' boats to prepare for service.

It is our desire that you inform all Gar Wood Boat owners in your territory in accordance with the information contained herein, if possible, by furnishing them with a copy of this bulletin, a number being enclosed for that purpose.

All Gar Wood Boats are of the batten seam construction. Technically this only applies to the sides and decking, the bottom being double planked, of course does not have battens back of the seams of the fore and aft planking. Nevertheless, the planking of the bottoms as well as the sides and decks is laid edge to edge and after the boat is completed at our factory, atmospheric conditions will tend to alter the planking at the seams by expansion and contraction.

The mahogany which goes into the construction of Gar Wood Boats is carefully selected and kiln dried before using which gives a uniform moisture content throughout. Many years of experience in the building of quality boats shows that a moisture content of 10% at the time of planking is most desirable.

It has been found that regardless of thickness, a mahogany plank six inches in width when immersed in water for 24 hours will expand 1/8 of an inch, the plank of course containing 10% of moisture at the time of immersion. Therefore, a boat taken out of the water after a season's use and placed in a warm dry atmosphere will excrete its moisture content necessarily resulting in opening of seams, the openings depending upon the amount of moisture excreted.

If inspection of the boat before preparing for launching discloses a slight opening of seams, DO NOT PLUG THEM WITH CAULKING because after the boat is placed in the water the seams will close through expansion by reason of moisture being absorbed. Caulking would prevent this action and cause the planks to buckle which might result in serious damage such as pulling the screws from the frames or pulling the heads of the screws through the planks.

A boat which has had reasonable care during the boating season should not require caulking. By reasonable care we mean if the boat has been taken out of the water when not in use and still has not been allowed to completely dry out by leaving it in a hot dry atmosphere for a great length of time. Being left continually in the water during the boating season thereby absorbing its maximum of moisture and then being left in a warm dry atmosphere causing it to excrete its entire moisture content will in time take the life out of the mahogany after which it will not expand and contract normally.

If after the boat has been in the water for 24 hours the seams will not close sufficiently to prevent excessive leaking, caulking may then be used. But only as a last resort should caulking be placed'in the seams between planks.

Yours very truly,

GAR WOOD, INC.

When this 1931 Gar Wood factory-to-dealer memo was written, the factory had only been in business for six years.

SURVEYING TRADITIONAL CONSTRUCTION

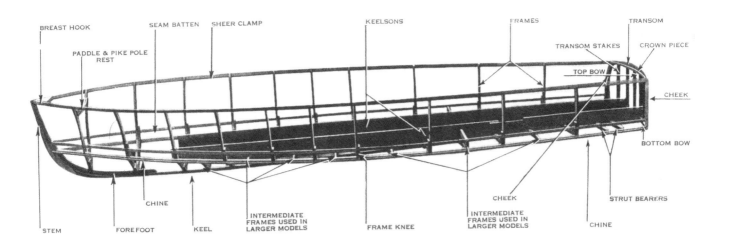

CHRIS-CRAFT FRAME CONSTRUCTION

Chris-Craft referred to the gripe as a "forefoot," a term that generally refers to the entire forward stem-gripe assembly as the forefoot of the keel.

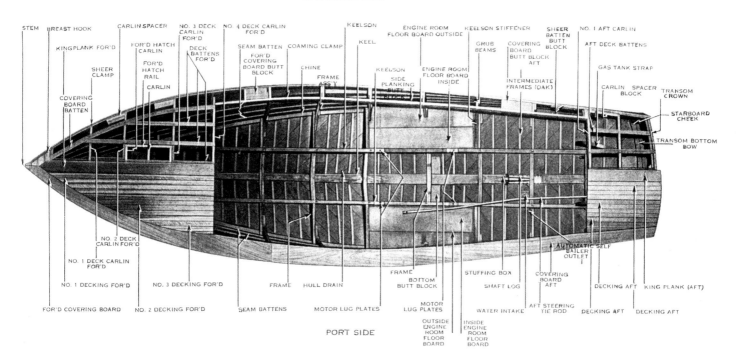

PLATE 5

CHRIS CRAFT HULL DETAILS

Chris-Craft referred to the bilge stringer or engine bedlog as a keelson. This term usually refers to a keel-stiffening piece mounted directly above the keel. This illustration also shows the deck beams labeled as "carlins," a term that usually refers to fore-and-aft deck framing (carling).

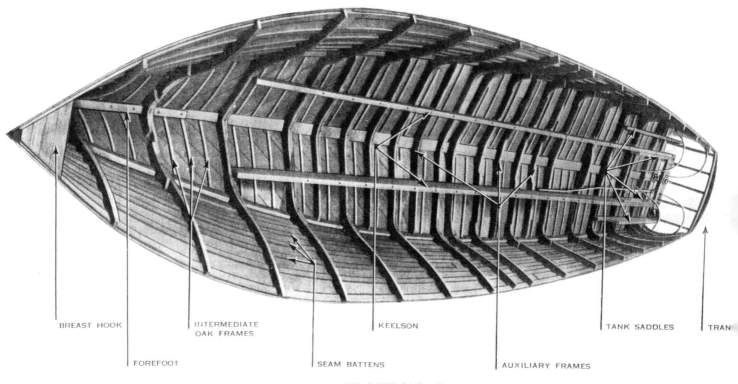

BREAST HOOK INTERMEDIATE KEELSON TANK SADDLES TRAN
OAK FRAMES

FOREFOOT SEAM BATTENS AUXILIARY FRAMES

PLATE NO. 6
CHRIS CRAFT HULL DETAILS
28 FT. MODEL ILLUSTRATED
IN PERSPECTIVE

Once again, the gripe is referred to as forefoot and the bilge stringers as keelson.

framework needs the same attention as that of the gray boat. These boats may look good, but you will probably find many broken frames and fasteners. Unfortunately, it has become common wisdom that wooden boats are supposed to leak, supposed to swell up, before they can be used—this misunderstanding became the greatest cause for their early demise.

The culprit of early hull aging is over-saturation of the wood. As excess moisture soaks into the wood, it expands like a sponge, and causes the planks to buckle and warp, stretching the fasteners out of their tightened positions, elongating the screw holes, and cracking the planks. Where the plank edges meet the force of this expansion crushes the wood cells, referred

to as "compressive set." Once the hollow cellulose wood cells become compressed, they remain that way and this causes gaps in the plank seams.

While in this condition, the still-watertight hull is over-tightened with wood weakened by water absorption. The flexing and pounding across waves stretches fastener holes even more, causing stress cracks in the planking and compressive set under the screw head. Should the moisture content of the wood climb above 25 percent, the rot spore already present in the wood will begin to grow.

When removed from the water for winter storage, not only will the excess moisture evaporate from the hull, so will some of the wood's natural rot-preventive

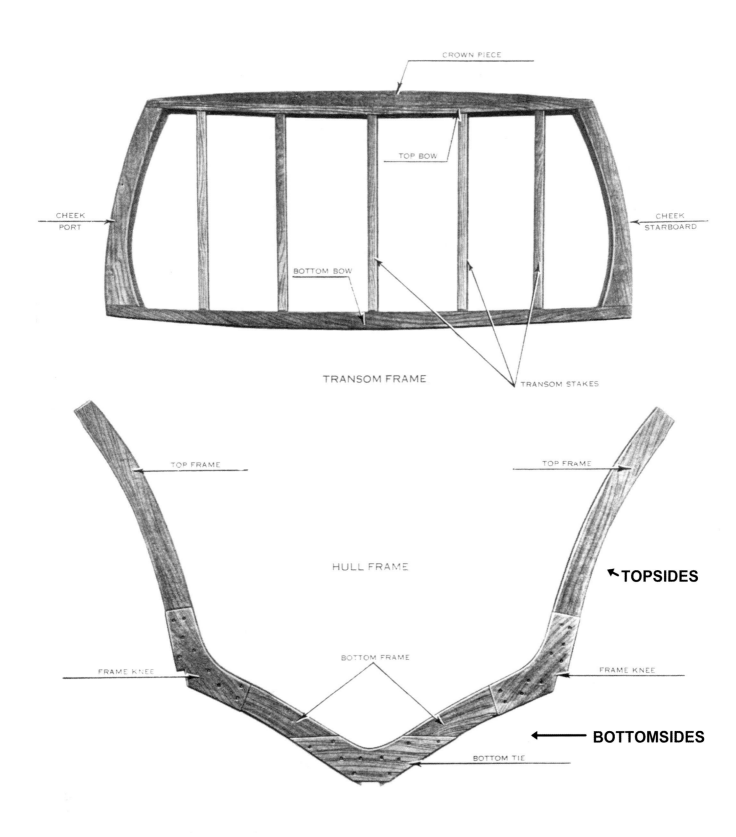

CROWN PIECE

TOP BOW

CHEEK
PORT

CHEEK
STARBOARD

BOTTOM BOW

TRANSOM FRAME

TRANSOM STAKES

TOP FRAME

TOP FRAME

HULL FRAME

TOPSIDES

FRAME KNEE

FRAME KNEE

BOTTOM FRAME

BOTTOMSIDES

BOTTOM TIE

Many confuse the term "topsides" to mean deck, because it has the word "top" in it. The bottomsides, port and starboard, run diagonally from the keel to the chine. The topsides, port and starboard, run vertically from the chine up to the sheer. The deck is the top horizontal surface of the boat.

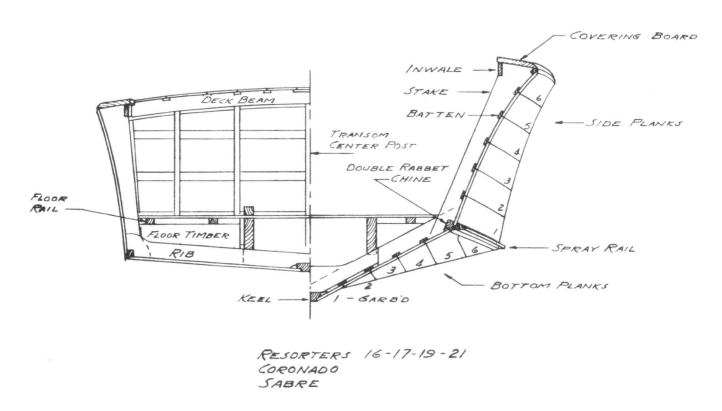

RESORTERS 16 - 17 - 19 - 21
CORONADO
SABRE

This illustration from "The Care and Feeding of a Thoroughbred" illustrates the general construction of the Century models indicated at the bottom.

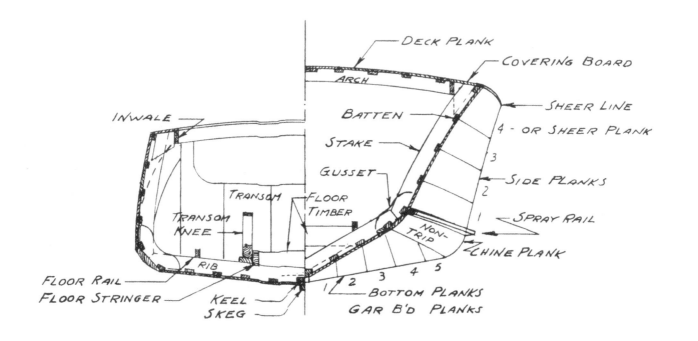

PALOMINO - ROAN - COLT

Century boats of the models listed employed heavy chine planks in place of separate chine timber to form a "non-trip" chine.

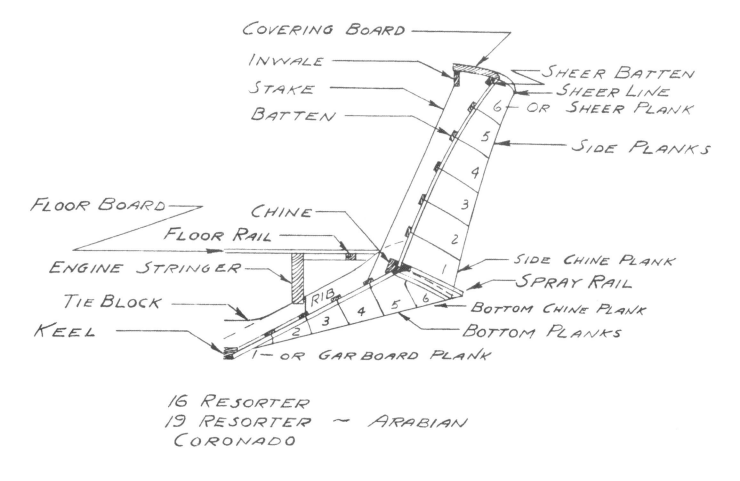

COVERING BOARD
INWALE
STAKE
BATTEN
SHEER BATTEN
SHEER LINE
OR SHEER PLANK
SIDE PLANKS
FLOOR BOARD
CHINE
FLOOR RAIL
ENGINE STRINGER
TIE BLOCK
KEEL
SIDE CHINE PLANK
SPRAY RAIL
BOTTOM CHINE PLANK
BOTTOM PLANKS
1 — OR GARBOARD PLANK

16 RESORTER
19 RESORTER ~ ARABIAN
CORONADO

Century boat construction employed fore and aft plank battens in their bottom construction rather than the double-planked bottoms favored by other manufacturers.

oils. Due to both these losses, the planks contract slightly smaller than original size. Gaps appear wherever compressive set occurred at plank edges or frame landings or fastener heads. Not only does this leave the entire structure weakened and loose, the resulting gaps between planks and frames—as well as the plank seams—collect dirt, debris, and rot spore. Plus, such gaps hold moisture that never fully evaporates in storage, feeding rot spore growth.

During the following seasons, these same conditions feed upon themselves as the hull requires more water to swell tight when more and more natural oils are lost and due to damage from compressive set.

The increasing gaps collect additional dirt and debris, which causes even more spreading of the components and dislodging fasteners. These clumps of dirt and debris also hold moisture all season long and are the main source for rot growth.

After enough seasons of this kind of abuse, the tropical hardwoods have lost most of their natural rot-preventative oils and the wood becomes brittle and lifeless. Like an unseen cancer, rot tendrils are growing throughout the interior mating surfaces of planks and frames.

Manufacturers never intended these wooden boats to last for half a century. In 1931, Gar Wood put out a factory-to-dealer memo on replacing worn-out bottom planks, after they had been producing wooden boats for barely six years. The operators were told to keep the boat out of the water "when not in use," warning against water-logging the wood. One simply cannot decide today that these boats can be treated as if they had fiberglass hulls, which we have also learned that after a few decades of use will absorb water and blister the gel coat if left in the water for extended periods. Clearly, there was an expected operational lifespan, after which repairs would be required.

In short, a $15,000 purchase can very often require the same amount of work as a $1,500 purchase for the same type of boat. Scary, huh? This is why I personally prefer the gray boat—I know exactly what I've got when I'm done. I know that nothing is hidden.

Surveying a Boat

So how do you figure out how much work a particular boat might take in order to rebuild it?

One answer is marine surveyors, who can be located through marinas, marine insurance companies, and on the Internet. The marine surveyor you choose should be certified. Costs for this service typically are in the range of $10 to $20 per foot of boat length. Your marine insurance company should also be able to provide you with a list of marine surveyors whose work they accept.

Several magazines and books also cover the subject of determining the cost to rebuild a boat. *Classic Boating* magazine has been the benchmark in this area since 1984. Not only does it provide views of all different types and makes of wooden powerboats, it also includes advertisements from parts suppliers, procedural and material advice for all aspects of boat operation, and classified ads that can prove handy. You can join organizations that will help you network your project. Finally, in addition to the Appendix of this book, which lists supplementary sources to help you in your search, the worksheets in this chapter can prove useful when looking at boats.

SURVEYING TRADITIONAL CONSTRUCTION

The following is an example of a worksheet that a professional might use to survey your potential purchase.

1) WATER TEST Launch and retrieve with operator and mechanic to determine engine and running gear condition; fuel, oil, or exhaust leaks; determine the condition of the bottom in water and locate through-hull leaks; examine stuffing boxes and the function of switches and gauges, lights, bilge pump, etc.

2) VARNISH AND PAINT General condition of finishes. Inspect wood condition for checks, cupping, rot or seam discoloration, raised bungs, etc.

Repair or replace hardware, prep, sand, varnish $ _____
Strip, fair, sand, stain, seal $ _____

3) CHROME AND STAINLESS STEEL Repair or replacement of damaged, missing or incorrect hardware and fasteners

Repair or replace, refinish stainless $ _____
Repair or replace, rechrome hardware $ _____
Replace pieces $ _____

4) GAUGES AND SWITCHES Restoration or replacement of incorrect or malfunctioning items or wiring $ _____

5) UPHOLSTERY AND TRIM Repair or replacement of seat covers, crash padding, linoleum, rubber flooring, windshield gaskets, towing cover, waterline cover, etc. $ _____

6) PLANK CONDITION Survey for likely structural repairs or refastening. Look for cracks, cupping, joint movement, raised bungs, discoloration or indications of mold or rot inside as well as outside. Look for incorrect repairs such as plank shorts or wrong type of wood replacement $ _____

DECK Strip, repair, bleach $ _____
Plank replacement $ _____
Mill, install new planks $ _____

TOPSIDES Strip, repair, bleach $ _____
Plank replacement $ _____
Mill, install new planks $ _____

BOTTOM Sand, repair, paint $ _____

Bottom reconstruction with new inner existing outer planks. Take into account disassembly and flipping expenses. Note possible exposure of previously unseen frame repairs

New ply inner-old outer planks $ _____
Individual plank replacements $ _____
All new exterior planks $ _____

7) STEM, GRIPE, KEEL AND CHINES These items are estimated in conjunction with complete bottom job as the vessel must be upside down and opened up to address them

New stem $ _____
New gripe $ _____
New keel $ _____
New chines $ _____

8) HULL FRAMES This portion of the estimate can only be guessed at until the bottom planks are off exposing the bottom surfaces. Obviously broken or rotten frames as seen from inside $ _____

9) FUEL TANK, ETC. Additional running gear problems noticed after opening up the bilge $ _____

10) MISCELLANEOUS Anything noticed but not previously covered. Ancillary items such as dock lines, fenders and cleats, flare kits, fire extinguishers, PFDs, paddle, and spare engine parts $ _____

11) RECOMMENDATIONS - Trailer repair or replacement, etc. $ _____

Exterior Hardware Catalog

BOAT	OWNER	DATE	HULL #

ITEM	NOTATION	STORAGE/ESTIMATE	# OF

STAINLESS
Rubrails
Quarter rails
Cutwater
Transom guards
Hatch hinges and trim
Miscellaneous trim
Fasteners above

CHROME
Stemhead fairlead
Chocks
Cleats
Fender cleats
Deck vents large
Deck vents small
F&A lift rings trim
Windshield frames
Step-pad frames
Bow light
Stern pole base
Hatch handles
Handrails
Gas cap and trim ring
Gas tank vent
Exhaust trim ring
Transom vents
Spotlight
Deck horn
Air horn and siren
Bilge pump through-hull
Steering wheel trim
Steering column bracket
Dashboard trim
Upholstery trim
Gear-shift lever

NOTES

Exterior Hardware Catalog

BOAT	OWNER	DATE	HULL #
ITEM	NOTATION	STORAGE/ESTIMATE	# OF

FURNITURE

Seat cushions _____

Seat backs _____

Seat bottoms _____

Seat back assemblies _____

Seat bottom frames _____

Engine box _____

Engine room hatches _____

Floor hatches _____

Floorboards _____

Dashboard _____

Ceiling planks and panels _____

Rubber flooring _____

Miscellaneous _____

ACCESSORIES

Windshield glass
    and gaskets _____

Gauges _____

Gauge panel _____

Step pads _____

Battery _____

Bilge pump and hose _____

Stern pole/globe/flag _____

Bow pole and burgee _____

Spare propeller _____

Dock lines _____

Fenders _____

PFDs _____

Flare kit _____

Fire extinguisher _____

Paddle _____

Anchor and line _____

Boat hook _____

Engine spare parts _____

Siphon _____

Miscellaneous _____

RUNNING GEAR

Steering wheel

Throttle and choke levers

Throttle and choke linkages _____

Steering column and sleeve _____

Steering linkage and arms _____

Reverse gear linkage _____

Rudder _____

Rudder stuffing box _____

Rudder sternpost brace _____

Prop shaft and coupler _____

Propeller _____

Shaft stuffing box _____

Shaft log _____

Strut and cutlass bearing _____

Siphon through-hull _____

Drain plug through-hull _____

Raw water through-hull _____

Fwd lift ring hardware _____

Aft lift ring hardware _____

Fuel tank and straps _____

Fuel lines and valves _____

Fuel filters _____

Fuel fill tube and locknut _____

Fuel gauge sending unit _____

Vent fan and hose _____

Electric horns _____

Air horn and pump _____

Electronics _____

Miscellaneous _____

NOTES _____

_____

_____

_____

OVERVIEW OF RESTORATION METHODS

The conventional mahogany runabout bottom had a diagonally laid layer of 1/8- to 1/4-inch-thick mahogany, 4 to 8 inches wide, applied to the bottom frames with tacks. Over this, a layer of canvas or muslin was laid, saturated with a boatyard bedding compound with a linseed oil base. The purpose of the canvas was to hold the bedding compound in place over the seams of the inner and outer bottom planks and to keep the action of the water pressures from washing the bedding compound away. This was the usual production procedure of manufacturers such as Chris-Craft, Gar Wood, and Hacker, among others less well-known.

Emphasis at Chris-Craft was on economy production, which meant employing the speed of production lines with individual workers specializing on one aspect of construction. Boats were not expected to last as long as they have. Today, with better materials, we can make hulls last 30 years or more. *Courtesy of The Mariners' Museum, Newport News, Virginia*

The outer bottom planks were laid fore and aft over the canvas and screwed to the frames, chines, and keel as tightly as possible. The canvas and bedding compound kept out the water until enough seasons of use caused edge-set gaps in the planking. No caulk of any kind was used because the friction between tightly fitted planks contributed greatly to the formation of a taut and structurally sound bottom.

Century did not use this inner layer of bottom planking in its production boats. Instead, it employed fore-and-aft plank battens with a boatyard bedding compound—the same technique used with the topsides planking of nearly all makes. This made for an initially stronger bottom, but the fore-and-aft plank battens held water that caused earlier wood deterioration than the two-part bottoms with athwartships plank battens that allowed water to drain to the keel.

Mahogany speedboats were very lightly built in order to attain their advertised speeds and, as such, were not expected to last any longer than the average automobile of their day. The scantlings were so light that the thin (7/8 x 2-1/2-inch) Philippine mahogany frames would break or split due to the action of so many closely spaced fasteners. In addition, the linseed oil-based bedding compound would volatilize and either soak away into the surrounding wood, which in most cases was not sealed in any way, or would eventually evaporate, leaving the dry solids of the bedding compound and the unprotected canvas to hold water and actually

As originally built, Chris-Craft bottom planking went on tight without any caulking. If an old original bottom appears to need excessive caulking to fill gaps, it could be indicative of other problems. *Courtesy of The Mariners' Museum, Newport News, Virginia*

Annual expansion and contraction of the planking stressed these Chris-Craft fasteners back and forth, creating split plank ends, loose or broken fasteners, and split bottom frames.

At the factory, bottom planking was fastened without any sealants. At best, topside plank edges were sealed with varnish, which was better than nothing. Then again, life expectancy was only six years. *Courtesy of The Mariners' Museum, Newport News, Virginia*

Original canvas in 1964 Chris-Craft bottom. The linseed oil has soaked into the wood, leaving dried compound behind.

An example of the dirt and debris that can collect in bottoms and prevent plank expansion the following season, forcing components farther apart.

The rubber caulking in this bottom was so heavily applied that when the bottom swelled, the chines were pushed nearly a full inch out of their landings.

SCHOOL OF HARD KNOCKS

Lessons from a Super Sport

A recent customer of mine took his 1964 Chris-Craft Super Sport to a preservation-oriented boat restorer because the bottom would not stop leaking. The "preservationist" did a fine job of cleaning the bottom plank seams and a very professional job of filling the seams (without voids) with 3M 5200 (a polyurethane rubber product that I, incidentally, have used for 30 years—and am very glad was invented). The customer could now drive this 210-horsepower hot rod of a boat without constantly running his little bilge pump. If he wanted, he could pull skiers and scream over somebody else's wake feeling safe and secure—for about a month, that is. By the end of the season he had installed a second bilge pump and ran them both constantly whenever the boat was in the water. Soon the water would not stay below the floorboards. One day he felt very lucky just to get back to the beach.

A mutual friend gave the owner my number and he called me concerned that the caulking was not done properly and asked me if I could caulk his hull for him.

I responded that, no, I would do no such thing to his boat, but if he could come over to my shop I would show him exactly what to expect from his framework.

As it turned out, when I removed the bottom of his Super Sport, the port chine had broken all of the carriage bolts and auxiliary frame screws from frame one to frame six. The bottom was attached to the topsides only by the outboard bottom plank, which was torn and split in several places. Because this major frame section was no longer securely holding the ends of the bottom frames and transferring the forces imparted on them to the topsides, he now also had eight bottom frame sections broken at the bilge stringer. That year's quick fix had cost him an additional $1,800 in replacement frames and chine.

I can fully understand the view of the "preservationist" who wants to retain all of the antique's original wood, fasteners, and construction procedures. Just don't expect to strap a motor to it and throw it in the lake.

Over-caulking planks that were never meant to be caulked causes a wide array of damage.

foment rot. It was a common boatyard service to replace the canvas and bedding compound in these boats every six to ten years. Accordingly, if you restore your classic runabout in the original manner, with a canvas and bedding compound bottom, you should expect to replace the canvas and bedding compound every six to ten years—or even more frequently if you don't replace the bottom planks with sound new wood.

That said, I feel that these collectibles are of such great value now that they are cared for much differently than they once were. They do not sit out in the sun without a cover. They are no longer stored behind the barn but in it. They are never put away with water in the bilge. They are kept carefully ventilated. The kids do not use them every day for water-skiing. The proper use of materials unavailable to the factories of the time and the knowledge of the weak points in this type of construction allow for better reconstruction. They are, in short, far too valuable not to be very carefully cared for.

I believe that if somebody invests thousands of dollars in something, it should last more than six years—and with correct restoration, maintenance, and use, it will. Key elements of a long-lasting rebuild include starting with the framework, and using appropriate materials in a proper manner.

An interior view of a Gar Wood utility shows the extent of damage caused by the six bottom planks spreading just 1/8 inch each.

The Dangers of Improper Caulking

After having repaired the framework of over one hundred wooden hulls, I can say without reservation that the single greatest cause of frame damage is improper caulking of the planks. If your planked wooden hull was not built with a caulking bevel in the plank edge, it should never be caulked. To date, I have not seen a single mahogany runabout that was designed to have its seams caulked.

The hulls that I have repaired with the worst frame damage are the ones where the owner mistakenly applied any kind of caulk—rubber, putty, or, in the very worst cases, a hard epoxy—to the seams of the bottom planks. Perhaps they felt they would make it last just one more season before paying for that bottom job. Perhaps they were amateur restorers who trusted too much in a product to properly research its correct use. Whatever the reason, putting any kind of caulk in the seams of the bottom planks is by far the worst thing you can do to the structure of your hull—worse even than applying fiberglass or epoxy.

When the planks swell they have no gap to fill, no place to go. If the chines are still sound, the planks may just cup and split. More often than not, the chines are shoved out and away from their frame landings, breaking the dezincified brass chine bolts or tearing out the frames or chines. The keel itself may be pushed out, breaking its bolts, as well.

Dunphy molded MAHOGANY plywood construction

How the 1958 Dunphy's were built.

The Dunphy 7-ply boat is virtually seven hulls in one, bonded together with waterproof plastic under heat and pressure. The result is a perfectly contoured hull—seamless, light and extremely strong. All superfluous weight is eliminated in the finished product. All stems, keels, gunwales, and the mahogany hull, are treated with a rot-resisting chlorinated phenol.

This illustration of "molded construction" from a period Dunphy ad illustrates how completely different it is from traditional plank-on-frame construction.

When _five_ bottom planks want to swell 1/8 inch or so each, you end up talking about 5/8 inch of travel for the outermost bottom planks and chines. The action of 20 or so frame fasteners spaced every inch and a quarter along a 7/8-inch-wide frame tends to split the frame like so many wedges. When the frame members push out of their proper landings and the fasteners stretch out of their holes or break, the structure is definitely not what the naval architect designed. Driving the boat in such a condition can cause far more damage than if it were not worked on in the first place.

All traditionally constructed wooden hulls must allow for some flexing and motion in the frame components; this is inherent in the nature of the material. This is, after all, what gives wooden boats the "sea-kindly nature" in their ride. Expansion and contraction of the individual wooden components must also be expected due not only to the absorption of moisture but to temperature differences, as well. Imagine your wooden hull laid up for the winter in the boathouse or garage at 10

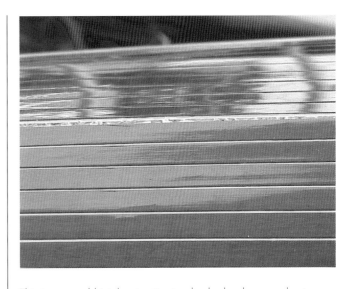

This two-year-old total restoration involved a hard epoxy glue to laminate 1/4-inch planks to 1/4-inch plywood. With only staples as fasteners, it's easy to see why such de-lamination could occur. It is not the glue that fails but the wood fibers that are torn from the wood's surface when dimensional lumber expands and contracts.

degrees Fahrenheit. Now imagine it moored in a 70-degree lake with 120-degrees of summer sun on the deck. The wood is going to expand and contract, no matter how well you feel it is sealed or "encapsulated." If you strap a motor to the boat, put

600 pounds of people in it, and go racing across the wave tops, you are going to cause a great deal of additional flexing of the integral parts. If your sealers and bedding compounds are flexible, you stand a much better chance of maintaining seal integrity. It is predominately because of this component motion that I strongly recommend against the use of any type of hard epoxy glue in traditionally constructed wooden hulls.

Other Kinds of Wood Boat Construction

Molded construction has been around for a long time. Dunphy Boat Manufacturing Company of Eau Claire, Wisconsin, advertised molded plywood hulls in 1946. These hulls were formed of 1/16-inch veneers of spruce or mahogany. The veneers were thin enough that even though not fully saturated with glue, their expansion or contraction (at 5 to 10 percent of their thickness of 1/16-inch) could not possibly affect their bonding glue line. These hulls were vacuum-bagged, so as not to puncture this multiple lamination with screw holes that could pump water into the small amount of still-absorbable wood, and then cooked in huge ovens to set the glue, which required enough heat to actually congeal into a final waterproof adhesive.

Cold-molded construction is basically the same system as above, except that heat is not required to set the new glues available after World War II, such as Resorcinol or epoxy resins that set catalytically (chemically produce their own heat in setting). The other parameters of this system are basically the same, especially the thickness (or thinness) of the wood, since outside heat is no longer introduced to help melt and spread the glue into the surface of the wood.

The cold-molded technique is a wonderful method for new boat construction but requires the use of multiple laminations of wood veneers of no more than 1/8-inch thickness so that any expansion and contraction of the wood cannot effect the glue line.

Completely different framing techniques were used because the single-sawn "sistered" frames of these older runabouts were too flexible for this type of skin. Cold molding was designed for round-bilged boats, not hard-chined speedboats. The only decent compromise I have seen to date was the procedure used at Riva of Italy. The hull topsides and bottomsides were laminated of thin mahogany veneers as individual sections on molds. These beautifully curved hull sections were attached to the hull framework with flexible bedding compounds at the keel and chines.

Epoxies

With hard epoxy glues, many people fooled themselves into believing that they have plasticized their lumber into stability. This could not be further from the truth.

Epoxy saturates the wood to a depth of about 1/100 inch. This is less than the 1/4-inch-thick piece of mahogany that expands or contracts due to seasonal temperature differences. Because it is stronger than the wood, the epoxy does not fail at the joint. What it *does* do, however, is tear the surface fibers off of one of the wood surfaces, especially weakened old wood, exposing one completely bare face to moisture. Once moisture enters, the problems really escalate. The surface "encapsulation" now holds moisture in and forms "zipper cracks" as the wood expands. When moisture builds up inside this encapsulated piece of wood to about 30 percent, it's great enough to incubate rot spore.

One epoxy manufacturer recently sent out a flyer explaining that their product should not be used with white oak because of the inherent dimensional instability of the wood, as if the wood were at fault. Unfortunately, the recommendation to frame the boat with ash, which sticks well to their hard epoxy glue, ignored much more important factors such as fastener holding capability or rot resistance.

I see no good use for epoxy in these older boats and have replaced epoxied bottoms either because of delamination caused by improper construction or simply because with the older flat-bottom designs they make for such a darn hard ride. I have used hard epoxy glues myself on a round-bilged sailboat in Hawaii. I used 1/16-inch veneers as in the original cold-molded construction. I may use this material again, but only in new, true cold-molded construction. It simply has, in my opinion, no place at all in classic-boat restoration. As Aime Ontario Fraser put it in *WoodenBoat* (Issue #84), "[E]poxy can never replace the caulking or fastenings in a traditionally built boat. This is what epoxy promoters mean when they say that epoxy not only makes a new kind of boat building possible, it makes it imperative."

However you proceed, if you are going to restore this valuable piece of property by yourself, please research the materials and their proper uses before more damage is caused than can be fixed by the next owner.

The Danenberg Solution

Now that I have upset the "preservationists" and the "epoxyists," what possible solution could there be? Mine is to take the best components of all the procedures and combine them with the materials, tools, and procedures available today. I believe that

This six-year-old "contemporary classic" mixed traditional construction and scantlings with assembly and encapsulation with hard epoxy. Original factory construction would have lasted far longer.

if the original builders had any idea that these vessels would become the extremely valuable antiques they are today, and had the materials and knowledge available to us, they would have taken a similar approach in their construction.

Because traditional construction allows for flexibility in the entire structure, which in turn provides a soft, comfortable ride (and the show judges really like original appearance and scantlings), restoring these vessels to their exact original construction is admittedly the loftiest goal. Unfortunately, I believe that boats preserved thusly should then go into a museum and not into the water, where we all want to use them. Undergoing a full, original restoration every six to 10 years would be prohibitively expensive for all but a few boat owners. And, eventually, nothing of the original wood would be left anyway.

The bottom technique favored by the author has each bottom plank sealed with Smith's CPES and bedded directly to the inner bottom ply with 3M 5200. Planks are sealed, yet the bottom remains flexible like the original construction.

The concept of encapsulating the wood has several good effects on hull structure. The wood retains strength and dimensional stability when it is kept dry. The lack of seasonal expansion and contraction of the planks protects not only the plank stock but avoids yanking the fasteners back and forth in the frames. Decreasing the movement of the framework and planks helps keep dirt, debris, moisture, and rot spore out of the joints. And decreasing the movement of the planks at their joints saves finishes like paint and varnish. Unfortunately, hard epoxy resins will not last on hulls built with traditional scantlings. This is not just my opinion, it's my experience after restoring several hulls that had been epoxied within the previous 10 years.

My solution is taken directly from the many shipwrights who were kind enough to teach me the traditional methods of wooden boat building in the shipyards of Newport and Bristol, Rhode Island; Norfolk, Virginia; Ft. Lauderdale, Florida; and Nassau, Bahamas. All wood surfaces must be sealed; and all joints must be bedded to exclude moisture. All bedding compounds and sealers must be flexible and, if possible, tenaciously attached. The one product that fills the bill for sealer is Smith's Clear Penetrating Epoxy Sealer, or CPES. This is an epoxy, but of an entirely different nature: it cannot be used as glue; it is a one-to-one mixture that brushes on like water and immediately soaks into the surface of the wood; and the more coats you apply, the deeper it goes. I seal all wood with it including the stain before varnish.

CPES was developed for saturating and stabilizing wood. When it sets, it remains flexible so that the surface encapsulation does not easily crack and admit moisture, while the hull works to provide a smooth ride. It also promotes the adhesion of paints and varnishes, and because it seals the pores of the wood, it makes the prospect of the future removal of 3M 5200 easier while still maintaining a viable bond. In addition, CPES slows the migration of moisture far more than oil-based paints, but less than a hard epoxy. And this is the most important point: spray and rain will not immediately absorb into the wood, yet, should excessive absorption occur, the moisture could eventually evaporate. CPES is a semi-permeable membrane of sealer, not a non-permeable membrane, such as a hard epoxy or even 3M 5200. When internal, hull interior surfaces are coated with non-permeable moisture barriers, excess moisture cannot evaporate from the wood, and that can incubate rot spore.

The exterior of the boat's bottom should be further sealed with a non-permeable barrier coat but the bilge and interior must be allowed to gas excess moisture through proper hull ventilation. The only way to keep water from wicking into a wood joint is to pay the joint with a compound that will remain in place to displace the water (dirt, rot spore, etc.) This compound must remain flexible and well-attached in order to take the jarring vibrations generated by these small speedboats. By far the best long-term bedding compound I have used is 3M 5200. This one-part polyurethane adhesive/sealant provides strong flexible bonds, yet, if repairs need to be made, is easily cut with a sharp knife. I have used this product for 20 years for frame and plank installations on hulls more than 100 feet in length, and have never seen a joint failure. I believe this and similar products immensely improve plank-on-frame construction by helping to create a flexible monocoque structure, distributing hull stress and loading rather than fracturing individual frame members. This type of adhesive bedding is also the only thing that will stay in place while allowing expansion and contraction to occur.

Bedding planks in 3M 5200 is not a new idea—it was the standard method of construction at the Trumpy yacht yard going back to the 1960s. The method met government specs in the construction of 80-foot fast-attack gunboats built by the yard in 1967 and 1968. As I write this, in 2002, a few of these 35-year-old hulls are currently for sale in *WoodenBoat*. A bare hull can be had for $48,800, or $198,000, complete with twin 3,100-horsepower engines and running gear. This should tell you something about the strength and longevity of double-planking mahogany with 3M 5200.

In short, this approach is what I call "enhanced traditional construction." All of the wood scantlings remain their original sizes. Fastener placement and sizes also remain original. The entire vessel is encapsulated, as with epoxy, but with flexible materials. As you may surmise, I am attempting to find a happy medium; something that allows traditional construction to coexist with current materials and provide established service with extended life, while the boat remains "re-restorable" by a future generation with better materials, tools, and knowledge.

Chapter 3

PREPARATION AND DISASSEMBLY

This information is presented in the general order necessary to prepare the standard-production antique or classic wooden boat to be flipped over for bottom plank and frame repair. It may also give you some idea of what you are getting into, and help you decide whether or not to have it restored professionally.

The first and extremely important step is to photograph everything on the boat, including details. Have those photos developed before you begin disassembly so that you know for certain that they came out. Of course, digital photography can be a big help and can speed up the process, but be sure to back up your digital files—the information contained within the photos will be critical later on. Three years—or even three months—after disassembly, details are hard to remember.

Hardware Disassembly

Remove all stainless hardware such as the cutwater, sheer and quarter rub rails, quarter guards and deck hatch hinges and trim, as well as hatches. Mark all for

All interior components must be carefully disassembled and marked on interior surfaces for location. Some boat interiors are still in very good shape, so great care must be taken.

placement and orientation—such as for "forward" and "up"—as necessary. I use a scratch awl on interior surfaces for this so the markings will still be there after the parts return from the metal shop. Keep all hardware fasteners in resealable freezer bags and mark the bags to indicate the hardware the fasteners are used for. You will probably not use these old fasteners again, but it is handy to know what size and amount to order on that magical day, just before the big boat show, when these items are reattached.

Remove all chrome hardware such as vents, lift rings, windshield frames, etc. Glass from the windshield should be carefully stored with at least paper towels between them. Use these for patterns and have them replaced. Bag and tag the fasteners as before and wrap the plated pieces in newspaper to prevent them from scratching each other in the box. It is a good idea to photograph all the chrome so you have a picture to send to the plating company as proof of which pieces were sent. Keep a copy and a list for yourself. It is best to have all chrome plating done at the same time to ensure the same color and hue.

Interior Disassembly

Remove all upholstered seatbacks and seats and mark hull numbers and placement on interior surfaces if necessary. A Magic Marker works well for this.Remove the floorboards and mark them as necessary. Remove the seat bottoms as a unit and mark them. Finally, remove the ceiling planks or panels and mark their backsides for replacement in the hull ("port 1 fwd", "starboard 3 aft", etc.).

Engine Removal

Unfasten all wiring to the engine after placing a piece of masking tape on the wire and marking where it goes. Put all the screws back in place.

SCHOOL OF HARD KNOCKS

Camera Overboard

I once totally restored a 68-foot ketch over a three-year period with a full-time crew of seven highly paid craftsmen and a budget of $440,000 in 1980 dollars. The very first thing I did was shoot six rolls of film of everything—inside and out and from every conceivable angle—with a brand new, very expensive 35mm program camera. I was certain I had covered every detail for re-assembly. I sent the film in and proceeded to put eight people and two rented trucks into high gear. We disassembled everything from the interior cabinetry to five diesel fuel tanks and their plumbing to sophisticated Satnav and Weatherfax electronics and their wiring harnesses, and moved it into two rented warehouses so we could get busy with broken frames and planks caused by an untimely grounding.

That's right—the shutter stuck halfway, on every shot, on every roll. That particular brand new, very expensive camera body went overboard in front of the entire crew as a lesson to them and to myself.

Close-up photos should be taken before engine removal to show linkages and connections. Photos will not only help you but will guide others who will be helping during installation—especially if the rebuild ends up taking years longer than you had planned, making it difficult to remember details

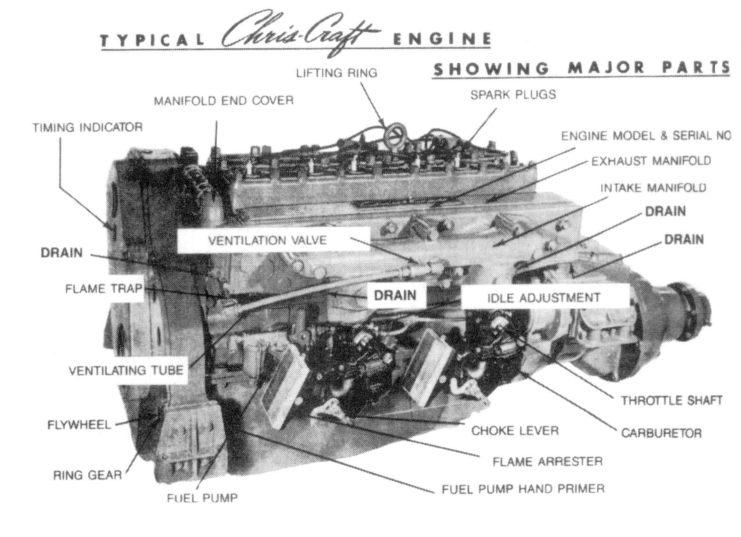

TYPICAL *Chris-Craft* ENGINE   SHOWING MAJOR PARTS

LIFTING RING

MANIFOLD END COVER   SPARK PLUGS

TIMING INDICATOR   ENGINE MODEL & SERIAL NO

EXHAUST MANIFOLD

INTAKE MANIFOLD

DRAIN

VENTILATION VALVE   **DRAIN**

DRAIN   DRAIN

DRAIN   IDLE ADJUSTMENT

FLAME TRAP

VENTILATING TUBE

THROTTLE SHAFT

FLYWHEEL   CHOKE LEVER   CARBURETOR

FLAME ARRESTER

RING GEAR

FUEL PUMP HAND PRIMER

FUEL PUMP

In addition to close-up shots, overall views show everything in relation to each other, as seen in this Chris-Craft factory illustration.

Shut off the fuel line valve and remove the fuel line—be prepared with a can and rag to clean any spill. Be careful not to kink the copper line unless you know that size line is still readily available.

Disconnect the oil line to the mechanical oil pressure gauge and plug the line to prevent leakage.

Disconnect the water temperature-sending unit and carefully coil the spring-protected line, being very careful not to kink it.

Disconnect the mechanical tachometer cable from its drive. Do not force these fittings. You may have

to spray them with penetrating oil and come back to them later.

Disconnect the raw-water intake hose.

Disconnect the throttle and choke linkages. Be sure to photograph these, as some are quite complicated with bell cranks and such. If you don't photograph them, at least take notes and make sketches.

Disconnect the exhaust pipe. Be very careful here; in fact, apply penetrating oil days in advance. Heat and water can really corrode things together. If your

A typical propeller removal tool. Gear pullers may work on some propellers but may not clear the blades on some, which could bend the thin edges.

A simple engine cradle built of 2 x 10s keeps the engine upright and makes moving it into storage or to the machine shop a snap.

Details such as proper orientation of linkage bell-cranks can be awfully difficult to figure out months or even years after disassembly.

View showing factory installations of the steering column and gear, throttle linkage, and wiring runs.

Photograph factory wiring to show overall layout. Label individual wires, as well as gauge terminals, with tape and a written code. Draw a rudimentary diagram if you intend to replace the wires.

This shot of a factory wire loom shows original installation with upholstery scraps and can aid in determining original upholstery colors.

exhaust elbow is cast iron, it can break with surprising ease. It may be best to unbolt the forward end of the elbow from the exhaust manifold. Put the bolts back where they belong. Exhaust elbows are much in demand and cost $300 to $400 each.

Disconnect the propeller from the shaft while it is still attached to the engine. With the engine in gear you should be able to unscrew the shaft nut. Do not beat on the end of the shaft to get the propeller off. Rent or borrow a wheel-puller—it's cheaper than a new shaft. Disconnect the propeller shaft coupler from the gear and bag and tag the bolts. Unscrew the large lag bolts at the motor mounts (8- or 12-point sockets work well on square bolt heads).

On most runabouts it may be necessary to use an engine equalizer to remove the engine, as the engine-gear assembly may be longer than the hatch opening. If you cannot obtain one of these, two

chain-falls will suffice. One is attached to the lifting ring at the center of the head; the other is usually attached to a line tied to the forward motor mounts. Do not use the convenient-looking water pipe at the forward end of the head: these are often made of cast aluminum and break off under the weight, tearing out deck beams and teeth.

As the engine is lifted, the forward end is raised so that the fore and aft aspect of the engine-gear assembly is small enough to fit through the hatch opening. In extreme cases it is wise to drain the engine oil first.

Bag and tag the motor mount wedges and any shims.

From a piece of 2 x 10 lumber, build a simple motor cradle as shown on page 33. If it is to remain in your shop, put wheels on it or it will always be in the way. You may also have to notch a section to provide clearance for the carburetor.

Steering Wheel Column and Gear Disassembly

If the steering column and gear is not removed before flipping the hull over it will most likely leak oil onto the inner foredeck. As with all other systems, photograph and take notes before disassembling this unit.

First, disconnect the horn grounding wire from the horn. This wire comes out of the forward end of the steering gear in the forepeak of the boat. Where the horn wire comes out of the tube, you will find a small clamp attached to the throttle linkage that secures the tube. On some boats there are two such clamps: one for the throttle, one for the choke. When these clamps are removed the throttle and choke levers can be pulled straight out of the center of the steering wheel, exposing a nut that holds the wheel onto the column. In later models additional horn ring assemblies must be taken apart next. The shaft is generally tapered with a key and will probably need penetrating oil before you remove the wheel; sometimes a wheel-puller is necessary. Be careful not to break or chip the wheel.

Next, remove the rudder linkage from the side of the gear assembly by means of the very large nut. The toothed shaft is generally tapered and you may have to tap the swing arm with a hammer to release it. Replace the nut and washer.

The gear and column assembly is usually attached to the top of the bilge stringer with two 3/8-inch nuts. Remove these and replace them when you have removed the gear.

Some boats have a column bracket screwed to the back of the dashboard. If this is the case, remove this and replace the screws. On some other boats the column simply protrudes through a hole in the dash. In this case just lift the gear off of the two

Fuel tanks are generally strapped in place on a shelf or cradle. Most older fuel tanks have pinhole leaks and are much cheaper and easier to have made new than to clean and seal.

bolts coming out of the bilge stringer and slide the column forward out of the dash.

Fuel Tank Removal

Siphon or drain the gas out of the tank.

Disconnect the engine fuel line if it hasn't been done already.

Disconnect the tank breather line if it has one.

Loosen the large locknut on the filler tube just above the tank. Unscrew the filler tube from the tank, remove the locknut, and slide the tube up out of the deck and replace the locknut on the tube.

Disconnect the fuel gauge sending unit wires and tape and mark them.

Finally, unfasten the tank straps and push them to the side. Slide the tank out and remove it from the vessel.

Detail of rudder linkage and rudder stuffing box. Months or years later, photos take the guesswork out of reassembling the boat.

Gauge and Switch Removal

Remove any electrical wiring necessary making sure to tape and mark where the wires go. Replace any screws or nuts as the wires are removed.

Switches are disassembled by first removing the knob. Some have tiny setscrews while others simply unscrew, sometimes with a tiny locknut. After the knob is removed there will be a knurled or hex nut and washer that must be unscrewed and removed from the face of the dashboard. The switch is now pulled out the back of the dash, and the washers, nuts, and knobs are replaced on it. Tape and mark what they were used for and what hole they came from.

Gauges are generally held in place by means of one or more brass brackets held to the back of the case by small nuts and lock washers, which when removed, allow the gauge to slide out the face of the dashboard. In the case of the mechanical water temperature gauge, the spring-protected sensor line is not removable and must be carefully fed through the dash and loosely coiled to prevent kinks.

Cables for mechanical tachometers unscrew from the back of the gauge.

The oil line to the mechanical oil pressure gauge should be plugged to prevent leakage.

Running Gear Removal

After the propeller and engine are removed and the stuffing-box locknut and stuffing nut are loosened, the shaft with coupler should slide forward out of the shaft log, which is screwed to the top of the keel with panhead woodscrews. If this unit has been bedded with an adhesive, oak wedges and heat will release it.

Remove any retaining pin or bolt on the rudder linkage swing arm on the rudder shaft and loosen the rudder stuffing box locknut and stuffing nut. The rudder should just slide out the bottom of the boat. Prepare the rudder with some blocking so that it does not fall and get dented.

The rudder stuffing box is usually mounted with two or four through-bolts with the nuts inside the vessel. Remove these nuts and drive the bolts out

An unusually clear view of the installation of the rudder stuffing box.

with a suitably sized drift pin and bring the stuffing box into the vessel for removal. Do not attempt to drive this unit through the keel with hammer blows, as this will mushroom the soft bronze housing, making it harder to remove and possibly damage the keel. Small oak wedges should be evenly placed under the unit flange inside the boat to draw it up. If this or other through-hulls have been previously assembled with an adhesive bedding such as 3M 5200, carefully apply heat to remove it.

The propeller shaft strut is fastened by four to six through-bolts with nuts on the inside of the vessel. Remove the nuts, drive the bolts out, and again be prepared with exterior blocking to prevent the unit from falling.

The strut holds a rubber-lined propeller shaft bearing called a "cutlass bearing" which needs occasional replacement, generally by means of a hydraulic press. If you have had vibration in your drivetrain, a bad bearing was probably the cause. Check to see if the strut has been mounted with shims. This may indicate some previous alteration such as an engine change or possibly realignment due to a "hogged" hull (one that is sagged, twisted, or spread). If so, the shims will likely need to be reinstalled or the planing surface brought back into shape.

The bilge pump through-hull is usually mounted with a large nut threaded to the inside of the fitting. Once this nut is removed, the through-hull slides outboard of the hull. The bilge pump and automatic float switch are usually attached to the keel with small woodscrews. Disconnect, tape, and mark the wires.

As for the drain plug fitting, it is generally screwed to the outside of the bottom and removed outboard.

Hull Interior Cleaning

At this point, with the hull pretty much opened up, I degrease and pressure-wash the entire interior. If your boat is still on its trailer you can drive it to a car wash that allows engine cleaning.

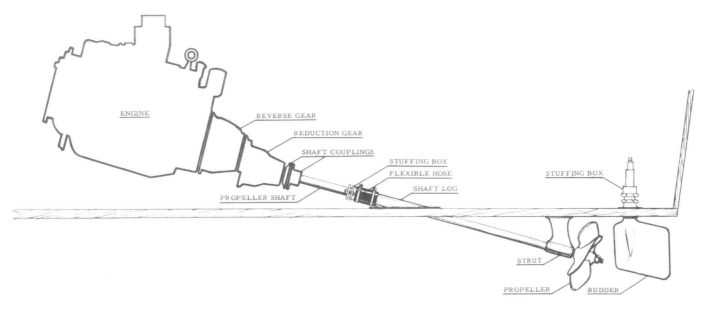

This illustration from a Chris-Craft owners' manual shows the alignment and location of the drivetrain and running gear components.

Courtesy of The Mariners' Museum, Newport News, Virginia

Temporary Internal Bracing

Before flipping a boat over you must install some bracing athwartships to keep the ropes or straps that will be used to flip it from deforming the hull. I use three or four 1 x 4s screwed to the exposed frames as closely to the sheer clamps as possible. This also helps the hull keep its shape during reframing. If you have an especially weak hull you can attach this bracing to frames at the keel to form rigid triangles. Even if you intend to replace the deck and topsides planks, it is wise to leave them on for now to hold the hull shape while the bottom is being rebuilt.

Flip-Over Rigging

This procedure must be approached carefully as the center of gravity shifts dangerously quickly. The old method that requires 12 strong friends, four old tires, two old mattresses, and two cases of Heineken should not even be considered.

The minimal approach requires two 1-ton chain-falls suspended high enough to allow the boat's widest beam measurement, multiplied by a factor of 1.2, to exist between the chain-falls' lower hooks and the floor. Remove the vessel from its trailer with ropes or straps and set it upon the floor. Use fore and aft lines, tied between the lift lines, to prevent the pointed shape of the bow from causing the forward lift line to slide forward.

Two substantial lines are attached at each lift station, crossed with one line wrapped completely around the hull, and met in a tied loop just below the sheer to be raised. This must be done at two points along the hull, each leading to its own chainfall. Lift only one side of the hull from these two points. The lowered side must be pulled under the raised side to effect turnover—as one sheer is raised, the center of mass shifts relative to the lifting points. Be very careful here—if you have allowed enough room, you can use some wheeled

When working with unrestored boats, never trust the lifting rings. Use wide nylon towing straps.

Before attempting to flip over a weak old hull, the installation of 1 x4 -inch cross-spalls help to distribute loads and avoid crushing the lowered side of the boat.

dollies to control this movement. If not, you should use some scrap carpet or similar material to keep your sheer from grinding along the cement. As the lowered sheer comes off the floor it must be pulled past the center of gravity and held until the boat is lowered enough to hold this orientation. As the raised sheer is lowered, the center of mass will continue to shift back and the lower sheer will have to be pulled or dollied out relative to the lifting points. The boat is now lifted straight up onto its blocking or frame rack.

The method I use for flipping a hull requires at least a 12-foot ceiling for boats of up to a 9-foot beam and 30-foot length. The forward chain-fall is hung from a car on a 10-foot I-beam allowing for length adjustment. The aft chain-fall is hung from substantial eyebolts mounted 12 and 18 feet from the forward end of the I-beam allowing any measurement from 1 to 18 feet between chain-falls.

A separate car runs along the I-beam carrying a cable wheel for the actual flipping maneuver. The chain-falls hold a bearing with a 3-inch inside diameter. These bearings are obtained, secondhand, from a machine shop where they no longer can hold true .0001-inch tolerance at 30,000 rpm, but which work just fine at any tolerance at 1 rpm. The bearings cost the shop owner about $900 each when new but they did their job and he regularly replaces them and throws them away anyway. So buy him lunch and offer him a ride in your boat when it's done. You will have to take them to your local welder and pay upwards of $15 each to have a piece of old pipe cut and welded with a lift ring and stops to hold the bearings. I would have a lower lift ring added as well.

The next item you will need is a standard 21-foot length of 3-inch black-iron plumbing pipe. Do not use old pipe, as it is often corroded in places you cannot see.

The lifting and rolling straps are sold as "tow straps"—yellow, woven, nylon things that are sold in every discount store. At this point your precious antique probably weighs about 900 pounds or so, but you want the widest strap you can afford to keep from crushing that tired old wood. I use 4-inch x 30-foot straps.

Detail of a 3-inch x 21-foot plumbing pipe running through large bearings supported by chain falls.

With straps around the plumbing pipe, the hull is lifted and one side is lowered with a power winch.

Adjustable sawhorses used to support and level the boat from the bilge stringers. These need to be assembled inside the overturned hull.

A frame rack used to straighten badly warped hulls. Height and half-breadth measurements can be easily taken from this.

The lifting bearings are positioned over the boat so that the straps can be run just inside the bearings and around a frame station with temporary cross-bracing, usually three or four frames in from either end. The pipe is set as low as possible and the straps simply tied tightly. If the pipe is set too low the sheer will not clear under the pipe and will have to be re-rigged. If the pipe is set too high before tying the straps the opposite sheer will not clear the floor. Plan on a good deal of stretch in the straps as the knots tighten. If something does not clear, set the boat down and re-rig it.

The last, and most important item in this rig is the flipping unit. I use an electric winch; I can push a button and not risk life and limb. The cable from the winch is attached to a sheer or chine. I lower one side and then re-rig the winch to lift that side up. With this rig I can flip a 24-foot boat by myself in 30 minutes.

Set-Up on Floor with Frame Rack or Blocking

If you are setting the hull on the floor you want to get it as low as possible to make your work easy to reach. The bilge stringers are a perfect place to support the bulk of the hull's weight. You can set the boat down upon sawhorses or on dollies if the hull has to be wheeled away from the lifting station.

Support blocking must be temporarily fastened at the stem, transom corners, deck beams, and at a couple of frame stations along the sheer. Along with the cross-bracing, the blocking is necessary to keep the hull from sagging or spreading while important frame members are removed and replaced.

Now is the time to make sure the hull is straight and plumb. While setting up the blocking you must use a spirit level or water level at the chines and sheer to make sure the hull is not wracked or hogged from some earlier episode of improper storage or snow load. A taught centerline strung above the keel and plumb bobs help keep things straight and give a point of reference from which to measure heights and half-breadths. (The Mariners' Museum in Newport News, Virginia, has original "lines" drawings available for many Chris-Crafts. If one of these drawings—essentially a set of measurements that defines the shape of a hull—are not available for your boat, you may ask the owner of a similar boat if you can take lines off of it when it is on its trailer.)

If you plan on restoring more than one boat, I suggest you build a frame rack like the one I use. It costs about $200 for materials and takes a couple days to build, but it makes all aspects of framing so much easier and quicker that mine paid for itself the first time I used it. It is mounted on low wheels so I can free up the lift station. When rolled into position it is a simple matter to level by jacking it up onto numbered blocks positioned on marked stations on the floor. This gives me a dead-level surface to measure from or attach to, and with upper and lower cable centerlines half-breadth measurements are a snap. The cross-framing is spaced every 24 inches on center, as are most classic boat frames, and makes straightening hulls very easy. In addition, the spalls and cross-spalls used to support the bilge stringers are simple to install. I have used this frame rack on hulls ranging from 12 to 24 feet in length and I am still finding new uses for it.

Removing the Bottom Planks

I always replace the weakened, oil-soaked, cracked, lifeless original bottom planking with new mahogany. If the boat owner wants to re-use the old planking, the labor involved is about twice the cost of simply using the old planks as patterns for new lumber. Also, the sealers and bedding compounds used today to construct bottoms intended to last 30 to 40 years will have questionable bonds if used with weakened, old lumber.

If you know that you are going to replace all of the bottom planks, the quickest method of exposing the screw placement is to run a large grinder down each row of screws using a very heavy knotted wire wheel. This machine will remove the putty and the wood between the screws, and clean the majority of the screw slots. This definitely destroys the planks for use as anything but patterns, but it is far more cost-effective than the alternative. With this method we expose the screws along the main frames, the chines, and the keel. After removing the screws in these areas only, the bottom is lifted off in two sections, one side to be pried apart later for use as patterns. The average 18-foot Chris-Craft bottom is removed in five to six hours. After the removal of the topside chine strakes and the lower transom plank, the entire bottom framework is exposed for repair.

Removing the Old Bottom for Re-Use

If you are going to re-use some or all of the existing bottom planking it is easiest to strip it all before the putty has been removed from the screw holes. Stripping will also expose the screw placement. I recommend using chemical paint stripper. For a horizontal surface like the bottom, the best stripper to use is the relatively inexpensive liquid as opposed to the semi-paste. Do not use a heat gun because it will damage the old wood, take far too long, and create a potential fire hazard with the thin, dried-out, oil-soaked mahogany. Also, do not attempt to grind all the old bottom paint—the paint dust is poisonous and the method is a lot of hard work.

When the chemical paint stripper is properly applied, stripping the bottom planks is quick and painless. First, cover the topsides with 6-millimeter plastic that's double-taped at the waterline with duct tape over easy-to-remove masking tape. Even if you plan to strip the topsides, do not do it now. You don't know how long the bottom framing and planking will take and you do not want the topsides to dry out and open seams. You also do not want sealers, paints, and glues getting into the grain of the wood. If you plan to replace all of the topside planks then you can forget the plastic.

If you are stripping the old waterline at this point, be sure to mark both top and bottom lines with a sharp chisel at various points around the hull, especially at stem and stern. Do this *only* if it is an original factory-scribed waterline. If there is some question about it's originality, then just record measurements for now and set a true waterline later with a laser level or water level.

A clutched screw gun allows you to set torque far more accurately than do cordless types. This makes the work easier and helps avoid stripping or breaking screws and splitting thin plank stock.

Next, lay a carpet of overlapping newspapers, at least three pages thick, from stem to stern and across the transom so that it lies a few inches under the edge of the sheer.

Prepare to complete the job in one session and have at least 4 gallons on hand for the average 20-footer—more if it looks like the bottom has many layers of old paint. Follow all safety instructions supplied with the material you are using. I like to pour the liquid straight from the can onto the keel in a controlled fashion and then spread it toward the chines with a cheap 6-inch bristle wallpaper paste brush. Do not be cheap here; remember, this stuff is going to do all the work for you, so apply as much as will stay put without running. Apply too little, and you will end up scraping. With this method it should take about 15 minutes per coat. As soon as you have completed one application, go back to where you began and apply the next coat. *Do not* scrape between applications of stripper—multiple layers help keep the stripper from evaporating.

After the third or fourth application you should notice large sections of bare wood as the stripper

The removal of screws in keel, chines, and main and auxiliary frames allows removal of entire bottomsides sections. The better of these two sections can be disassembled later for the new plank patterns.

literally falls off, taking the old finish with it. When it is all ready to come off to the bare wood, use a 6-inch putty knife to gather the gunk from the keel to the chine and into a bucket. Don't slop it onto the floor, as you will have to walk on it. When your work with putty knife is done and the bottom is still wet with stripper, use a wire brush to remove any remaining gunk from the grain of the wood, making sure to scrub *with* the grain.

Start at one end of the boat and roll the newspaper up and properly dispose of it.

Now, following the instructions on the stripper can, hose down the boat bottom to neutralize it and let it dry. Peel the plastic from the topsides and dispose of it. If you are not going to work on the topsides planking you may leave the plastic in place to help protect it. On the average 20-footer, this entire procedure should take about four hours from beginning to end.

The next step is to remove the putty from the screw holes. The quickest method involves making a bung-removal tool. Start with a regular slot screw bit and grind or file back the shoulders until you have a center point that is as deep as your screw slot. Experimentation will tell you when you have the setting right, shallow for slotted screws, deeper for Reed & Prince (Frearson) screws. Get the setting right so that it just exposes the screw head without cutting into the metal. After all, you have a few thousand screws to expose and you want the tool to last. If it doesn't, regrind it or make another. The second step is to expose the actual slot of the screw by cleaning it out with a sharp ice pick followed by a blast of air.

Mark the planks for position and orientation with plank number one at the keel. The planks are marked "S1F" (starboard one forward), "S1A

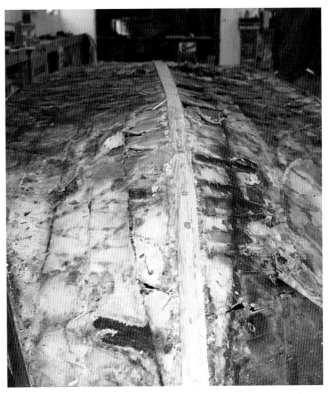

Remnants of canvas and bedding compound used as an early waterproofing gasket layer. After the mineral spirits vehicle in the bedding compound evaporated, the canvas held water that promoted rot.

(starboard one aft), "P3F" (port three forward), etc. I also include an arrow for up (in this case, inboard) and an arrow for forward.

Removing the screws comes next. By far the most important tool for restoring a wooden boat is an adjustable-clutch screw gun—not the kind for Sheetrock installation, but the kind with an adjustable torque setting and variable speed. This type of screw gun can cost anywhere from $150 to $200. But since you will have 5,000 or more screws that have to be replaced, you might as well make it easy on yourself and save twice that amount of money on labor. Use the lighter torque settings to remove the old screws—it gently jars them loose instead of stripping or breaking them, which requires drilling them out. Likewise, the correct torque setting on installation enables the screws to be properly seated without splitting the planks you have spent so many hours preparing. Believe me, this tool is a must.

Make sure you have the correct drive tips. Before 1941, planks were almost always fastened with slotted screws. After that time, most boats were assembled with Reed & Prince (Frearson) screws. Although these look very much like Phillips screws, their points and shoulder angles are different and the wrong tip will definitely strip them. Now that you have the correct screw gun, you can begin the removal of all those nasty old crystallized brass fasteners.

If you strip the head slot of a screw, just mark it with a piece of chalk so you can drill off all the stripped heads at the same time. Use a drill bit that's just slightly larger than the screw shaft—reverse-cut drill bits work best, as they most often reach a point where they stop drilling and the screw simply backs out.

If the head is not stripped but the screw just spins without coming out ignore it for now, it will come out with the plank. It is either broken or the threads

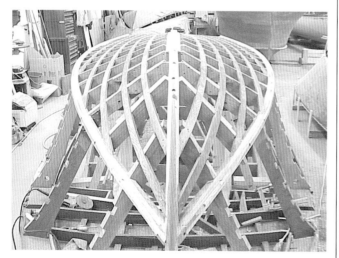

Century bottom construction showing fore and aft plank battens instead of inner bottom and canvas.

are stripped in the hole. Keep track of the percentage of broken bottom fasteners—this will tell you what to expect of the condition of the brass in the carriage bolts and topsides fasteners.

After drilling off any stripped screw heads you should be able to peel off the planks using a flat Wonder Bar-type pry bar and wood wedges. Remove the broken screw shanks from the frames later with Vise-Grip pliers and save all old planks for now, at least for patterns and through-hull placement. After the planks have been removed and all broken fasteners removed from them, clean their inside surfaces with a grinder and a 40-grit disc. Clean the edges with a scraper, being careful not to scrape away too much wood. You may now decide whether these planks can be salvaged or used as patterns.

You will not be reusing those old brass fasteners, but collect them in a bucket, anyway. Around here it is a tradition to sell them for scrap and buy lobsters and beer for the crew.

Most boats, except for a Century, have an inner planking of about 1/8 to 3/16 x 6-inch mahogany laid diagonally and nailed in place. Between this diagonal layer and the fore and aft planking you will find the remnants of a gasket layer of canvas, originally soaked with boatyard bedding compound. Tear out this inner layer of wood and properly dispose of it. This wood is generally oil soaked and extremely flammable.

If your boat *is* a Century, you will find only fore and aft plank battens laid into the frames. If you plan to do any frame repairs these battens must come out and be degreased and resealed if they are sturdy enough to be reused. If they are shot, it is a simple matter to cut new 1/2 x 1-1/2-inch battens and save yourself a good deal of work while providing new wood to which to screw your planks.

Remove the topside chine strakes—which is the first line of planks in the sides of the hull above the chine—from stem to stern so you can get at the real problem area of frame knees. Be very careful if you intend to use these planks again, as the varnished bungs are more likely to tear chips from the surrounding wood. Under the bottom painted areas of these planks you can use putty to fill these chips but in varnished areas you will only want clean bung lines. You can always tape off and strip just these areas.

Remove the lower transom plank, also being careful of varnished surfaces.

Even though you already degreased the heck out of the bilge, you will probably find a layer of black gunk on the frames. Scrape this stuff off and remove any nails or broken screws. The broken screws in the frames can be turned out with Vise-Grips, or by using a drill with a keyless chuck. Tighten down on the screw shank, reverse the drill to unscrew, grab the keyless chuck for a second to drop the screw, switch to forward and go down on the next one. This method is much faster than the pliers and will even work if the screw head is still in place.

Clean and degrease all framework thoroughly.

Chapter 4

INSPECT AND STRAIGHTEN HULL FRAMEWORK

Now that your boat is turned over and the bottom planks and topsides chine strake planks removed, all of the bottom framing is exposed for inspection and repair.

The first consideration is to determine whether the hull is straight, plumb, and level. Hulls that have sagged, twisted, or spread are said to be "hogged." Having repaired more than 100 wooden hulls, I can say that I have never seen one that did not need to be pulled or pushed into shape somewhere. This is not surprising given that these wooden boats have outlived their intended lives by many decades, most without minimal care. Even proper blocking will distort a hull if it sits there for decades.

I have heard many times from people who have found a boat they want restored and proclaim proudly that the boat has been "in storage" for 20 years, as if this has somehow preserved it. On the contrary, phrases like "long-term storage" ring alarm bells. All boat hulls are designed to displace water in order to support their weight. This means that

Extreme hogging from prolonged or improper storing not only misshapes the keel but also causes planking to buckle. *Courtesy of* Classic Boating Magazine

the hull was built to be supported at all points of its bottom surface. Out of the water, hulls are inevitably supported at only a few points.

Temporary winter blocking, as directed by the factory owner's manuals, generally puts all the weight on three points of the bottom. If left too long in this position, the weight of the transom, fuel tank, and running gear typically causes the stern to drop, creating a longitudinal *concavity* in the supposedly straight planing surface. When run in this condition, the bow is forced down and can cause plowing and dangerous attitudes when cutting across waves or wakes.

If the support blocking is set farther aft to support the transom and left this way for years, the weight of the engine causes the center of the bottom to drop creating a longitudinal *convexity* in the supposedly straight planing surface. When run in this condition, especially at higher speeds, the boat keeps trying to climb up on it's curved planing surface only to reach a point where the weight of the vessel drops the bow back down, over and over

A bottom hogged 1 inch in from the intended planing surface, as indicated by the transom.

Check for chine spreads at ends of auxiliary frames. Topsides frames have to be brought in until this gap is closed.

again. This performance is usually referred to as "porpoising" or "hobby-horsing," which is not only maddening, but leaves you half out of control and unable to see over the bow. Many have tried to correct this condition by adding wedges or shingles to the after-edge of the planing surface at the transom to force the bow down. This method works to some extent but is analogous to using water brakes and really only creates the concave planing surface previously mentioned.

If your boat has an original bottom and frames and is more than 20 years old, even a single season of improper storage could cause these conditions to appear. These are just a couple of reasons why it is so very important to properly address the framework of the hull when restoring a boat. With the boat upside down and the bottom planks removed, frame repair is about as easy as assembling Lincoln Logs with screws. These boats are merely large models; think of them as such.

Straightening the Framework

If you do not have a frame rack, set the boat on two or more sawhorses with the weight of the hull on the bilge stringers and the deck just inches above the floor. Temporary blocking should be placed at intervals along the sheer line and at the stem to keep the hull from hogging out of shape.

The main bottom frames are attached to topsides frames. I number these with a marker starting from the first frame aft of the stem and continuing back to the transom frame. The frame ties are also so marked, and port and starboard indicated (be careful here, your hull is upside down). If you write your numbers on a forward face of a frame, mark that also. An example would be frame "3pF" (third port forward) or "4sA" (fourth starboard aft). With this method you should easily find the correct place and orientation for any piece you have removed from the hull.

The auxiliary bottom frames are attached from the keel to chine only and do not have a corresponding

In this case, the vertical legs are screwed through the topsides planks into the sheer clamps in the area that the rub rail will cover.

The misalignment of this hole, drilled after assembly, shows the obvious spreading movement of the frame and frame tie.

topsides frame. I number these in reference to the main frames. The auxiliary frames following the above examples would be "3.5pF" and "4.5sA". This may look silly, but I know exactly what it is and where it goes.

Intermediate frames are the small battens that run athwartships and are not attached to the keel or chines, except in some Gar Woods, where they are boxed into the keel and chines. Centurys do not have these intermediate frames but use fore and aft plank battens as in the topsides.

Note the gap usually found between the auxiliary frame and the chine. These were assembled tightly, and any gap indicates the amount of spread in the bottom.

Inspect also the carriage-bolt hole from the bottom of the bottom frame to the bilge stringer. Although this hole should be in the bottom frame or the frame tie, sometimes the factories were less than careful and the carriage bolt ended up between the bottom frame and the frame tie. If this bolt hole is skewed out of round, it indicates further spread of the frames.

Clean the gunk out of any gaps between the chines and the chine landings. Using long bar clamps attached to the bilge stringers, pull the topsides frames back into line until the chine is tight against the auxiliary frames. This may involve wedging the keel and frames upward to allow the frame ends to move inboard. Adjust any blocking at the floor and bilge stringer supports. These frame components must be pulled or pushed back into their original positions and temporarily clamped or fastened in place before leveling or straightening.

A 6-foot spirit level is required to level the framework from side to side. This job will require two people, one on either side. There are many spots where the keel or bilge stringers will be in the way so you will have to mill identically sized blocks of wood to set upon the chines to provide clearance to set the level on. Level across the hull at each frame station and adjust your supports and blocking accordingly. This process will help to take any twist out of the hull shape.

With chine landings clean and chines brought back into original placement with bar clamps, the hull can be water-leveled at each frame station and support blocking can be attached to sheer.

An 8-foot I-beam and 6-foot levels should be used to determine a flat planing surface. Do not duplicate bent frames.

Start leveling the hull from frame stations closest to the sawhorse supports. Choose a similar point on each side of the boat at the chine landing and carefully hold your end of the level in place. No matter what point you decide is easiest to read, make sure you are both reading the same point. When one side shows out of level, place spacers under the low end and clearly mark how far up or down that side of the boat must go. Use wedges between the sawhorses and the bilge stringers and level again. Do this at all sawhorses first and continue at all frame stations, blocking between the deck at the sheer line

Some boats can be terribly warped out of shape. It is best to determine this while the boat is still upright and easy to see. Continue this multi-level procedure before attempting any frame work.

This interior view of a hull shows spalls, cross-spalls, and bracing used to force a hull into shape and hold it there during frame replacement.

With cross-spalls attached to hold the frame in position and the hull straight, level, and sturdily supported, the bar clamps, keel, and chines can be removed.

Carefully inspect the chines for cracks where they are bolted to the frame knee. When you have removed the chines, pick them up from either end. If they break under their own weight, replace them.

and the floor. This procedure should remove any twist in the hull, but further fore and aft battening must be applied to determine if individual frames still have to go up or down evenly at both sides to remove any hogging.

Sight down the keel and chines from both ends of the boat. Look for "sweet lines," or obvious unfairness. Lay a straightedge parallel with the keel along the bottom frames in the planing surface. The size of this flat planing surface varies with the design and length of your model of boat. You must research this to get it right. Chris Smith (grandson of the founder) says that Chris-Crafts were straight for at least 8 feet at the keel, or approximately half the length of the hull. The "V" shape of the actual planing surface means the flat would be shorter at the chines. Forward of the planing surface, the hull surface should gently and uniformly curve up to the stem. A number of limber battens laid across the forward frames will help you to see these curves.

As previously mentioned, the Mariners' Museum in Newport News, Virginia, has "lines" drawings for many Chris-Crafts and some other boats. Most of these drawings include a "table of offsets," a set of measurements for any point in the outside shape of your hull. These measurements indicate a point at the outside of the planking so you must deduct the plank thickness from them to locate the frame's dimensions. With a set of these measurements you can blueprint your hull: that is, put it back in exactly the shape the factory intended. If lines cannot be obtained, you will have to do the best you can with straight edges, battens, and as much knowledge as you can obtain from books or trade journals. You might even hire a respected professional in your area to survey the shape of your hull. Re-framing and re-planking a warped or skewed hull will only leave you with a warped or skewed boat that is worth about as much as a "gray boat" to a serious buyer.

Once you have gotten your boat back into shape and made sure everything is plumb and level, apply temporary athwartships bracing to connect opposing topside frames just below the frame knee. I use 1 x 4 pine stock with three screws in each end. This should be done at every frame station to help hold the hull's shape during disassembly. This bracing may also be used to push or pull a particular area into shape. The hull should now be sturdy enough to remove the keel and chines. Remember to take notes and many photos as you proceed.

Frame Disassembly

Remove the putty or bungs covering the keel and chine fasteners, then remove the chine fasteners, starting at the stem. The chines are generally fastened at the stem, the first one or two frame stations, and the auxiliary frame ends with woodscrews. They are also usually quite large, #12 x 2-1/2 or so. On most hulls the chines are also through-bolted to the frame knees with #20 x 1/4-inch carriage bolts (20 threads per inch and 1/4 inch diameter). Larger vessels have larger bolts. A 7/16-inch or 1/2-inch "deep socket" may be necessary here because of the bolt length and because some of the nuts may be recessed into the wood. Old carriage bolts will quite often spin the head in removal attempts. I have altered a

SCHOOL OF HARD KNOCKS

Close Call with Oil-Soaked Chris-Craft

I once restored a Chris-Craft that was seriously oil-soaked. All bottom frames, keel, chines, and even bilge stringers were replaced, leaving only the topsides frames and deck beams to carry on the tradition. These remaining topsides frames were degreased three times with strong stuff and the wood heavily sealed with a penetrating sealer. But the new plank fasteners, 2-inch screws, opened up paths to the centers of the frames and pumped oil to the interior and surface of the new planks. Luckily, the problem was noticed before the hull was varnished.

Until such an oil-soaked frame is replaced or runs out of oil—expect the new planking that's attached to it to always have trouble holding paint or varnish. Imagine, when this boat was down to its frame, an extra 30 minutes of work and four dollars' worth of wood could have prevented the substantial amount of work necessary to remove and replace the topsides frames and new planking. Now, imagine if this problem was not noticed until ten expensive coats of varnish had been applied.

Oil-soaked keels can be terribly weak.

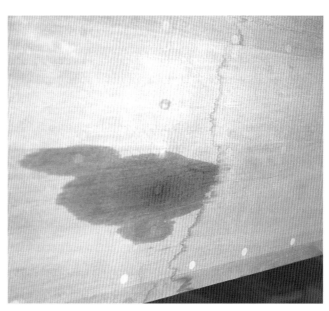

Oil-soaked frames can cause problems many years later. Doing it right the first time is far cheaper in the long run.

Probe for rot, especially at the frame end grains at the chine landings. Attempt to slide the ice pick in between the frame pieces as well.

Chines are very often cracked at the frame landing along the line of the carriage-bolt hole.

A typical stem/gripe joint with stem knee.

A typical stem/gripe joint.

mid-sized regular screwdriver by filing vertical grooves in the blade, leaving teeth to grip the head of the carriage bolt as I turn the nut. I tap the screwdriver in alongside the bolt head with a hammer, making sure to place the blade across the grain to avoid splitting the wood. Prying the screwdriver against the head of the bolt is usually enough to hold it as I turn the nut with the socket. If it cannot be held, saw it off—it's time to replace this bolt anyway.

Using a 3/16-inch drift pin and hammer, carefully back the carriage bolt out of the hole. An ice pick may be needed to direct the bolt head out and keep it from splintering the wood. Note the sizes of all the carriage bolts because no matter how good they look, they are brass and are probably dezincified, so replace them.

Carefully remove, degrease and inspect the chines, especially at the ends and frame landings where dirt and moisture were held. Watch for cross-grain cracks indicating weak wood due to brown rot.

If small areas at frame landings are rotten or crushed less than 1/4-inch in depth and the wood underneath is sound and has healthy color, it is acceptable to route the area and apply a graving piece. After a thorough cleaning and repairs are made, re-used chines should be well-sealed with Smith's CPES or a similar product.

If the damage affects more than 30 percent of the thickness of the piece, it should be replaced. A real-life test of the strength of the original chines is as simple as holding the chine aloft, by either end, and shaking it vigorously. If it falls apart under its own weight, it's long past the time to replace it. Weak old chines in new construction will soon break, so replace it now while it's cheap and easy.

If your chines need replacement (and most do), set them aside for reference until the new chines are in; you will need to take angles and measurements from these.

The keel and gripe should be removed in the same manner as the chines. In the area of the propeller shaft log and engine oil pan, where the frames are very shallow as they cross the keel, there are likely to be woodscrews in place of a keel bolt. Sometimes these come up from the frames into the keel. The keel and gripe should now be degreased, inspected, repaired, and sealed. Again, if your keel needs replacement, set it aside because it can be used as a pattern for the placement of the strut, shaft log, and rudder log.

Remove all broken fasteners from keel and chine landings and clean and degrease everything.

Surveying Frame Condition

Use a fine, sharp ice pick (a 6-inch blade no more than 1/8 inch in diameter) and scraping tools to inspect the framework. Probe the end-grains of the frame members and all joint lines with the ice pick. The surface of the joint may look sound; however, its interior was most likely unsealed, unbedded, and without equal in its ability to wick and hold moisture. Wood joints are almost always partially end-grain, where the rot spores can quickly gain a foothold and cause great damage by following the vessel structures of the wood. Mark repair areas with brightly colored chalk.

Rot is a term that describes wood that has been partially consumed by wood fungi, which are naturally abundant agents that exist as airborne spores.

Watch for frames that are split from the expansion and contraction of the bottom planks.

This 22-foot utility was totally restored in the early 1990s. It was given a new engine, new leather, new chrome…the works. It was also encapsulated with what was then called a "bulletproof" bottom. Three layers of 1/4-inch plywood and two layers of fiberglass (to the waterline) were epoxied to a new keel and new bottom frames—as well as to rotten chines and rotten topsides frames. Luckily, it was at the dock when it sank two years later.

Carefully inspect bilge stringers with a sounding hammer and ice pick.

OTHER POTENTIAL HULL AND FRAMEWORK PROBLEMS

STEM
- Rot at stem-head or chine attachment
- Broken on grain at joint with gripe
- Splitting in plank rabbet due to over-fastening

GRIPE
- Excessive wear from grounding. If no other condition exists, a graving piece or "dutchman" can be applied here provided it's outboard of the plank rabbet or inboard of the bearding line Cut a new plank rabbet
- Broken on grain at joint with stem
- Deterioration due to stress cracks or over-fastening

STEM KNEE
- Mounted inboard, attaches the stem to the gripe (or stem to keel in the absence of a gripe)

KEEL
- Cracks, breaks, or bowing due to improper shoring in storage
- Longitudinal cracks at plank rabbets
- Split or crushed ends at fasteners
- General weakness due to oil saturation
- Cracks or crushed wood at the rudder stuffing box and lower transom bow

CHINES
- Cracks or breaks, usually amidships at the leading edge of the planing surface, at frame landings
- Rot or crushed wood at frame landings
- Weakness due to age
- General weakness due to over-fastening at plank rabbets or frames

FRAMES
- Split on sided surface caused by plank fasteners and years of expansion and contraction
- Split on molded surface caused by hull wracking
- Weakness due to oil saturation
- Rot at frame ends, especially where topsides and bottomsides frames are attached to frame knees and frame ties

BILGE STRINGERS
- Rot or excessive cracks at frame fasteners
- Bowed or broken due to improper shoring in storage

LIFT RING SUPPORTS
- Any frame member where these are attached should be carefully checked and probably replaced with white oak

TRANSOM
- Frame and fastener problems, especially at the after sections of the hull where torque forces are concentrated

Brown rot consumes mostly the cellulose that comprises the cell walls of the wood, and is evidenced by a brown powdery residue and cross-grain checking similar to that in fire-charred wood.

White rot, on the other hand, eats the cellulose and the *lignin* that binds the cells together, leaving a whitish residue and obvious softening of the wood.

For the ever-present rot spores to find a niche and grow, consuming and weakening the wood, four factors are necessary:

1. The food source, cellulose and lignin;
2. The correct temperature range, between 40 and 100 degrees Fahrenheit;
3. Adequate oxygen content, at least 20 percent air volume (waterlogged wood will not rot); and
4. Moisture content of 30 percent or more ("dry rot" is a misnomer).

Stopping any one of the above four conditions will halt the growth but will not kill all of the fungi,

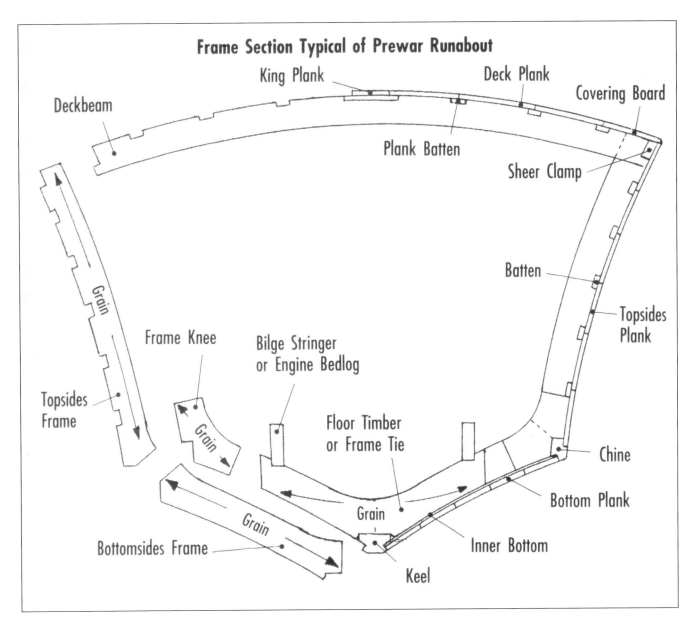

Frame Section Typical of Prewar Runabout

A cross-section of typical framing shows grain orientation to maintain the strength of each piece.

which simply become dormant until the conditions are once again right. The offending piece of wood should be removed from the boat and be replaced with a properly sealed new piece of wood.

The short grain of the stem/gripe joint almost always fails. Chines are very often broken just under the driver's seat at the leading edge of the planing surface, where pounding occurs. The frames in this area are also more likely to flex athwartships and loosen the fasteners and futtock joints. In addition,

lower transom bows almost always should be replaced because, due to the rotational forces of the propeller and rudder, all the surfaces that are attached to this piece get constantly wracked from the vibrations. These and all the rest of the wood-to-wood joints in the hull are the perfect place for moisture to accumulate and not dry out as well as the exposed surfaces of the wood.

Another condition to watch for is oil-soaked wood. While oil saturation is toxic to aerobic fauna

Since the owner of this 1932 boat intended to replace the original 85-horsepower flathead six with a big-block engine producing four times the horsepower, this hull was rebuilt with doubled bilge stringers.

Typical transom framework.

and does not host rot spore, it does leave the wood equally weakened. The oil breaks down the cellulose in the cell walls or melts the lignin that binds the wood cells together. Whatever the reason, the oil-soaked wood is no longer strong enough to do the job, and should be replaced. In oil-soaked wood, even properly drilled holes do not hold fasteners. Glues, sealers, and bedding compounds are not likely to stick very long to this kind of surface. Future failure is guaranteed.

Other Potential Hull and Framework Problems

Frame ends are by far the most likely places in wooden boats to find rot. I know of no manufacturer of small, mass-produced wooden speedboats that covered these adjoining surfaces with either putties or paints prior to World War II. The precut frame futtocks were removed from the mill delivery cart and assembled on the form, but apparently not treated with bilge paint until planked. According to Chris

Smith, his father-in-law, who also worked at Chris-Craft, framed four 19-footers every day by himself. These did not include coatings of any kind. If you unscrew a frame knee you will most likely find bare wood on the inside surfaces except where thinned bilge paint has wicked itself in by capillary action. It is exactly this capillary action that wicks and holds water into these joints.

The best method of preventing rot in this kind of wood construction is to seal all surfaces, especially the end grains, and pay bedding compound on any surfaces that meet in order to displace moisture.

As for bilge stringers, it is rare to have to replace these large pieces as they are generally suspended high enough in the bilge to stay dry. Most likely, all you will have to do is install a few dutchman repairs at the top edges where moisture and dirt were trapped under the floorboards. If there was a great deal of leaves or trash in the hull over a long period of time it is possible they could have rot at the bottom edges where they meet the frames. Probe these areas well with the ice pick or a sounding hammer. If there is rot, either cut out the affected area and fit a repair piece with adequate through-bolts or replace the entire piece. Bilge stringers were usually clear, vertical-grained fir. If you do find a knot, cut it out and fit a graving piece. Knots are a perfect place for rot to start.

If you intend to re-power your boat with two to four times the original horsepower, as so often is the case these days, you should consider replacing these pieces with larger stock or sistering the existing ones. Your engine is attached to these stringers, or "engine bed logs," and propels them across the lake—the rest of the hull is just hanging on to them. If you do replace the bilge stringers, wait until the keel, chines, and bottom frames are all replaced or refastened, and are properly braced and supported by temporary framing.

Finally, transom framing consists of topsides frames, often called "cheeks," a "transom post" from keel to deck, and upper and lower "transom bows" with vertical "stakes" between them. Look for frame and fastener problems, especially at the after sections of the hull. The rudder swings the transom from here and the rest of the hull follows from in front, causing a rotational torque on the after-quarters of the hull, which is generally why you will see the varnish crack at the topside seams here first. Because of this torquing, transom frame fasteners are likely to be loose or broken—and loose joints hold moisture. The transom cheeks are very often cracked or broken along a grain line 6 inches or so above the chine. Watch for this.

The lower transom bow is very often in bad shape because of the number of plank fasteners it has held from two directions: two rows of screws from the transom plank and two rows of screws up from the bottom planks. If you dislike running the bilge pump, make sure this piece is sound. If your boat is a Century, you are likely to find this lower transom bow laminated of three pieces of oak that have since come apart. I always replace these with solid, steam-bent white oak. The stakes are end-fastened and if otherwise sound, probably only need to be re-drilled and refastened with a larger screw.

The upper transom bow should be dealt with after the hull is once again upright, as it is fastened from above. I also prefer to straighten all deck beams at the same time with fairing battens. Similarly, cheeks, post, and stakes are fastened from above (through the top of the upper transom bow). If they must be replaced, I toenail them (with a screw) to the upper transom bow at this time in order to keep them from moving during the return flipping.

Chapter 5

MATERIALS FOR REBUILDING

While I favor certain materials over others for rebuilding a wooden boat based on my experience and research, you will ultimately need to make your own choices. Do as much research as possible on whatever materials you might use, with an emphasis on how they are properly used. All too often I see the correct materials used incorrectly.

Wood

The best way to protect your investment is to use the best materials you can obtain, especially with the wood. Since you are rebuilding a wooden boat, I suggest you buy or borrow every book you can find on wood. Get to know how wood expands and contracts relative to its grain direction so you will know what to expect before you install it. If you own a wooden boat you must obtain the book

Understanding Wood (The Taunton Press) by R. Bruce Hoadley. In it, the author not only explains wood's properties, such as stability and rot resistance, but also explains, in depth, how to work with it.

Traditional plank-on-frame construction has for thousands of years depended mainly on white oak *(Quercus alba)* for all frame construction. This is due to compression and shear and tensile strengths, combined with high rot resistance and unsurpassed fastener-holding capabilities. Do not confuse *Quercus alba* with red or black oaks, or even with some of the lesser white oaks, which do not have anywhere near the same degree of rot resistance. Your local lumberyard probably does not make these distinctions, so you will have to do some research to find the real thing. You may even have to purchase and ship your lumber from a marine lumber supplier.

One method of testing wood is to cut a small sample across the end grain to expose the vessel structure. Very carefully slice this surface clean with a razor blade until the vessels can be clearly seen with a 10-power hand lens. If the large pores appear dark, it indicates a type of red oak that will transport water too well for use in boat construction. If the large pores appear white, they are likely filled with bubble-like structures called *tyloses* that make it very difficult to pass liquids and contribute significantly to rot resistance. For more specific information on different wood types, read *Identifying Wood* (The Taunton Press), another book by Hoadley. Chris-Craft seems to be the only notable

ROT-RESISTANCE OF WOODS

Rot-Resistance of Woods Commonly Used in Classic-Boat Frame Construction

VERY RESISTANT
White oak

MODERATELY RESISTANT
Honduras (American) mahogany
African mahogany
Douglas fir

SLIGHTLY OR NON-RESISTANT
Red oak
Philippine mahoganies
Ash

SCHOOL OF HARD KNOCKS

The Real Skinny on Mahoganies

The true mahoganies are of the family Meliaceae and include the American mahoganies (*Swietenia sp.*), the African mahoganies (*Khaya sp.*), and even the misnamed Spanish cedar (*Cedrela odorata*), which was apparently, very early on, given the erroneous taxonomic name because of its cedar-like aroma. It has since been found to be of the *Meliaceae* genus, not of *Cedrela*.

The so-called "Philippine mahoganies" (*Shorea, Parashorea,* and *Pentacme spp.*) are not related at all to the Meliaceae family and, as such, are not true mahoganies.

In my research in the Chris-Craft archives at the Mariners' Museum I found wood orders dating back to 1927 for millions of board feet of lumber placed with the Indiana Quartered Oak Company. The only "mahoganies" ordered were "good dark" or "fine wormy dark" Philippine "mahogany." See, isn't it fun to learn that the only mahogany boats built by Chris-Craft were the Spanish cedar-planked hulls built just after World War II?

exception to the use of white oak in frame construction. While they usually used white oak for stems and lower transom bows, only on some early models was it used for gripes, keels, chines, and transom framing. The bottoms, topsides, and deck frames were almost always Philippine mahoganies, as was the plank stock. If replacing Chris-Craft frames with mahogany, I recommend Honduras, (also known as American) mahogany over Philippine for reasons of better fastener holding capabilities and rot resistance.

Lumber Basics

Once you have completed a survey of your bottom framing and marked all those pieces you intend to replace, it is time to add up the materials you will need to order to replace them. Lumber is sold in "board feet," a unit of measurement equal to one square foot that is 1 inch thick, or 144 cubic inches. One board foot, therefore, can be 12 x 12 x 1 inches, 6 x 24 x 1 inches, 6 x 12 x 2 inches—just as long as it's 144 cubic inches. To determine board feet in a piece of stock, multiply its length (in inches) times its width (in inches) times its thickness (in inches) and divide the result by 144 (the number of cubic inches in one board foot). For example, for a board 10 feet long, 8 inches wide, and 1 inch thick:

First, transfer length to inches:
10 x 12 = 120
Next, multiply length by width and thickness to arrive at cubic inches:
120 x 8 x1 = 960
Finally, divide by 144 to determine board feet:
960 ÷ 144 = 6.67 board feet

Multiply this amount by the figure the lumberyard will quote, per board foot, and you will know how much your lumber will cost. The lumber is usually sold "rough sawn" and will need to be dressed to the finished thickness your boat requires with a surface planer (called "surfacing"). If you do not own such a tool (costing from $400 to thousands), a good lumberyard can usually provide this service at an hourly rate or at a specified price per board foot. Lumberyards measure thickness in quarters of an inch:

- 1 inch thick is called 4/4, read as "four-quarter";
- 1-1/2 inch thick is called 6/4, read as "six-quarter"; and
- 4 inches thick is called 16/4, read as "sixteen-quarter."

Another service your lumberyard should be able to provide is "re-sawing," that is sawing the board on edge lengthwise to change the thickness. For example, to obtain 1/2-inch-thick plank stock, I usually buy 6/4 mahogany and have it re-sawn and surfaced to two pieces 1/2 inch thick. This is cheaper than buying 4/4 (the smallest size usually available) and throwing away half of what you paid for in surfacing it to 1/2 inch. This also produces "book-matched" planks, which will allow you to mirror the grain of the deck and hull planks as they are placed outboard from the king plank.

When ordering lumber I always figure what I need and add at least 30 percent to the order. This allows me enough room to avoid knots or cracks or other weak or undesirable areas in the lumber. One weakness you must always watch for is "wind breaks" or "compression failure," evidenced by very fine lines of fracture across the grain of the wood and can be seen only after the wood has been surfaced. These fractures were caused when the bole of the tree was overstressed in bending either by wind or snow load or even in felling the tree. These areas are extremely weak, sizable planks can be broken over your knee.

During the drying process, either kiln or air drying, the lumber must give up a great deal of moisture, and in so doing shrinks in size, causing considerable stresses in the structure of the wood. The planks are stacked and weighted during this process to keep them straight and flat or they would warp and crack and check and bow all over the place. These stresses usually cause small fractures and weaknesses in the first 6 inches of either end of the planks. So, do not use these plank ends; throw them away and sigh, or make bookends or something of them. Check your lumber to make sure these cracks do not extend farther. Remember when you are ordering

your lumber that this amount cannot be used and order lengths accordingly.

The sistered-frame technique was developed hundreds of years ago in order to keep the grain direction of each futtock as straight as possible for the strength of the piece. Note the shape of the piece you are replacing and pattern your pieces accordingly. If you have a curved frame, try to find appropriately curved grain in your frame stock. Ideally, the grain of any piece should not be out of line more than five degrees. Short lengths of grain create weak spots in the frame. Likewise, do not include any knots.

Also, once you receive your lumber to be used for planking, you'll want to select the best of it for use above the waterline. For example, when you receive your lumber, first select the most beautiful pairs of plank stock to complete the deck, transom and ceiling planks. This is 90 percent of the wood you will see at a boat show with the boat in the water. Mark this wood and set it aside for later. The next group of planks to be selected for color and grain, etc., will be for the topsides. The least beautiful and poorly matched planking can be used for the bottom, under paint.

Fasteners

As far as I have seen, most antique and classic wooden boats were assembled with brass fasteners, at least until the mid-1960s. There are some notable exceptions to this, but they are worse. I have, for example, restored a few late-1920s Chris-Crafts that had iron fasteners in the decks. In such cases, the planks generally have to be cored with a hole-saw to remove them. In many 1930s and 1940s Chris-Crafts, the auxiliary frames were attached to the bilge stringers with #16 x 5-inch steel screws, and the lower transom bow attached to the sternpost with a steel lag bolt. These are generally badly corroded and must all be removed. Also, the iron-sick wood around them should be cored out and fitted with a graving piece, or the entire piece should be replaced.

You may have noted during disassembly of the planking, keel, and chines how many of the old brass fasteners were broken. In one 1938 18-foot Gar Wood utility I restored, eight of the 11 keel bolts were broken. In one 1941 17-foot Chris-Craft barrelback, an astounding 60 percent of the topsides plank-to-frame screws were broken. Look carefully at the ends of these broken fasteners with a magnifying glass. Does it look porous or crystallized? Is there a green or blue powdery residue of oxidized copper? If your brass fasteners are more than 30 years old, then this condition exists whether you see it or not. The old brass fasteners

that haven't yet broken are porous, crystallized, brittle, and just waiting for you to make the hull tight again so that they too can break. Brass is an alloy of copper and zinc (the least noble of all metals). Over time, through a process known as galvanic corrosion, the zinc leaves the alloy (dezincification) creating a brittle, spongy copper so reduced in strength as to be useless. The mass of bronze below the waterline aft (propeller shaft, strut, propeller, rudder, stuffing boxes, through-hulls, etc.) is very high on the nobility table and is likely responsible for drawing much of the zinc from the brass alloy.

If you want to understand this better, go to your local library and study galvanic corrosion and electrolytic corrosion. This is the fun stuff—no, really. You will learn about the nobility table, or which metals are anodic (less noble), willing to give up their ionized molecules to more strongly atomically

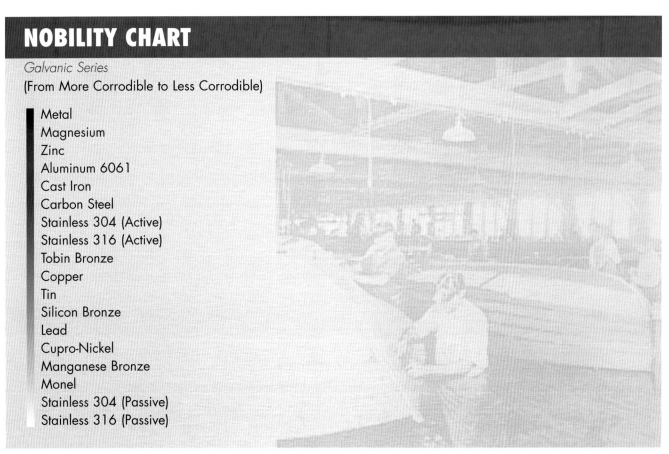

NOBILITY CHART

Galvanic Series

(From More Corrodible to Less Corrodible)

Metal
Magnesium
Zinc
Aluminum 6061
Cast Iron
Carbon Steel
Stainless 304 (Active)
Stainless 316 (Active)
Tobin Bronze
Copper
Tin
Silicon Bronze
Lead
Cupro-Nickel
Manganese Bronze
Monel
Stainless 304 (Passive)
Stainless 316 (Passive)

CLEAR PENETRATING EPOXY SEALER

by Steve Smith

The original Clear Penetrating Epoxy Sealer was developed for restoration of wood in the marine marketplace. The highly aggressive marine conditions proved the acid test for this new technology. It gave paint and varnish that actually stuck, and sealants and adhesives that did not tear or crack where all other products readily failed. Some boat owners were also painting contractors, architects or similar, and began to use these products in the architectural field for restoration as well as an adhesion-promoting primer for paint on new wood buildings. It proved far more workable than any other practice for "restoration" of deteriorated wood and soon became apparent that enamel or latex house paints applied to wood treated with this product did not readily fail. Without this treatment, failure of paints typically occurred in half the time and rot soon started up again behind wood repair with a filler.

The new technology departs from old wood treatment practices, even with epoxy products, with the discovery that the fungi that cause decay in wood actually penetrate into wood far beyond the visible region of total decay. The extent of this penetration is not obvious and may be many inches or feet. The old-technology practice of removing visibly decayed wood leaves an infected region below the "repair" and any water intrusion or diffusion that brings the humidity above roughly fifteen-percent triggers germination of fungal spores in the infected region, and rot begins anew.

The genesis of the new technology was the development of a product that would selectively impregnate the entire infected region of wood with a water-repellent resin system derived in large part originally from wood. This brings about restored mechanical properties similar to wood and a water-repellent characteristic leaving a natural porosity in the treated wood so it could "breathe" as does natural wood. This prevents the accumulation or condensation of liquid water in the wood behind old-technology filler repairs, a leading cause of failure of such repairs. This product is marketed as Clear Penetrating Epoxy Sealer to a wide range of consumers, from homeowners or boat owners to painters, contractors, and maintenance personnel of property managers. A

high performance version, Lignu Impregnating Resin, is provided under license to trained applicators.

All of the versions of Clear Penetrating Epoxy Sealer are designed to dissolve not only the saps and oils in the wood but also the natural water, and to keep the impregnating resin dissolved "in solution" in the presence of those saps, oils, and moisture of the wood. This permits the solvent-resin mix to efficiently penetrate the natural porosity of the wood. Fungi and bacteria produce an additional porosity that is especially penetrable by this product.

The resin system is formulated primarily with resins derived from wood, and therefore, this resin system is compatible with the chemistry of wood in a way that no other resin system is. The resin system is very hydrophobic to inhibit liquid water accumulation in impregnated regions while allowing (via the designed porosity remaining in the wood) the diffusion of water vapor through the impregnated region as well as the natural porosity of the wood. Wood impregnated with this system has a toughness and flexibility comparable to the original wood, because the resin system itself has a toughness and a flexibility comparable to the original wood.

When fungi and bacteria eat their way into wood, they destroy the material and create porosity on a gradient between the sound wood, the slightly porous (but apparently sound) wood with fungal spores in that region, and the more obviously deteriorated wood until, at the extreme, there is wood so porous and so obviously deteriorated you could stick your finger into it. When wood is impregnated with this material, the penetration extends all the way through the zone of deteriorated wood containing bacterial and fungal spores, and on into any available porosity of the sound wood. This impregnation helps the wood resist further deterioration such as might be caused by fungi or bacteria.

Because the primary purpose of the product is not to kill fungi or bacteria or encapsulate fungal spores in epoxy, thus possibly stopping them from hatching (even though it might do that), the Federal EPA and the California EPA do not allow such claims to be made unless the product is registered as a pesticide. Since the primary purpose of the product is the mechanical restoration of deteriorated wood, the product is not registered

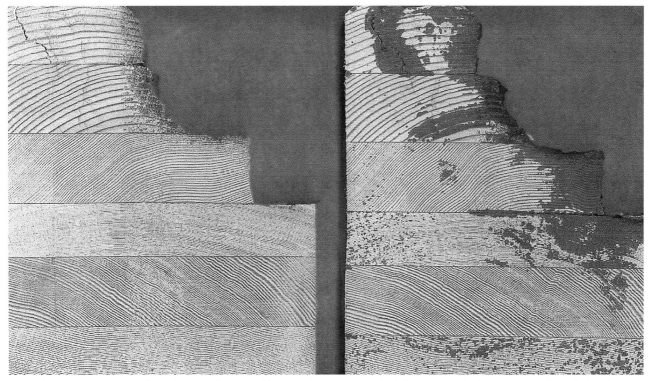

Two adjacent cross-sections from the same laminated beam. The section on the left is untreated, the section on the right has been treated with CPES. The dark regions indicate areas of abnormal porosity that have wicked up the CPES. *Photo ©2000 Steve Smith, All Rights Reserved*

as a pesticide. Consequently, no such claims are made by the manufacturer and others are discouraged from making such claims.

The sole claim for this product is that it can improve the physical properties of wood in some circumstances, and that it can help the wood resist further deterioration such as might be caused by fungi, bacteria, etc. Contributing to this claim is the fact that varnish, oil-base enamel paint and most latex paints stick better and last longer when applied to wood that has been treated first with Smith & Co. Clear Penetrating Epoxy Sealer. This has been a consistent observation by thousands of Smith & Co. customers, since 1972. Improving coating adhesion directly helps the wood resist decay.

The reason for the foregoing discussion of decay-related issues in the context of new construction is that wood does decay, even new wood. Under coatings, under sealants, adhesives caulks or glues, there are microscopic air interfaces. The spores of fungi are everywhere, with a minimum of one in each and every one of those microscopic air pockets. Given only sufficient humidity and warmth, which does occasionally happen everywhere, the spore hatches, becomes a fungal cell, and that cell eats a little bit of a wood fiber for a while, then dies and leaves behind a dozen spores, each the egg of another fungal cell. On wood houses, the paint fails because the wood rots under the paint, releasing the paint film. Rot starts up and continues under putty or plaster repairs over nail holes on houses, giving rise to the plugs of filler you may have noticed rising up under a paint job done on that house a few years earlier. Wood actually rots faster under such "repairs" than if left bare, as the "repair" retains water, which accelerates fungal activity.

The reason a small crack in a moisture-protection barrier is bad, on something completely encapsulated, is that the volume of water vapor is about a thousand times the volume of that small amount of water in liquid

Clear Penetrating Epoxy Sealer, continued

form. Thus, a small amount of liquid water may leak in where it should not, but if water vapor may only leave through the entry crack, it requires a thousand volumes of vapor to pass. This usually takes long enough that excessive dampness accumulates behind the protective coating, and with the warmth of a day, rot starts in a matter of minutes.

Under new coatings, under new sealants on new wood, failure is common for this reason. This failure mechanism can, by experience and observation of 30 years, be largely prevented by improving the ability of the wood to resist this sort of degradation. The elimination of the microscopic air-void interface seems to be the key, for when a sealant has a strongly attached non-porous surface to which to bond, there simply does not exist the microscopic air void made of wood cells, each space containing a spore awaiting hatching conditions. With treatment with Clear Penetrating Epoxy Sealer, the surface air void is filled with a resin system, which coats any wood fibers at or near the surface. This resin system tastes bad to the fungi that would normally attack the wood fibers, and this treatment helps the wood to resist deterioration. The extraordinary deterioration resistance of wood-adhesive interfaces treated in this manner contributes to the high quality and long life of restoration and construction of both sail and powerboats by the Danenberg method.

Because this resin system is so flexible, similar to wood itself, there is no abrupt mechanical discontinuity in the transition from sound wood to sound wood with some impregnated porosity, whether natural as in new wood or fungally induced as in aged wood. The transition from natural wood to the resin system of Clear Penetrating Epoxy Sealer allows natural wood movement and water vapor passage similar to the properties of natural wood. There are commercially available "epoxy" products made from petrochemicals (very small, inexpensive molecules). These are extremely stiff, do not impregnate wood to any significant depth, have negligible water-dissolving capacity (wood may have 10 to 30 percent water, or even more), and result in an abrupt mechanical transition and an effective water-vapor barrier at the interface. When these products are used for treatment of wood, and the wood is subjected to mechanical flexure or seasonal humidity cycles or in-and-out-of-the-water use (as with boats) cracks can develop at the wood-epoxy interface. When these run the length of seams in planked boats, which have been glued with such rigid materials, the cracks are called "zipper-cracks."

charged cathodic (more noble) metals. This molecular transfer takes place in an electrolytic solution such as saltwater or fresh water contaminated by mineral salt—and soaked bottom planks make a nice electrical conduit. This, in effect, imitates the electroplating process except that there is no requirement for energy input other than the position of the components on the Periodic Table of Elements. Please read "A Close Look at Wood-screws" parts one and two, both by Ed McClave, in *WoodenBoat* issues #54 and #55. Another good source of information is *Boatbuilding Manual* (McGraw-Hill) by Robert M. Steward.

The bottom line here is that, in our shop, we replace every fastener in the bottom, including all of the frame screws as well as all of the carriage bolts in the keel, chines, and bilge stringers.

The question now becomes, what do you refasten with? What is nearest to bronze on the nobility table and least likely to react unfavorably with that mass of bronze that hangs below the waterline? The answer is silicon bronze! Sure, stainless steel is available in many different grades: 304 (which I have personally seen bleed red rust), 308, and very rarely, 316. Still, they are very low on the nobility table, near cast iron. And although they are available with a surface treatment called "passivation," which leaves them oblivious to the electrical charges of galvanic corrosion, this method only works if the fastener is exposed to oxygen, which is obviously not the case in a boat hull, where they are covered with varnished bungs in the topsides and painted putty in the bottom planks. Unexposed to oxygen, the stainless steel fasteners lose their passivity and revert to active, bringing them back down in nobility.

I have two major suppliers for fasteners and, when asked directly about the intended use of stainless steel, both admit that they should probably not be used below the waterline. Instead, they offer silicon bronze that is only five percent more expensive than the stainless steel.

One final note: when buying carriage bolts, make sure they are the cut-thread type rather than the rolled-thread type.

Wood Sealer

I have been using Smith's CPES as a wood sealer on all wood surfaces, whether new or old, even over the stain before varnish, for 12 years now. I will not do woodwork without it simply because it has so improved the longevity of paints and bedding compounds far beyond what my first 20 years in the business taught me to expect. I highly recommend its use, and refer you to the explanation of its properties by its inventor, Steve Smith (See sidebar, page 62).

Bedding Compound

If you have chosen to rebuild your hull with a boatyard bedding compound, as the factories used in the bottom construction, be certain that you use it in all of the hull's wood-to-wood joints. Seal all of these surfaces before applying the compound, or the mineral spirits vehicle will quickly absorb into the wood, leaving only the solids of the bedding compound behind. This would then allow the wood to absorb and hold moisture, fomenting rot growth. This will likely happen in a decade or two anyway, but, since you've made it easy to repair, you can plan on repairing it often.

I use and recommend 3M 5200 as an adhesive bedding compound. This is not only because of its four decades of proven service life, but also for its ease of use. The average small runabout in this class uses some 2,000 to 3,000 wood screws in the bottom alone. Drilling this many countersunk holes and placing this many screws, as you apply the bedding and install the planks, takes, on average, 30 to 50 man-hours. It takes 3M 5200 up to seven days to cure, allowing plenty of time to accomplish this before the adhesive sets. There are less-expensive products on the market, but will they allow this amount of time for application?

I have replaced a number of expensive new bottoms for this reason alone. The quick-set compounds or hard epoxy glues had simply set up before the components could be screwed tightly together, and thus no bedding or adhesion took place. These bottoms were filled with voids, one surface bare and unbedded that collected and held moisture. This leads to very early bottom failure.

Some have begun experimenting with the relatively new 3M 4200 fast-set temporary bond adhesive/bedding, ostensibly for ease of repair. This product sets in one to two hours and is certainly contra-indicated in this application.

Chapter 6

STEAM-BENDING WOOD

Steam-bending wood is a very simple operation that you will need to learn to apply chines, transom bows, forward bottom planks, covering boards, and topsides planks where extreme bends occur. Once a piece of wood is steam-bent into shape, it will not fight to spring free of its fasteners and will be far less likely to cup or crack in the future.

The Structure of Wood

A cross-section of a log shows darker, finely spaced growth rings from the center of the log out to within a few inches of the bark. This darker, harder wood is called heartwood. The last couple of inches, much lighter in color, out to the bark, is called sapwood.

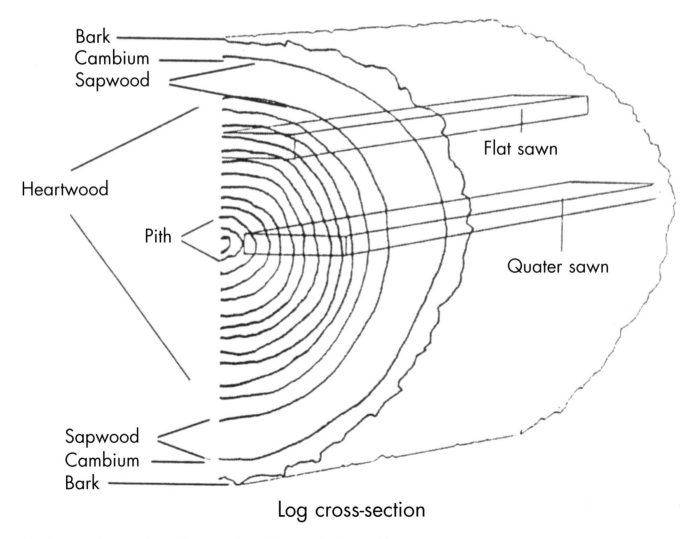

Bark
Cambium
Sapwood

Flat sawn

Heartwood

Pith

Quater sawn

Sapwood
Cambium
Bark

Log cross-section

This illustration diagrams the useful areas within the heartwood of a typical log.

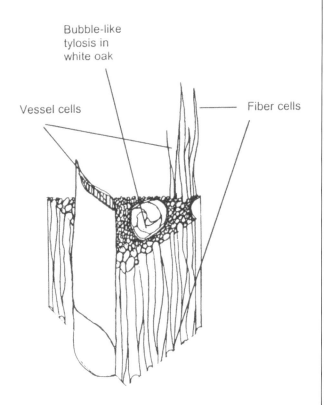

Bubble-like
tylosis in
white oak

Vessel cells

Fiber cells

Hardwood cell structure

An illustration of hardwood cell structure notes the tyloses that plug the vessel cells of white oak (*Quercus alba*). This feature, coupled with high rot resistance due to tannic acids, has made white oak the premier choice for marine construction for thousands of years.

The sapwood is still a part of the living tree. Its vessels still conduct moisture and food within the tree, and its cells are full of sugars used in the growth of the tree. Maple syrup, for example, is simply sap that is drawn from the sapwood of a sugar maple and boiled down. Sapwoods of any species contain these sugars and simply beg to be eaten by bugs and rot spore that have evolved to do just that. Never use any part of the sapwood in boat construction.

Every spring, a new layer of cells is added to the sapwood at the cambium layer just beneath the bark. This is the only place where the tree grows. This one layer of specialized cells then splits, adding one new layer (ring) to the sapwood and one

to the bark. As this new growth ring is added to the outside of the sapwood, the innermost sapwood ring loses most of its free water and shrinks down in size, becoming the outermost ring of heartwood. As this new heartwood ring loses most of its water and shrinks, minerals and cellular matter are concentrated and integrated into its cells. These materials are referred to as *extractives* and give the heartwood its distinctive color, hardness, and rot resistance, among other attributes. When you buy lumber of any sort, watch for a noticeable transition to lighter-colored growth rings, and either cut it off or do not purchase the wood. It's like adding a Holiday Inn for rot spores to your boat.

Hardwoods mainly comprise a variation of cells arranged in an end-to-end alignment within the tree. These cells are hollow structures, much like

When selecting lumber, always watch for a distinctly lighter section of wood at the edge of the plank. This indicates the possibility of sapwood. Do not use this in the boat.

A simple temporary soaking tank. Use only similar wood under the bricks and for spacers between the lumber. Placing dissimilar woods in the same tank, such as white oak used for spacers between mahogany, can cause deep stains in the lighter wood.

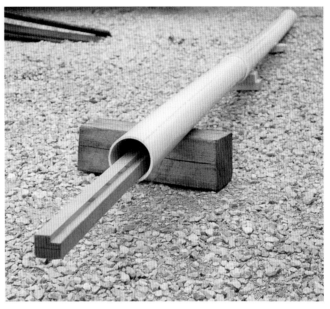

Long, thin pieces such as chines can be soaked in lengths of capped PVC pipe. Stay away from metal pipes, which can stain the wood.

drinking straws. Some of these cells are vessel elements; they form in the tree like fat straw pieces arranged end-to-end and create continuous pipelines for the transfer of fluids in the tree. The *xylem*, for example, transports water and mineral salts from the roots to the leaves, where photosynthesis in the chlorophyll creates sugars that are transported back down, in the *phloem*, as food for the growth of branches, leaves, and roots. These cells can be distinguished in white oak with the help of a 10x magnifying glass.

The more numerous cells are called *fibers*, which are much smaller in diameter and longer in length with closed ends and thick walls. These do not transport fluids but provide strength for the tree. These straw-like cells are mainly composed of cellulose, the carbohydrate that forms the framework of the cell wall and 75 percent of the wood substance.

The cells on the concave side of bent wood plasticize (melt) and can be compressed. The length of the piece is hence made shorter on that side, holding the new shape.

The remaining 25 percent of the wood substance is *lignin*. This forms a bonding agent that is the cementing layer immersed in and between cell walls. Without this "glue," the cells would separate and the tree could not stand. With *lignin*, however, the multitudes of tiny, overlapping fibrous cells become staunch timbers for boat construction.

Moisture Content

In the live tree, cells are not empty but filled with mostly water and protoplasmic matter. In order to be stabilized for use in construction of any type, the majority of the water must be removed. The traditional method of drying wood is to cut it into lumber and carefully stack it in piles so that air can circulate in, around, and through the lumber. The moisture content (MC) will slowly drop until it reaches the average for the geographic area. This might be 18 percent in New England or 10 percent in Arizona. This may take years, depending on the size of the stock. An important factor to remember is that rot spore can grow in any wood with an MC of more than 30 percent.

"Free water" is moisture held in the cell cavities of the wood. Free water may come or go without affecting the dimensional size of the cell or the lumber as a whole.

"Bound water" is the moisture absorbed, or bound, in the cell walls. When all of the free water is removed (the cell cavity is empty) and the cell walls are still full of bound water, the wood is said to be at its "fiber saturation point" (FSP)—approximately 25 percent MC. This is when the wood is at its weakest shear and dimensional strength and the best condition for bending. Many people think that fully green wood (100 percent MC, i.e., cell cavities full) should be used for bending, but this is not so. It will bend but, in doing so, will rupture the cell walls because the water will not compress. The piece will be bent but will remain terribly weakened because of the

For steam boxes, metallic-coated insulation can be easily shaped and is far easier to use and store than a couple hundred pounds of soaked wood. They can also be used in place on the boat and will last for a dozen uses or so.

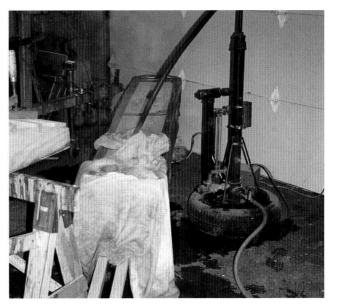

Temporary steam boxes can be quickly and inexpensively made from Celotex and duct tape. They can be made to any size you need and altered easily.

The foamboard steam box is also light enough to hang in place for quickly bending planks onto the boat.

A wooden steam box wrapped in insulation and made from plywood and 2 x 4s wide enough to take curved plank stock.

Either spacers must be built into the steam box or sticks of the same wood temporarily taped under and between the pieces being steamed. The heat must be allowed to circulate freely around the piece to heat it uniformly. A thermometer should be inserted into the box to verify that as close to 212 degrees is provided and maintained.

ruptured cell walls. Further, wood that has more than 25 percent MC will host rot spore.

When bound water is removed (below 25 percent MC) the extractives in the wood mineralize and the cell walls become brittle and the wood gains strength and hardness. In addition, as bound water is lost, the cell walls shrink in size and the piece of lumber, as a whole, becomes dimensionally smaller and more stable. These are qualities you want in the wood but not until it has been bent into the desired shape.

Kiln-dried wood, at 6 to 10 percent MC, can be used if it is soaked long enough to bring its moisture content up into the 12 to 20 percent range. This does not take that long. For 1/2-inch mahogany planks, one to two days seems to be enough. We used to soak 8/4 planks for two weeks before steaming. A temporary soaking tank can easily be made with some spare lumber and 6-mil plastic sheet. I was taught, long ago, to stir rock salt into the soaking water.

Bending with Steam

Now that you can understand the structure of wood, it will be easy to comprehend the bending mechanism.

To begin with, there is nothing magic or necessary with steam. Steam does not add moisture to the wood; in fact, it dries it out. Many commercial kiln operations use steam heat to remove moisture from wood in the kiln-drying process.

All steam does is use molecular water to transfer heat. The same effects can be achieved by boiling the lumber or placing it in a very large oven. The moisture in the wood simply acts as a conductor for the heat.

In kiln-dried wood, however, 6 to 10 percent MC acts more like insulation than like a conductor. Air-dried wood of about 20 percent MC is preferred.

BUILDING A DANENBERG STEAM GENERATOR

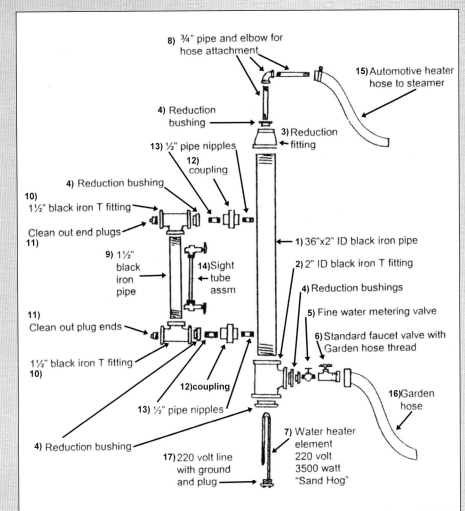

8) ¾" pipe and elbow for hose attachment

15) Automotive heater hose to steamer

4) Reduction bushing

3) Reduction fitting

13) ½" pipe nipples

12) coupling

4) Reduction bushing

10) 1½" black iron T fitting

Clean out end plugs

11)

9) 1½" black iron pipe

14) Sight tube assm

11) Clean out plug ends

1½" black iron T fitting

10)

12) coupling

13) ½" pipe nipples

4) Reduction bushing

17) 220 volt line with ground and plug

1) 36"x2" ID black iron pipe

2) 2" ID black iron T fitting

4) Reduction bushings

5) Fine water metering valve

6) Standard faucet valve with Garden hose thread

16) Garden hose

7) Water heater element 220 volt 3500 watt "Sand Hog"

The parts are as follows:

1. 36 x 2-inch ID black iron pipe
2. 2-inch ID black iron "T" fitting
3. Reduction fitting
4. Reduction bushings
5. Fine water-metering valve
6. Standard faucet valve with garden hose thread
7. 220-volt, 3,500-watt Sand Hog water heater element
8. 3/4-inch pipe and elbow for hose attachment
9. 1-1/2-inch black iron pipe
10. 1-1/2-inch black iron "T" fittings
11. Clean-out end plugs
12. Couplings
13. 1/2-inch pipe nipples
14. Sight tube assembly
15. Automotive heater hose
16. Garden hose
17. 220-volt line with ground and plug

The starting point is a 36-inch black iron pipe with a 2-inch inside diameter. In my construction the main tube and the stabilizer tube need to be drilled and threaded into the sides of the pipe. Perhaps you or your plumber can select fittings that make this unnecessary. The stabilizer tube calms the violent water level movement so that it can be read at the sight tube.

The unit will not stand up on its own, so I had mine welded to a tire rim. Make sure that your unit is well-grounded. Just about any straight water heater element will work, even 110-volt, but the Sand Hog, made by State Industries, outlasts the others by far and produces the greatest volume of steam. The pipe fittings and drilling and tapping service may cost about $100, the heater element around $30, the sight tube $30, and the wire and plug another $30.

An 8-foot-radius bending jig handles most curved transom bows.

The cell walls contain nearly moisture saturation levels, aiding the heat transfer and plasticizing, yet not enough moisture to host rot spore. The fiber saturation point at which the cell walls are still saturated with moisture and transmit the heat easily to the interior of the piece of wood, is approximately 25 percent MC.

Whatever lumber I attempt to bend, I soak it at least a day before heating. This soaks the entire surface, which aids greatly in transferring heat to the interior of the piece. I have no trouble bending kiln-dried 1/2-inch mahogany plank stock this way. Soaking the wood, even for a short time, will cause it to expand somewhat, so let it dry for at least one week for every day of soaking before trimming it to fit.

When enough heat is applied, the cells walls plasticize and can be compressed into smaller cells, as long as the original free water is gone. To a lesser extent, the lignin also plasticizes and allows the cells to slide alongside each other, as this compression occurs.

Almost all cell deformation in bending occurs on the inboard, concave surface of the piece being bent. When hot enough, these cells can compress in length some 20 percent without cell wall fracture. When clamped in place and left to cool, the compressed cell walls solidify and hold their new dimension. The measured length of the plank on this inboard, concave surface will be less than it was before bending, due to the deformation (compression) of the cells.

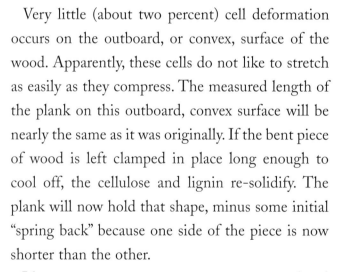

After two hours steaming at 212 degrees, new oak chines bend easily onto the boat.

After cooling overnight, the new chines will hold not only their own shape but will also keep your boat in shape.

Very little (about two percent) cell deformation occurs on the outboard, or convex, surface of the wood. Apparently, these cells do not like to stretch as easily as they compress. The measured length of the plank on this outboard, convex surface will be nearly the same as it was originally. If the bent piece of wood is left clamped in place long enough to cool off, the cellulose and lignin re-solidify. The plank will now hold that shape, minus some initial "spring back" because one side of the piece is now shorter than the other.

I have seen some restorers attempt to steam bend 1/2-inch, kiln-dried mahogany plank stock with a wet towel and a household laundry iron held to the exterior surface of the plank. This method could not possibly effect the interior and inboard surface of the plank, where cell compression needs to occur. You have to apply enough heat for a long enough time to raise the temperature of the entire board, all the way through, to as close to 212 degrees as possible. In order to do this, you must be able to maintain 212

degrees in your steam box. Use a meat thermometer stuck through a hole in the top of the steam box farthest from steam entry. You may have to wrap insulation around your box or tube to accomplish this. The traditional rule of thumb has been one hour of steaming for every inch of lumber thickness. This must be tempered somewhat by how many pieces of lumber you put in and how efficient the steamer and box is. If you are heating a bunch of frames at one time, add a few test pieces and check them until they are wobbly and somewhat rubbery. What you expect to take an hour could very well require two.

Building a Steam Box

The steam box need be no more complicated than an insulated piece of ductwork or a simple pine box. The box or pipe should be only slightly larger than the pieces you are steaming, and the steamed pieces should be propped up when inside the box so that the steam can fully circulate. Temporary steam boxes can be quickly made of Celotex, a

Simple clamping jigs and wedges are all that is needed to hold planks in place while they cool.

Pre-bent planks are much easier to fit in place.

Steam-bending removes the stresses in the lumber and keeps them from cracking long after they are installed.

Wooden blocks should be used when clamping steamed wood. This not only helps distribute the point-loading forces imparted by the clamp face, avoiding cracks along grain lines, it also avoids crushing the wood while it's in a softened state.

home insulation foamboard. Cut it to size with a utility knife and tape it together with duct tape. This construction works very well for planks. Avoid steam boxes made of ferrous metals, which can stain the wood.

For steaming transom bows and chines I prefer lengths of "B-vent" pipe of the sort used to vent gas water heaters. This is a lightweight aluminum double-walled vent pipe available at building supply stores. Two 5-foot lengths work great. Plug the ends with rags. In building containers to steam planks, I have had great success with "reflective insulation," a new type of home insulation made of two layers of plastic bubbles between layers of mylar. It's sometimes sold under the trade name Reflectix. You can cut and staple these steam bags together quickly and they last a surprisingly long time.

In the past I have used the traditional wooden steam boxes but they usually take an hour just to get to temperature. They also cannot be easily altered to fit just the volume you need to fill with steam, which can lead to wasted time and energy.

Whatever type of box or bag you build, make sure it cannot build pressure. This can be extremely dangerous and is not only unnecessary, but also unwanted, for bending wood. Tests performed by the USDA Forest Products Laboratory have shown that temperatures above 212 degrees do not help in plasticizing the lumber and create more problems with over-drying and checking. A drain for condensation on one slightly lowered end of the unit will also help vent pressure.

The steam supply must be adequate in volume to heat the mass of wood you are steaming. The water

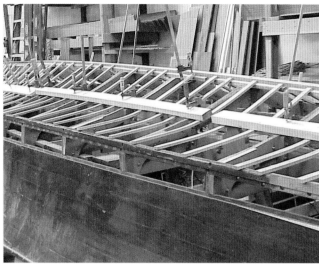

Intermediate frames can be steamed in place on the boat prior to the installation of the inner ply.

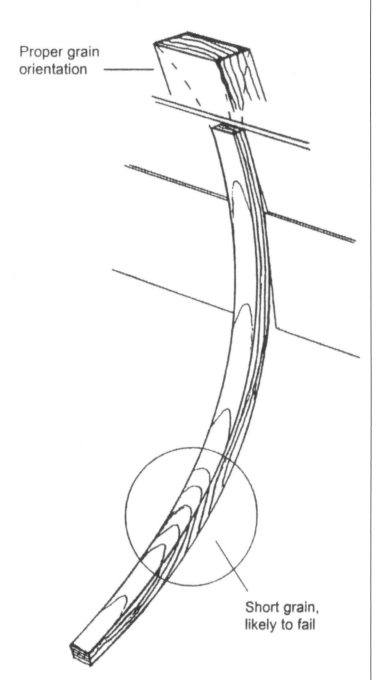

Proper grain orientation

Short grain, likely to fail

Frame grain orientation

Small steam-bent, intermediate frames should maintain vertical-grain throughout their length. Short grain parallel to the bend is likely to fail when bending or years later. The grain alignment should also remain perpendicular to the screw-line to avoid being split by so many closely spaced fasteners.

supply must be great enough to last until the wood is thoroughly heated. Adding cold water to a boiling bucket will not maintain high temperatures and can actually overcook and dry out the wood rather than uniformly heat it.

Steam generators can be rented from most rental stores in the form of tools such as a steam pressure washer or steam engine cleaner, and *WoodenBoat* magazine has 25 back issues that include articles on steam-bending wood, many of which feature descriptions for building your own steam generator.

The steam generator I have used for the last 10 years is quite easy to build (see sidebar, page 71). It is basically made of plumbing pipe and a standard household water heater element that operates on either 220 volts (recommended) or 110 volts for a lighter duty unit and smaller pieces of wood. The parts are available from your local builder's supply store with the exception of the sight tube, which can be obtained from almost any local plumbing shop through their Sexauer supply catalog. The water heater element can be almost any straight-loop

Intermediate frames can be installed to the plywood, on the boat, after the installation of the inner ply. After the rubber bedding has set, temporarily applied screws are removed from the plywood.

In areas where clamps are impossible, screws with washers can be used to temporarily hold the plank in place. This is a two-person job and the fasteners must be quickly pre-drilled and set.

design, but by far the longest lasting one is the "Sand Hog" (240 volts and 3,500 watts recommended) made by State Industries.

The heater element screws up into the bottom of the pipe casing and heats just 1 gallon of water instead of the 40 gallons it is designed to heat. This produces a great deal of steam and the water must be constantly re-supplied by means of a hose and trickle valve. Be extremely careful with this; it does after all, mix 220 volts and water. If it is properly wired and grounded it should be no more dangerous than the household electric water heater. After I had built mine, I had a certified boiler mechanic wire it for me. He warned that his profession would consider it an illegal process boiler. OK, I'll never tell who wired it.

Once you have the unit constructed and the sight tube shows that the element is submerged, plug it in and adjust the needle valve until the water being turned into expelled steam is being equally replaced with just the right trickle of water. You must check

this level often during the entire operation; failure to do so could result in a burned-out element.

Be very careful with steam! This unit will produce enough steam to flay the skin from your body.

Bending the Wood

Remember: You must apply enough heat long enough to raise the temperature of the entire board, all the way through, to as close to 212 degrees as possible. You must be able to maintain 212 degrees in your steam box in order to do this, which may require you to wrap insulation around your box or tube.

The rule of thumb for heating wood in the 12 to 20 percent moisture range is one hour per inch of thickness of the wood. One half hour for a 1/2-inch plank, two hours for a 2-inch chine. This must be tempered somewhat by how many pieces of lumber you put in and how efficient the steamer and box is. If the piece doesn't bend right, stick it in and cook it some more. You will have to experiment with your specific lumber, but follow the hour-per-inch rule to start.

The most important factor in successfully bending wood is selection. White oak is the recommended species for framework and has been the standard for boat frames for thousands of years. Very few expensive and exotic species can compete with it. Mahoganies of all species tend to bend very easily with little surface checking, as long as some pre-soaking has been done.

For wood-bending to be successful, the grain orientation of the wood itself must be spot-on. Your frames must end up in the boat with the flat growth rings parallel to the planking. If the growth rings were to end up perpendicular to the planking, the fasteners would quickly split the frames like wedges between the growth rings. Carefully mill your frame stock out of straight-grained wood with this in mind. There must be no indication of knots or grain run-out more than five degrees. It may be difficult to find such lumber, but it is important if you want to keep failures to a minimum. I always mill 20 percent more frame stock than I need because I know there will be some failures. Take it in stride—toss it and bend in another one.

While the lumber is cooking, prepare the work area. Have all clamps and braces at the ready, within reach and with the screws backed off. If you are bracing from the inside, have your bracing precut and screws started and a clamp or cordless driver

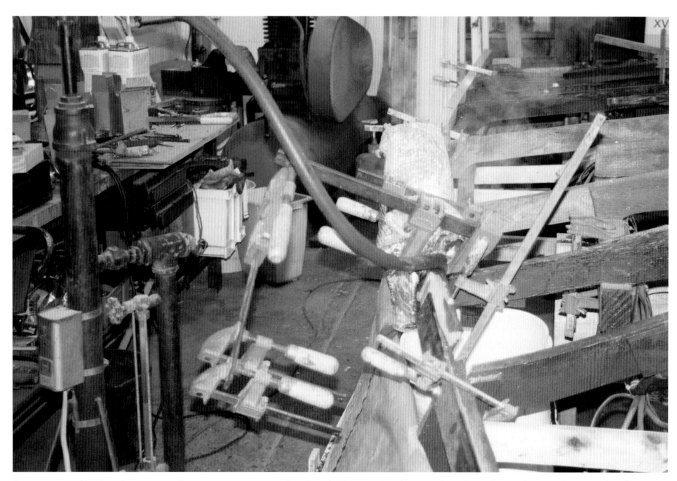

Some pieces, like this chine repair, have some twist as well as bend. This can be done in place by utilizing the metallic-coated Reflectix, stapled in place and weights hung from a clamp to encourage the twist. This must be watched carefully as the steaming progresses to avoid too much twist.

After two weeks of soaking and two hours of steaming, even the large, kiln-dried, 8/4 covering boards for this 1939 Chris-Craft barrelback are easily held in place with only three light-duty clamps.

close at hand. After your first few attempts you will learn what to have ready. Quickly installing a boiling piece of lumber can cause energy levels and tempers to rise.

You will want to position the steam box as close to the work as possible because you should have the piece bent in place in less than a minute. The steamed wood quickly cools and stiffens as soon as it's removed it from the heat—have good-natured, strong-armed help to wrestle these pieces quickly into place. Have hot rags ready to cover the piece, especially if it's white oak. This will help to keep it from cooling too quickly and forming checks at the surface. If it's not bent in one minute, forget it and cook it again. You'll get hot and sweaty (working around a steamer is like being in a rainforest) and you may even feel like yelling at yourself and your help. Keep plenty of cold drinking water on hand.

Steam-bent pieces should remain clamped to their form at least overnight to cool and hold their shape. Some spring-back is to be expected and can be overcome by experimentation with over-bending, if necessary.

Pieces such as thin planks that have to be soaked can swell and should be allowed to dry to normal moisture levels before they are sealed and fitted.

Chapter 7

FRAME REPLACEMENT

Presumably, your vessel is upside down with the proper supports applied to bilge stringers, sheer line, and stem. The hull should be tight, plumb, and level. The gripe, keel, and chines have been removed and all frames cleaned and degreased, as outlined in Chapter 4.

Use a taught line suspended over the hull to occasionally check your centerlines. If you have used straightedges and battens to get the bottom and planing surface back into shape and have found that some frames are still too concave in their midsection, it is very possible that these frames could be bent or edge-set. This could very easily have happened through prolonged or improper storage, especially if they were oil-soaked. Do not duplicate bent frames.

Repair vs. Replacement

I have seen many frame repairs made by simply removing an offending piece of frame and replacing it with another piece to fill the space and create something new to screw a plank to, a graving piece or dutchman. Glued or not, this is wrong if the repair piece is larger than one-third the molded surface measurement of the frame. It totally negates the purpose of a frame. Note the photo of the frame repair made by replacing the piece of frame and sistering it with a piece of 3/8-inch plywood. Like the weak link in a chain, this frame is essentially as strong as a 3/8-inch piece of plywood at the joint. The boat will depend on the planks holding the frames together here, which will not last long. And, this repair almost certainly took longer than patterning, cutting out, and installing a new frame would have.

In the case of a bottom frame that's split on its sided surface, you could try to clean the splits of oil, splinters, and broken fastener pieces and glue and clamp them together. You must realize, however, that you intend to put another 20 or so fasteners down this same (probably oil-contaminated) glue line, making it almost certain to fail again.

In any case, it is almost always easier and cheaper to simply unscrew the bad frame, trace it onto new frame stock, mark any bevels, walk over to the band saw and in about 15 minutes, overall, have a new sturdy frame to seal and install.

I recently replaced all the bottom and topsides frames in a very gray 22-U (22-foot utility). With one person removing frames and another assembling them while I patterned and cut them out, we were able to replace all bottom and topsides frame futtocks and knees in two days. In another six days I had fabricated and installed a new stem, gripe, keel, chines, and complete transom frames and bows. If I had been required to use glues and dutchmen to attempt to save those badly deteriorated old frame members, I'm sure it would have taken weeks to accomplish something with a very questionable lifespan, fairness, and strength. I would certainly have expected popped bungs and cracked varnish in the topsides.

This frame is only as strong as the 3/8-inch plywood butt sistered to it. Better to replace it with an all-new piece. Once more, the thin planking will have to hold this frame together.

When frame ends are missing or rotted away, simply shape the missing end out of posterboard and staple it in place before removing the frame from the hull.

Shaped blocks were glued in to replace missing frame sections. It is up to the planks to hold this "frame" together. This is certainly not the way to make repairs, as this will create a very weak area that will create far more problems in the future.

The angles are transferred to the pattern using an adjustable protractor or bevel gauge.

It is a good idea to replace every other frame section using the alternates to verify shape by means of battens across the adjoining frames. Be sure to batten entire sides of the bottom to locate entire low areas.

The end grain of the topsides frame may only appear slightly affected by rot on its surface, but this is end grain and rot tendrils can travel several feet past the affected area. If rotten topsides frames are left in the boat, they will soon effect the new bottom frames you've just installed.

In short, it is up to you how historically important a bad frame member is; and if it is important to you, you should probably have started with a different boat. You might consider the extra effort worthwhile in saving and restoring frames that contain hull numbers.

You will soon learn that whatever seems, at first, to be the hardest or most expensive choice in wooden boat repair is generally the cheapest and easiest in the long run. This is mainly due to the fact that doing it right the first time makes each of the successive procedures easier and quicker.

Replacing Frames

Cardboard or posterboard can be used to pattern missing areas by stapling a piece to the side of the frame and tracing the new frame to this added edge. If sections of frame ends are missing or incomplete

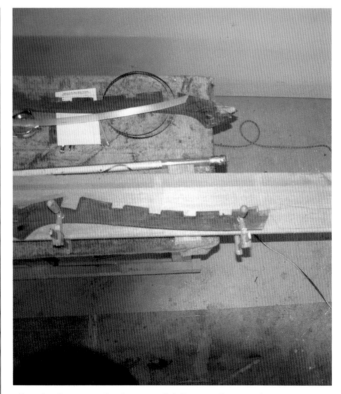

Align the frame on the framestock following the wood grain as much as possible. Frames are best made of plain-sawn wood.

FRAME REPLACEMENT

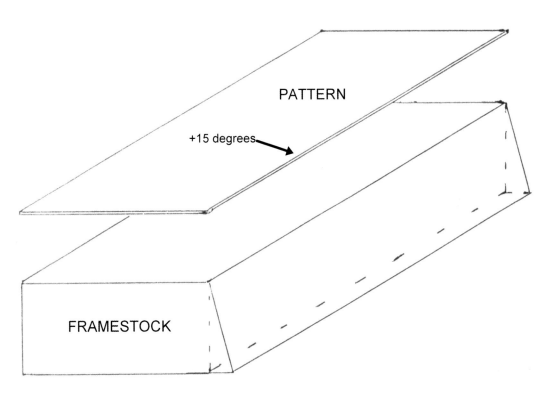

When patterning from the top of this piece, the angle is indicated to extend away from the cut line, thus adding to the size of the piece (+), as in "+15 degrees."

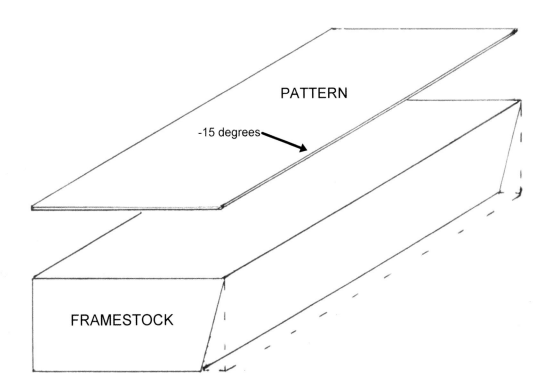

When patterning from the top of this piece, the angle is indicated to undercut from the line, thus negating the size of the piece (-), as in "-15 degrees."

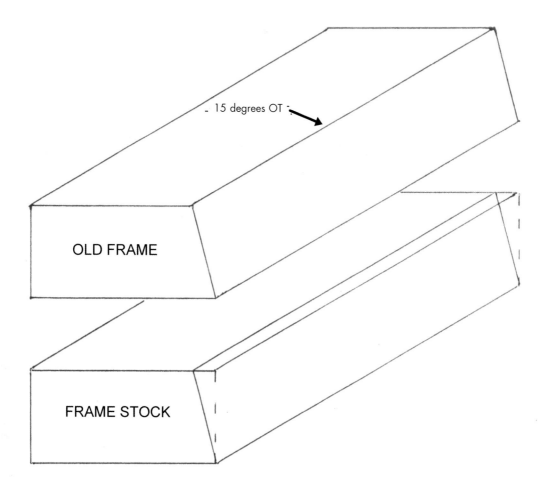

15 degrees OT

OLD FRAME

FRAME STOCK

When patterning from the bottom edge of this piece, as in directly tracing the piece to be copied, the angle is indicated to remove wood from the top of the piece, as in "-15 degrees O.T." (on top). This is accomplished by first cutting the piece out at 90 degrees in order to transfer this line to the bottom of the workpiece, and then flip the piece over and cut the bevel (as a minus) using the newly cut bottom edge as a guideline.

due to rot or breakage, I staple an appropriately sized piece of cardboard pattern material to the affected end and spile the missing section before removal from the boat. Be sure to mark any bevels on this pattern. By using battens from surrounding frames you can reproduce the intended shape of the missing piece.

If you really want to do the job correctly (you might as well, while everything is accessible), unscrew, degrease, seal, and pay bedding compound on all mating surfaces of all the frames and frame knees. You may even find it easier and quicker to

simply trace and replace the frames with sound new wood. Remember to replace the old brass fasteners with new silicon bronze.

I generally remove and repair or replace all of the even-numbered frames first, leaving the odd-numbered frames to hold the overall shape and give something to batten to when assembling the new futtocks.

If sections of frame are broken in two or more pieces, I fasten them together with small cleats before removal, using battens across adjoining frames to ensure the correct shape. Note the inboard ends of the bottom frames where they join at the keel. It is very important that this joint be tight. Make sure that bottom spreading does not cause this gap. I note this gap on the frame and extend the new pieces so that the joint is tight. This will make the assembled frame stronger and, with proper bedding, seals the end grain better. The outboard ends of the bottom frames can also be slightly altered to fit the chine landing better, if necessary. Note the bevel here and make it fit right.

Remember that the vast majority of these antique and classic runabouts were built from pre-cut parts on assembly lines. There were no master boatwrights on the line. You will, most likely, accidentally be rebuilding your boat far stronger than it was originally built, especially if you use sealers and bedding compounds that the factory did not.

If your topsides frames appear sound except for the very bottom edge at the chine joint, you may be tempted to remove the affected edge and alter the shape of the new bottom frame to compensate for the missing end. The remaining end of the topsides frame may look sound and may look absolutely free of rot, but it is not. Rot tendrils grow far past the visibly affected area. You may very well be doing this again in just a few years.

And, if a topsides frame needs replacement, do it now. Remove the bungs and plank screws in the topside planks along this frame line and possibly a fastener or two coming up from the covering board.

If entire sections are so bad that they cannot be reliably traced, sheets of plywood can be used and the shape battened from adjoining frames.

Frame alignment is continuously checked with battens, or straightedges on the planing surface to verify shape before committing to final placement.

This will leave the frame unattached except for the nail holding the plank battens to the frame. Use small wedges, and possibly a hacksaw blade, to disconnect the battens from the frame and remove and replace the frame.

The frames can be traced directly onto the frame stock. Check your boat's framework to determine the correct thickness (usually 15/16 inch) and duplicate this thickness for the new frame stock or you may have trouble correctly aligning the futtocks. If you bought wide enough frame stock you can nest the patterns to save on waste.

Using a protractor or adjustable bevel gauge, transfer the bevels of the original frame futtock to the new pattern. When a number of patterns are prepared, cut manageable portions of the frame stock with a jigsaw and cut out the new frames on a band saw.

Cut all of the 90-degree edges first and then cut the beveled edges in the order they go into the boat. This will help keep track of the bevels and insure you do not cut some of them backwards.

If you are replacing both frames in the same station you should be able to turn one over, trace it, and cut out the mirror image. The only place this cannot be done is on some of the larger boats, such as the Chris-Craft 28-foot upswept, which was built slightly fuller on one side of the transom to offset the torque of a large propeller.

If your boat is a Century, all of the bottom frames are notched to accept the fore and aft plank battens. You need not cut these at this time. You can leave

Frame sections forward of the flat planing surface must be kept fair as well. A long, 1/4-inch-thick aluminum bar battens this area in well.

the frames whole until the entire bottom framework is assembled and faired in. This job can be much more accurately handled with battens and a router.

You must be very careful when taking and marking bevels. You must visualize the angle from your pattern and mark whether your pattern is facing forward, aft, inboard, or outboard.

I use three kinds of bevel labels: + (plus), – (minus), and OT (on top); please note the illustrations.

There are many areas of the hull where the frames may have changing bevels at the planking surface. Make sure you check the frame bevels every few inches along the beveled edge and mark and cut them accordingly. You will have to either become very proficient at the band saw or cut these out to the largest size and then dress them with a hand plane.

The center frame ties or floor timbers in the area of the engine oil pan are very thin as they pass over the keel. These are usually broken or bent out of shape due to their small size and the weight of the engine above them. I do not cut these out until I have fit the frames in those stations and verified that the originals are not bent. I generally pattern these in place by tracing their shapes directly from the correctly positioned new bottom frames.

Re-Assembly

Chris-Crafts and many other makes had a straight, flat planing surface for 5 to 8 feet at the keel forward of the transom. I use a 3 x 3-inch x 8-foot aluminum I-beam as a temporary keel to clamp the frames to during assembly of the frames in the planing surface

Once the futtocks are all shaped and battened in, the locator holes can be drilled.

A single-sawn and sistered assembly fastened with bronze screws shows the frame knee grain orientation.

area. I also use 6-foot aluminum levels, checking at many points along the frames outboard of the keel and at the chine landings in the planing surface. The frames will have varying degrees of slope as you move outboard but should still fair in a straight line in the planing surface. Keep your straightedges parallel with the keel.

After the planing area is assembled, I replace the I-beam with a 1/4 x 3-inch x 16-foot flat aluminum bar to batten the correct curvature of the keel and properly set the frames. I also replace the 6-foot levels with 3/4 x 3/4-inch x 16-foot cedar battens in order to fair in the gentle curves of the bottom forward of the planing surface.

Trial-fit these frames in the hull and trim them as necessary using appropriate battens and straightedges. Clamp the bottom frames, the center frame tie, and the frame knees in each frame station together as you fit them and, when you are satisfied,

drill two locator holes in each frame overlap. I suggest clamping together all of the even- or odd-numbered frame stations before drilling the locator holes. This will allow you to use battens and the odd- or even- numbered frames to ensure fairness before you commit to the shape. Drilling all of the fastener holes now will make it very messy when the bedding compound is applied. On the other hand, if you do not drill the locator holes now while the frames are dry, the slippery bedding compound will make it very difficult to clamp them back into the proper position. Make sure you are using properly sized drills and countersinks to avoid splitting the wood.

For far-forward frames it might be wise to clamp the gripe back in place to verify the centerline and ensure proper alignment. At this point you may need to pattern some of the frame ties in the engine area as mentioned earlier.

Sometimes the screw's thread will catch on the piece being applied and wedge it a full thread width away from the piece it's being screwed to. You must back the screw out and reset it to pull the frame pieces together. Always watch to see the bedding compound ooze out as the pieces are fastened tightly together.

Once you have committed to the shape and drilled the locator holes, mark the overlaps with a pencil. This will show you where to apply the bedding compound later. You may now remove all of these frame futtocks and properly seal them. Do not use a hard plastic coating. Once the sealer is properly set you may apply the bedding compound at each overlap and assemble the frames. As mentioned earlier, the bedding compound makes these pieces very slippery and difficult to clamp into position. I use ice picks to find and set the locator holes and then replace them, one at a time, with screws.

Sometimes the screw threads hang up on the top piece of wood and force the two pieces slightly apart. Watch for this, especially with the first screws, as these can keep the rest of the fasteners from seating properly. It is very often necessary to back these first screws out as you watch the wood pieces fall together and then reset them. You may now drill the remainder of the fastener holes, following the manufacturer's original pattern, except where they put two screws on the same grain line—don't do that. Use the proper torque setting on the screw gun and watch the edges of the frame sections as you set the screws, making sure they bed together tightly as the bedding compound oozes out evenly all around the joints. It is better to have a little bedding compound ooze out than leave a dry spot that water and debris can collect in. You will soon learn the proper amount to leave with your putty knife, as you are the one who has to clean up the mess. Do this carefully and you can re-use the excess compound on the next frame. Wipe the joints clean with a suitable solvent.

Chapter 8

TRANSOM FRAME, KEEL, STEM, AND CHINE REPLACEMENT

With the main frames repaired or replaced, sealed and bedded, and refastened, you may be ready to install the keel, chines, and transom. But, are the frames properly set enough to determine proper placement of keel or chines? Improper placement can mean excessive hours using large, dangerous power grinders to re-determine the exterior shape. One must constantly sight down individual component landings and shaped surfaces. Crouch low at the stem and slowly raise your point of view as you follow the keel landing notches, with and without battens. You will soon learn to discern a sweet line or an obvious unfairness. Do this low crouch and slow rise tangentially with battens as you watch the bottom frames and chine landings transition from vertical to horizontal, as the water will address them. Truly sweet lines allow for speed, comfort, and safety.

The keel, chines, and transom frames are built much sturdier than the main frames because of the forces applied to them, and also because they

After all frame repairs are made and faired in, the major frames can be installed.

generally receive three or four rows of fasteners. Consequently, do not even consider using any kind of partial repairs on these members—they are just as easy to replace.

Transom Framing

I rarely find a lower transom bow in good enough shape to re-install (perhaps one in ten), as they are the most fastener-punctured piece in the boat and take a great deal of torque from the drive gear. The average lower transom bow has two rows of screw holes from the bottom planks (100 on average) and two rows of screw holes from the lower transom plank (60 on average) coming from a different direction. Refastening the planks using the old split, weakened screw holes is asking for trouble. Drilling all new fastener holes in the existing piece (average size is about 1-1/2 x 1-3/4 inches) will leave over 300 holes. How strong could it be? Ever heard of "tear on the dotted line"? The same is true for all frames and planks.

Chine and keel landings must be faired with battens to insure proper landing bevels are cut in the frames.

If your boat is a Century you will find that this piece was laminated with three pieces of oak that have since delaminated. This is due, in great part, to the number of fasteners coming up from the bottom and splitting the laminations like so many wedges. I always replace these with solid white oak that is steam bent, not sawn.

Make sure the hull is plumb, level, and properly braced before removal of any of the framework. Take careful measurements to insure that the hull is holding the correct shape. Using a tape, measure diagonally from the outboard point of the starboard chine to the outboard point of the port sheer. Make this same measurement from the port chine to the starboard sheer. If these measurements are not identical, your transom is skewed and must be braced into shape. Likewise, insure a plumb center-line and take half-breadth measurements from that, insure a level planing surface and take heights measurements from that.

Apply athwartships and diagonal bracing to ensure keeping the correct shape and remove and replace this bracing as you remove and replace the frame components. If your boat has a flat transom, the lower transom bow can be removed. And if it is not warped or bent, it can be traced directly onto appropriately surfaced stock.

If the lower transom bow is curved due to a rounded transom, you should pattern it in place. Temporarily staple a piece of stable pattern material

Lower transom bows are wracked with the forces exerted by the propeller and rudder.

to the aft surface and trace the shape. Be sure to mark any variations in thickness or bevels directly onto the pattern. Fold the pattern in half to verify that the shape is bilaterally symmetrical.

If your lower transom bow is curved, I highly recommend steam-bending the replacement rather than cutting the curve, which leaves short grain at the ends (note the original). When steaming transom bows, it is necessary to do so on a form built to match the radius of your transom's curve. This is the only piece that cannot be bent directly onto the boat because the only bending point is the stern post. This would create a V shape rather than a smooth curve. This form could be as simple as a half dozen blocks of 2 x 4s temporarily screwed to your bench top.

After steaming and fitting the curved shape of the transom bow, it can be temporarily assembled

and the bottom surface shaped. This is the most important area of the planing surface, so batten the shape from the bottom frames carefully before final installation.

The topside frames' cheeks are typically broken, rotten, or split at the ends; I almost always replace these. Remove the transom plank battens. Remove the topsides plank fasteners at these frames and topsides plank batten fasteners at least to the next forward frame. This will allow access to the batten fasteners into these frames. The upper ends of these frames are fastened from the upper transom bow under the deck. It may be necessary to peel back the covering boards enough to get at these fasteners or, if you know you will be taking the covering boards off later, sneak in at those upper fasteners with a hacksaw blade. Remove these cheeks and scrape them clean enough for patterning. If they are broken

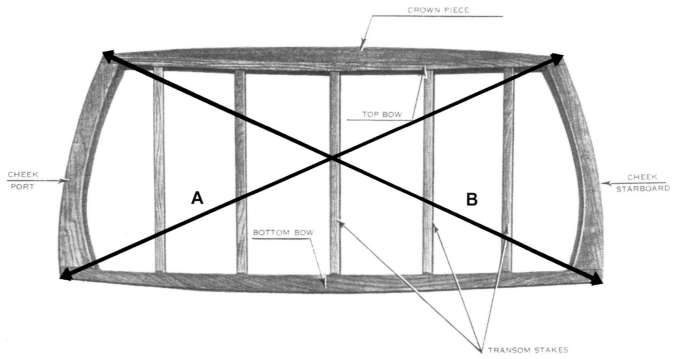

CROWN PIECE

TOP BOW

CHEEK PORT

CHEEK STARBOARD

A

B

BOTTOM BOW

TRANSOM STAKES

The length of line A should be equal to the length of the line B.

When re-framing the transom, diagonal measurements indicate whether it is square and bilaterally symmetrical.

in pieces, screw some cleats to the backside of them before removal, ensuring the correct shape.

The cheeks can now be traced directly onto prepared frame stock of the proper thickness and grain. In most classic boats this is 7/4 white oak. Use your adjustable ship's curve to continue a fair curve across the spaces left open because of the plank batten notches.

Check and mark the correct bevels at close intervals. The more tumblehome your boat exhibits, the more this angle will change. This changing bevel will require multiple passes at the band saw. Cut the lowest angle first and then enter the piece with succeeding cuts of greater angles. Make sure the chine landing is the correct bevel and depth as this is an important structural point.

After cutting out these frame blanks on the band saw, lay them alongside the originals and mark locations for the plank batten notches. I clamp the new frames to the face of my bench and address these notches with a small router (a laminate trimmer with a small base). After sealing, these frames are re-installed in the boat with at least one screw per plank to help with the turnover.

The remaining transom framework—the sternpost and vertical stakes—should be sound. If not, they are easily replaced with white oak. These usually have been fastened to the upper and lower transom bows with long screws into their end grains. Very often, even in brass-fastened boats, the stern post was fastened with steel screws, a situation that should be remedied.

Stem and Gripe

If the stem is rot-free at the stem head and has no fractures at the joint with the gripe or obvious

The topsides transom frames, often referred to as "cheeks," can have a great deal of short grain, depending on the amount of tumblehome in the design. Even if not broken, this short grain allows a great deal of moisture incursion and rot is often found here.

Transom frame components can be traced directly onto new stock. Rotten or missing edges are defined with an adjustable ships curve and angles transferred with a bevel gauge.

fractures caused by multiple screw installations, then you should be able to clean and seal the surfaces in place. The old screw holes should be filled with round wooden toothpicks and marine glue and ground flush.

If you cannot repair the stem in place and are going to replace it you will need to remove the plank bungs and fasteners from the frames and battens at least two frames back from the stem. Do not remove all of the topside planks as they help to hold the hull in shape while the bottom framework is being disassembled. Remove the fasteners from the plank battens at the stem and any fasteners that may be coming up from the covering boards or breast hook.

If your topside planks are in great shape and you intend to reuse them, you must be very careful not to break chips off the edges or at the bungs. If the

planks have heavy coats of varnish it might be wise to use chemical stripper to remove the varnish so that it does not pull any chips of wood from the surrounding areas upon bung removal.

If the stem is broken at the joint with the gripe you should temporarily re-install the gripe and bolt them together, making sure they are in the proper position. Remove the stem-gripe as a unit for patterning. If the gripe is to be replaced, it too can be patterned at this time. Set the stem-gripe unit on a bench top after scraping the surfaces clean. Make sure this is positioned so that you can sight straight down on all sections of the unit.

Place an appropriately large piece of glass on top of the stem-gripe assembly or individual pieces and support the corners of the glass.

Tape an adequately sized piece of clear Mylar plastic sheet (available at art supply stores) to the

If topside planks will be replaced, the batten notches can be cut with a small router, after installation and alignment is assured.

glass and trace the outlines and joint of the stem and gripe with a permanent ink marker. Make sure you are sighting straight down and not causing a parallax in lines. Trace the lines of the plank rabbet. These lines are referred to as the "rabbet," "back-rabbet," and "bearding" lines.

Note any other pertinent information such as the placement of the carriage bolts and the "stop-waters," the softwood dowels located at the stem-gripe and gripe-keel joints at the back-rabbet that are intended to swell more than the surrounding hardwood to make the joint watertight. Also note the placement of the waterline as well as the chine landing at the stem.

Transfer this Mylar drawing to the appropriately surfaced and grained stock of wood. For most classic boats this is 7/4 white oak. The stem and gripe will have to be done separately in order to maintain the proper grain direction. Also, I do not recommend laminating pieces of thinner stock, as they would be liable to delaminate along the line of carriage bolts.

With the Mylar pattern securely taped in place, simply trace over the lines with a pounce wheel, which is a multi-pointed wheel that pokes a line of small holes in the plastic and surface of the wood. Look for a good quality, heavy duty one at art supply stores (also sold at sewing stores as a "pattern wheel"). To help you further see the lines, rub carpenter's chalk along it.

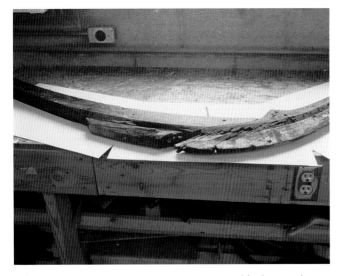

When stem or gripe pieces are missing, assemble them in the boat to assure proper shape. The entire assembly is secured to the bench with screws for tracing.

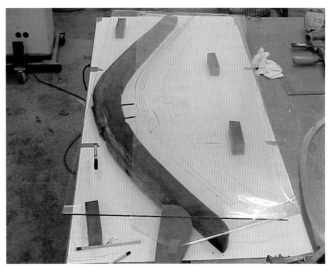

Lay a sheet of glass directly on top of the old stem and gripe to trace details of the rabbet, back rabbet, and bearding lines.

When all lines have been transferred, remove the Mylar pattern and cut out the outline of the stem (or gripe) blank on the band saw. Using a small square, transfer lines from the first side down the edges to the other side.

Flip the stem (or gripe) blank over and carefully re-apply the Mylar pattern to the reverse side, following the blank outline and the transferred lines at the edges. Use the pattern wheel to transfer the rabbet lines, etc., to the reverse side.

Use an adjustable ships curve and pencil or pen to connect these dotted lines to make them easier to see.

When both the stem and gripe blanks are cut out and have their pattern lines on them, draw centerlines on the blank edges and transfer the rabbet lines to the ends of the blanks. It's now time to carve out the plank rabbets.

Securely fasten the blank to the bench top, either with two clamps that have to be moved occasionally, or with two screws that do not. Run a 1/8-inch router bit down the full length of the back rabbet line. Determine the correct depth from the lines at the end of the blank, so as not to cut in to the rabbet faces. This may have to be done in more than one pass to be controllable. This procedure, of course, must be done to both sides of the blank.

The idea is to carve this rabbet out starting with a gouge chisel and mallet to remove the bulk of the material, and finishing with a flat chisel to connect the rabbet line and bearding line at the surface, with the back rabbet line at its intended depth. Use wood blocks of correct thickness to simulate the plank edge to check the depths as you carve. The plank rabbet may rotate in relation to the centerline of the boat but should always remain a 90-degree angle to the plank edge.

After carving 90 percent of the rabbet, the surface can be carefully cleaned up with a small grinder.

This may sound like a lot of work but with the average 22-foot Chris-Craft I can usually remove the stem and gripe, pattern and fabricate new ones, and have them installed before the end of the workday.

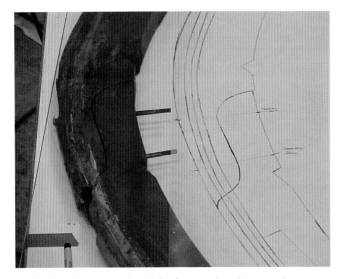

Mark these lines onto the Mylar from a directly vertical viewpoint and include details such as carriage-bolt placement and chine and batten locations.

After one side is transferred and the new stem and gripe cut out, the transparent Mylar pattern can be used upside-down on the other side.

These pieces can now be placed in the vessel and temporarily clamped in place along with the keel so that any slight mismatches of the stem-gripe or gripe-keel joints can be addressed with chalk, a hand plane or grinder if necessary until tight joints are achieved. Rub carpenters chalk on one of the meeting faces and when the joints are rubbed together the chalk will transfer to the high spots on the opposing piece, showing you where to trim. Clean this chalk off before sealing.

After final fitting of the new stem and gripe, you may completely seal these pieces. If you are going to re-use your old keel, then these pieces may be installed in the boat with the proper bedding compound and new fasteners. If you are going to replace the keel, do not permanently assemble the stem or gripe until the new keel is fit.

Keel

The lumber for the new keel should be plain-sawn or flat-sawn so that the growth rings are parallel to the widest face. The garboard plank fasteners, spaced every 3 inches or so from stem to stern, would eventually cause quarter-sawn grain to split. While some of the smaller or earlier Chris-Crafts were built with mahogany keels, I always prefer white oak.

I am lucky enough to live in western Michigan where there are many very large furniture factories. The supply of wood is excellent, both for imported mahoganies and local Michigan white oak. Finding straight-grained white oak in lengths greater than 16 feet is possible but rare. If you cannot locate a single length of stock long enough to make the keel in one piece you will have to scarf two pieces together.

Keels vary from one boat model to the next, so determine what your needs are. Some are 6 inches wide at the after end and 6/4 thick. Most prewar keels are 4 inches wide and 8/4 thick.

Determine exactly what you are doing and use this as an opportunity to alter from original if necessary. For example, when I rebuild a Century bottom I include a 1/8-inch plywood inner bottom to

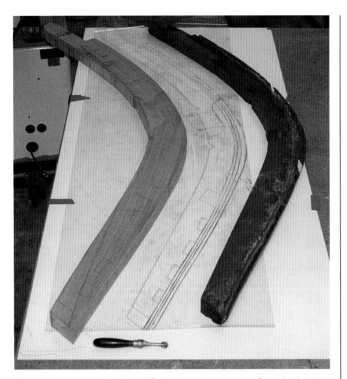

By using my method of transfering a pattern, a perfect duplicate should result.

extend the life of the rebuilt bottom. This requires adding a 1/8-inch cap to the outboard surfaces of the keel and chines to make up for the added thickness. If you are replacing keel and chines, make them 1/8-inch thicker than original.

A standard scarf is at least 6:1, that is, six times longer than the thickness of the stock. For 8/4 stock that means a scarf length of at least 1 foot. Plan the lengths of the pieces carefully so that the scarf ends up centered between two main frames. If you are planning for new chines, these too will have to be scarfed to obtain the necessary length, you should plan these at this time also so that the chine scarfs do not fall in the same frame bay as the keel scarf. If there is an intermediate frame in the same frame bay as the scarf it will have to be adjusted to fit the scarf-backing block.

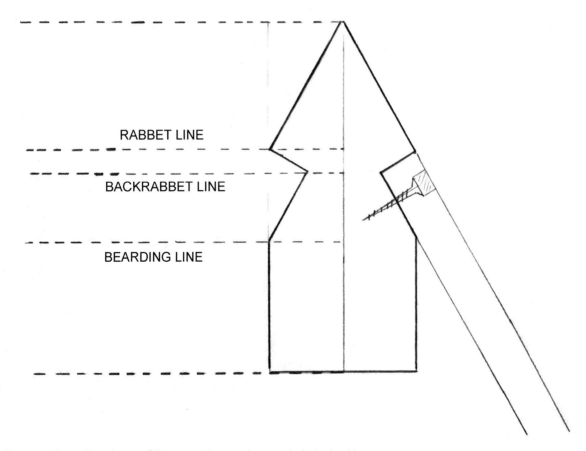

RABBET LINE

BACKRABBET LINE

BEARDING LINE

This illustration shows the relation of the pattern lines to the intended plank rabbet.

Profiles are transferred to the ends of the cut piece to insure proper alignment of both sides.

This stem head for a Gar Wood includes rabbet notches for the sheer clamp and plank battens.

Using gouge and straight chisels, the plank rabbets are carved to correct depths. The original is kept nearby to confirm proper depth and constantly rotating angles of plank rabbet. Note that rabbets are set deeper to accommodate the inner bottom ply.

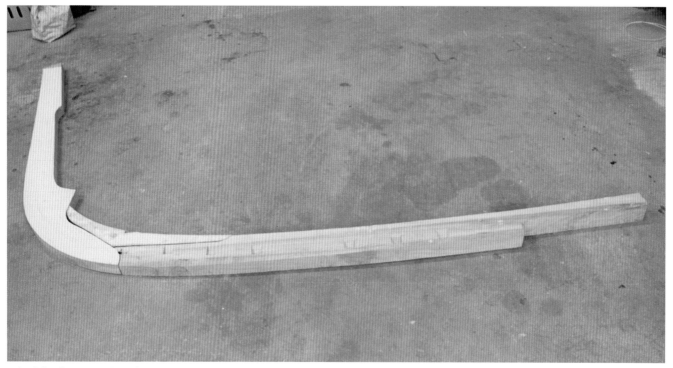

A keel forefoot assembly of stem, stem knee, and gripe.

To pattern the new keel blanks I do not simply trace the old one, as they are all too often not straight. I snap a chalk-line for the centerline of each piece and with the aid of a centering rule (a 15-inch steel ruler with "0" at the center, available at art supply stores). I transfer the greatest width at 1-foot intervals along the length of each piece. Remember to leave at least 1 foot extra length on the pieces to make up for the overlap of the scarf. I also leave a few inches extra on the outboard ends of both pieces until the scarf is finally fit.

Fit the forward keel blank to the aft end of the installed gripe by tracing directly from the gripe. You will need help with the other end of these heavy pieces as you trim the ends on the band saw. Cut this forward end and trim as necessary until you have a satisfactory fit. The chalk trick works well here. Make sure the widths of the keel blank are correct as it falls into the landings at the main frames. Clamp this piece in place and drill the holes for the carriage bolts in the gripe-keel joint. Put at least one carriage bolt in place to hold this position. Block the aft end of the forward keel blank up high enough so as not to interfere with fitting the aft keel blank. Fit the aft keel blank into the main frame landings and clamp into position for the scarf. Lower the aft end of the forward keel blank so that they can be marked for the scarf at the same time. Mark both sides of each piece with the leading and trailing ends of the scarf and note the depths of the lap. Draw the diagonal lines on both sides of each piece and mark, with Xs, the areas to be removed to avoid confusion at the band saw.

Again, get help at the band saw to make sure you are holding these perfectly straight as you cut the scarfs. It is better to cut outside of your lines and plane or grind these to fit rather than to accidentally remove too much. Cut the end and the short lap with a circular saw before making the diagonal cut on the band saw.

The stem and gripe are installed in the hull to fit the forward end of the keel.

An original keel scarf in a Chris-Craft 22-foot utility.

Bottom frames are battened and faired prior to cutting chine and keel plank rabbets.

Temporarily install the forward blank with the locator bolt and clamps and fit and fair this scarf until it is tight and the outside keel shape is correct.

Fabricate an appropriately sized backing block and pre-drill the fastener holes. Make sure these carriage bolts do not land in the area that will be cut for the plank rabbet. The backing block should be as thick as possible without being proud, or protruding above, the adjoining frames. Countersink the inboard surface for the nuts and washers so that they too do not end up raised above the block. Apply a couple of locator bolts to this assembly and clamp it tight.

Clamp the entire keel to all frame landings and mark the inside surface of the keel at the point at which it crosses the forward edge of the lower transom bow. The keel is very often stepped here, usually about 3/8-inch or so; refer to your original keel. Remove the aft keel blank and cut this step. Leave an inch or more overhanging the lower transom bow to be addressed after the keel is finally installed. The bottom planks, keel, and chines overlap the lower transom plank and a portion of each must be left overhanging until the transom has been planked—resist the temptation to trim these flush with the transom bow. Fit and install the after

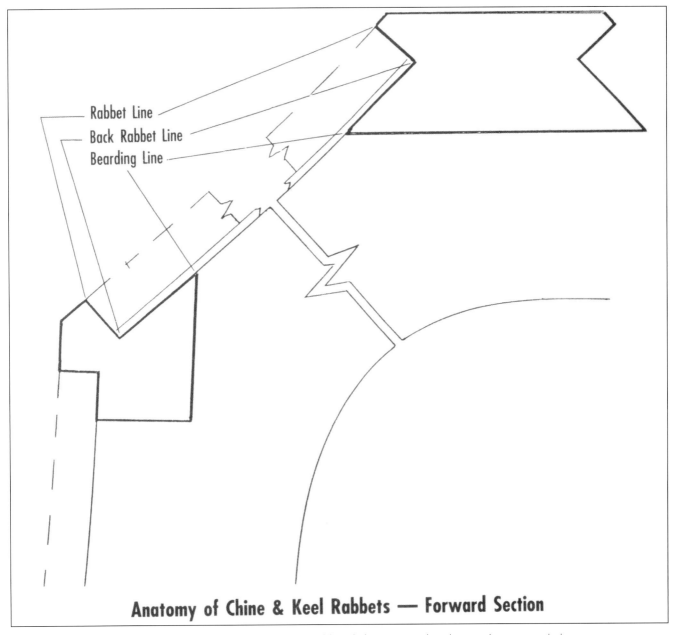

Rabbet Line

Back Rabbet Line

Bearding Line

Anatomy of Chine & Keel Rabbets — Forward Section

This cross-section of the forward section of the chine and keel rabbets helps you visualize the cuts that are needed.

keel blank using locator bolts at the scarf and clamp in position.

Note that we have not addressed the plank rabbets as yet. These are much more accurately cut after the keel is permanently installed. It is possible to cut the bulk of the material out of the plank rabbet before installation with a circular saw or table saw and then dress the remainder of the angled surfaces with a rabbet plane after installation to insure accuracy.

When you are satisfied with the fit of the new keel into the main frame landings and have verified that the planing surface is flat, drill all of the fastener holes. These are generally 1/4-20 carriage bolts. If you have original frame ties in the boat you should drill them up from inside following the

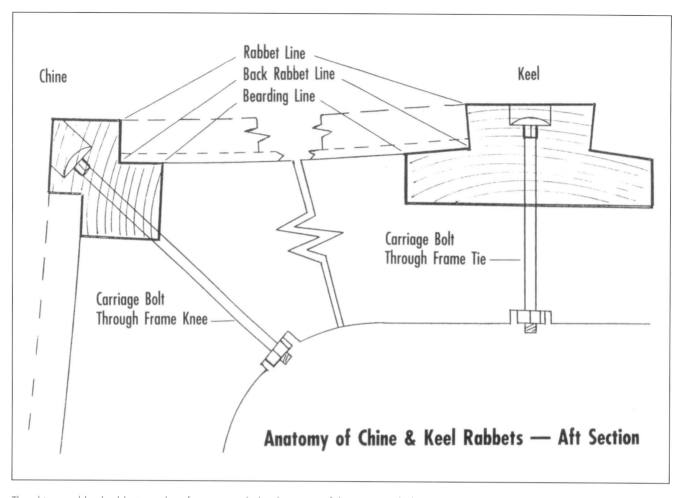

Chine

Rabbet Line
Back Rabbet Line
Bearding Line

Keel

Carriage Bolt
Through Frame Tie —

Carriage Bolt
Through Frame Knee —

Anatomy of Chine & Keel Rabbets — Aft Section

The chine and keel rabbets on the aft section include placement of the carriage bolts.

original hole. Remember that in the area of the propeller shaft the frames are attached with screws in the plank rabbet so as not to interfere with the shaft on the centerline; refer to the original and remember to fasten these after the rabbets are cut.

The keel bolts should be drilled through the frame tie, not through the butt joint of the bottom frames; take more care here than the factory.

Remove the keel blanks, gripe, and stem and clean and seal the surfaces well with a penetrating sealer. Make sure the frame landings are also cleaned and well sealed. This will be the lowest point in your hull when the boat is once again upright and the only place where water can accumulate. Make sure the weep holes or limber holes

are adequate and that they and the bottom frame end grains are well-sealed and painted.

Pay all meeting surfaces including frame landings with a generous amount of bedding compound. It is better to have to clean up the resulting "spooge" than leave voids in the bottom of the hull for water to sit. Do not use a hard glue with these large pieces of lumber; it simply will not last. I highly recommend 3M 5200.

Assemble the stem, gripe, and keel sections with appropriately sized carriage bolts and tighten them after everything is in place. The carriage bolts should be tightened enough to seat the wood firmly but not so tight as to crush the wood fibers. Place whatever screws are necessary and clean up the

After the forward end is temporarily bolted to the gripe, the two keel blanks are overlapped to mark placement of the scarf.

A sturdy keel scarf with keyed ends. The auxiliary frame is altered to fit the backing block. Make sure all items such as strut or rudder stuffing box support blocking are put in before installing the keel. Refer to your pre-disassembly photos.

mess. Be sure to clean all limber holes, where water drains to a low point in the bilge, especially the large square hole in the frames at the top surface of the keel. This can be done with a strip of terrycloth material, soaked with xylol, and run back and forth through the weep holes.

Carriage bolts should be of the cut-thread type, where the shank remains the same diameter as the threads, as opposed to the rolled thread type, where the threads require a 1/4-inch hole to pass but leave a 3/16-inch diameter shank to slop about in the 1/4-inch hole. This not only makes for weak construction but can also allow water to pass. Pay the extra pennies for cut thread.

Chines

The chines, like the keel, should be clear straightgrained white oak. Some models were originally constructed with mahogany and this is acceptable.

If you can locate single lengths long enough for your hull, it is best to do so. If you must scarf two pieces, make sure the scarf lands in a different frame bay than the keel scarf.

I measure the greatest dimensions of the original chines and surface the new stock 1/8-inch larger than this. Make sure the chine blanks are long enough to accommodate the scarf and some extra for fitting the ends. Be sure to remove the ends of the stock to avoid checks caused by drying processes.

I always steam-bend the forward sections before any fitting is done as this will change the landing bevel at the stem as well as allow you to put the proper twist into the piece for proper landings at the frames. After steaming, clamp the chine blanks directly onto the chine landings and hold them in place using clamps and weights to create the proper twist. Allow these to set 24 to 48 hours to assume the shape. Wet towels or burlap left on the pieces will

An original chine scarf in a Chris-Craft 22-foot utility. I much prefer the keyed scarf, which limits movement in at least one direction.

The proper twist put into chine utilizing steam and clamps (both clamping pressure and gravity) with additional clamps hung for weight. This must be watched very carefully so it does not twist too far.

help to keep checks from forming on the surface due to cooling too fast.

As shown in the accompanying photos, to cut the chine ends start by taking bevels and measurements from the forward ends of the original chines and transfer these lines to the new pieces. Leave the extra 1/8-inch on the outboard side for later trimming. Start back far enough from the end and take your measurements from the point created by the intersection of lines 2 and 3. Bring line 4 up from the bottom of line 3 with a square and use the same angle as line 2 to create line 5. The point created by the intersection of lines 5 and 1 must now be transferred to the bottom surface and connected to line 4 to show where the saw must exit the bottom side.

Cut line 1 (watching the bottom side as well) and then cut the 2-3 line. Set the chine in place and mark the hood end at the stem rabbet. Cut this line and fit in place with the aid of a chisel if

necessary. After cutting both chine ends, sight down the stem to make sure the ends are aligned vertically with each other.

Drill fastener holes at the forward ends, set locater screws, and clamp the forward chine sections in place long enough to determine and mark the scarf location.

The chine scarf should be made in the same manner as the keel scarf and backed with a through-bolted block of the same-sized material of nearly one frame bay in length. With the scarf temporarily screwed together, the curve of the joint should be traced onto the backing block and cut to fit. A flat backing block would transfer a flat section to the chine. If there is an intermediate frame in this frame bay it will have to be shortened appropriately to accommodate the backing block.

Fit locater bolts in the scarf and clamp the entire unit in place. You may now drill all of the screw and carriage-bolt holes, referring to the original. Make

To cut chine ends, lines are transferred from the original. Line 1 is cut first, watching the bottom cut line as well. Lines 2 and 3 are cut next.

The two cuts should produce a shape similar to this. Keep the original nearby to confirm the shape.

The correct bevel is verified and marked and the hood end trimmed until it fits.

Topsides chine rabbet locations are marked to assure clearance with the carriage-bolt holes.

Using a reference block of the same thickness as the intended bottom, kerfs are cut parallel to the block to indicate the outboard profiles of the keel and chine. Make sure you include the inner bottom ply in this measurement.

sure the chine bolts pass through the frame knees and not the butt joint of the main frames. If some of the original frame knees are still in the boat, you should drill the carriage-bolt holes from inside the hull following the original holes as a guide. Remember to leave the chines raised above the transom bow at least 1/2-inch to cap the lower transom plank. The chines may now be removed, cleaned, properly sealed and bedded and bolted in place.

Any uninstalled auxiliary frames may now be fit and installed using the keel, chines, and battens off of the main frames as a guide.

Fair in all finally assembled bottom frames with a grinder or plane as necessary. Use straightedges in the planing surface and limber battens in the forward sections. This is your running surface so take whatever time is necessary to do it right. Make sure the frames are beveled correctly so that the planks lie flat. If you have a frame that is too low, do not grind the others too low also. Instead, you may have to add a shim to the frame to bring it into line with the others.

Routing Keel and Chine Plank Rabbets in Place

The next step is to cut the keel and chine plank rabbets. The method I have devised is to set up router tracks and fences along the frames and rout these out with a powerful router and a 3/4-inch straight bit.

The keel and chine blank (shown) are shaped by reference to the kerfs. When the kerfs disappear, the desired shape has been achieved.

The original rabbet lines are transferred to the blanks. Router tracks are set to intended depths of cut: 1/2 inch for topside planks and 3/4 inch for bottom thickness is the usual.

After marking the depth of the router base cut, guide fences are installed.

Keel and chine plank rabbets rotate from horizontal (aft) to vertical (forward). There is no easy way to cut these on the bench other than hand-carving them with chisels and rabbet planes. Getting the changing bevels correct to the hull can mean a lot of on and off the boat trial fitting. I have found that the most accurate way to cut rotating keel and chine plank rabbets is to rout them in place using the hull itself as the router mold.

This procedure assumes that you have already made the hull plumb and level, all frames have been repaired, replaced, or refastened, and frame and frame landings have been faired in with battens. If the frames are not fair, the keel and chines will not be fair, either.

The first step is to shape the outboard profile. Prepare a block of hardwood the thickness of your intended bottom (for example: 1/8-inch inner ply + 1/8 inch for two rubber layers + 1/2-inch plank = 3/4-inch-deep rabbet). Place this block at the ends of each frame at the keel or chines and using a handsaw, cut a kerf just deep enough to indicate the intended final shape of the piece as shown in the photos.

The keel and chine plank rabbet for the bottom will be the same depth. The plank rabbet for the

After marking the depth of the router base cut, install a guide fence. The fence guides the router to a perfect cut in what would otherwise be an unwieldy procedure.

Hull contour determines the correct rotation of the continuously changing bevel.

topsides will likely be the depth of the plank stock and should be kerfed accordingly. Usually these can be cut on the table saw before the piece is steam-bent.

Using a power plane, I now plane in the keel and chines until the handsaw kerfs just about disappear. The keel and chines should exhibit the exact same angles as the adjoining bottom surface, only higher by the amount of the intended bottom surface. Sight these beveled edges carefully along the length of the boat for fairness. If there is any unfairness it will have been caused by an unfair frame end, which should be addressed as well as the corresponding area of the keel or chine.

Using the original keel and chines for reference, mark how far into the keel and chines you want the rabbet to go. This is the rabbet line. For a 4-inch-wide keel this is usually about 1 inch; for chines it is usually about 3/4 inch.

Then temporarily screw a set of reusable planks of the intended bottom thickness to the frames, down both sides of the keel, and, later, the chines. I use pine 1 x 4s surfaced to the correct thickness. The forward set of these planks will need to be steam-bent to accommodate the rotation of the rabbet at the stem.

Using dividers, determine the depth of cut of your router from the base edge to the outside of the cutting bit. Mark this distance from the rabbet line you determined on your keel and chines. Screw a router fence (I use 3/4 x 3/4-inch) to this plank using the marks at the inside edge of this fence. Place your router in position and check to make sure that the bit will cut to the desired line. It may be difficult on some bottoms to get this fence to feed properly into the rabbet at the turn of the gripe. Dress this heavily curved area with a chisel or grinder later if you have to.

I use a 3-1/2-horsepower router with 3/4-inch carbide bits and still have to make these rabbet cuts in as many as six passes of no more than 1/4-inch deep at a time. White oak is a tough wood—do not try to

The chine rabbet changes from horizontal aft to vertical forward, but the router just follows the fence, making it look easy.

take too much at a time. Also, this is a dangerous and tiring job, so pay close attention at all times and follow all appropriate safety procedures.

If you are using a 3/4-inch (carbide only) bit and cutting a 1-inch-deep rabbet you may have to make your first three passes all the way around to the required depth and only 1/2-inch into the rabbet. Move the router fence in 1/2-inch (or add an appropriately sized shim to the inside of the existing fence) and repeat the procedure to achieve the required back rabbet.

The fence set-up and routing procedure is applied to both sides of the keel and both bottom-sides surfaces of the chines. When cutting the chine plank rabbet for the topsides surface it will be necessary to replace the temporary router tracks with planks the same thickness as the topsides

With the proper set up, the router makes quick work of an arduous task, but cannot maneuver in the stem area. The last few inches of chine at the stem still need to be hand carved, which is a small compromise.

Plank battens should be fastened in the center of the batten as two plank-to-frame screws will be set through them on either side of the centerline.

Plank batten notches, or "pockets," are marked by using the actual battens, clamped in place. The sides of these notches should be cut with a fine saw to avoid splintering caused by the router.

The finished profile of the plank rabbets cut into a one-piece chine.

planks. The router tracks do not follow past the stem so there will be a 3- or 4-inch area at the stem where the rabbets will have to be carefully hand-cut with a chisel.

Dress any irregularities where the frames lead into the rabbets and where the rabbets lead into the gripe and stem with a chisel or grinder and you are ready to plank.

If your boat has fore and aft plank battens laid into the frames, such as a Century, you may address these now. Using a long piece of batten stock and referring to the original frames for placement, simply clamp this piece (usually 1/2 x 1-1/2-inch) in place and trace the edges along all of the frames. Using your router set at 1/2-inch deep, cut out the notches. After sealing the notches and battens, bed them in place with one small screw in the center of the batten.

Two-Piece Chines

Some boats, notably the postwar Chris-Crafts, used a two-part chine rather than one piece that required the routed rabbets. These are much easier to work with and replace. The inner portion of the chine can be installed and faired to the shapes directed by the outboard surfaces of the frames with a power plane or hand plane. Now, you can use

Two-piece chines are basically two pieces that are screwed together, offset, to create the plank rabbets. The outer piece is generally mahogany. These are notable on postwar Chris-Crafts.

The inner piece of a two-piece chine. These are much easier to mill and generally just get faired to the frame surfaces.

a rabbet plane to cut the rabbet to the depth of the inner planking layer.

The outer portion of the chine is essentially an offset piece that is attached with screws to form the rabbets. On some models, this piece is the same thickness as the topsides planking, albeit very narrow, and is basically applied the same way. On some models, this piece is 3/4- to 1-inch thick and is proud of the topsides planking. This forces the water, coming off of the planing surface of the bottom, away from the topsides to reduce spray on the boat's occupants.

For many Chris-Crafts, an illustration of cross-sections at each frame station is available from the Mariners' Museum. In most cases you can just duplicate the remnants of the original pieces from your boat.

Chapter 9

BOTTOM PLANKING

The most important aspect of wooden boat restoration is a sound hull, so the previous chapters have been the sermon before the meal, so to speak. It does not really matter what kind of bottom construction you choose, except with regards to longevity. Remember, the bottom planking is not, in any way, meant to hold the framework together; quite the opposite is true.

When doing a standard bottom restoration, the hull is turned over, the bottom planks and topsides chine strakes are removed and the framework and fasteners properly addressed. The original planks are saved for patterns only, as a standard bottom job includes all new mahogany planks; the labor to save the weakened old wood is more expensive than replacing them with new and the benefits are obvious.

As I have stressed repeatedly, it's critical that you eliminate weaknesses in the framework and fasteners in order to minimize failure rates in the bottom planking. The hull is brought plumb and level. The gripe, keel,

Boatyard bedding compound is troweled onto the inner ply with a toothed trowel to maintain an even application. The wood must be well-sealed or the mineral spirits vehicle of the compound will soak into the wood, leaving behind dry solids to absorb and hold moisture.

chines, and lower transom bow are removed from the boat, degreased, inspected, replaced if necessary, sealed, bedded, and re-installed with new silicon bronze carriage bolts. While these components are out, the bottom frames are likewise degreased, inspected, replaced if necessary, sealed, and bedded, and all fasteners, including the carriage bolts in the bilge stringers, are removed and replaced with silicon bronze.

If the hull is not straight, plumb, and level now, it never will be after it is planked—the planking will secure whatever shape the framework is in now.

Check carefully for all things that are easy to get at now before the bottom is applied. Make sure that all of the weep holes in the frames alongside the keel are adequately sized and sealed. The sides of the bottom frames are easiest to paint now. Surfaces in the bilge areas should be sealed with CPES and a light coat of bilge paint, usually an alkyd enamel. Too thick of a coat can keep excess moisture from gassing. I

After the canvas is applied, it must be completely saturated with a brushed-on and thinned mixture of boatyard bedding compound. This gasket layer is meant to waterproof the bottom layers of planking.

Even professionally built, molded construction can suffer from wood movement, creating delaminations. Expansion and contraction occur due to seasonal temperature differences alone.

make quick work of it with a 6-inch paint roller and a 2-inch brush in the corners.

I favor double planking with a bedding compound between the layers. The size and placement of the planking layers should be as close as possible to the original factory construction, with one exception. I use sheet plywood in place of the original inner ply of 6-inch diagonal slats, which are notorious for collecting dirt, debris, and moisture inside the bottom construction. Some manufacturers, including Chris-Craft, switched to plywood for the inner layer sometime in the 1950s. If you do not want to upset the judges, scribe diagonal lines on the inner face of the plywood and re-install the little panhead screws wherever the inner bottom can be seen through hatches. The size and placement of the fasteners should be as the factory installed them. The original brass fasteners should all be replaced with silicon bronze.

Bedding Compounds

The real debate is what kind of bedding compound to use. Originally, builders used linseed oil–based boatyard bedding compounds with a layer of absorbable canvas to hold it from being washed away. This method does have its problems, however. While some believe that it will leave the bottom planks easy to repair, it is still the same six-year lifespan bottom construction delivered by the factory. Even if the inner ply is bedded in rubber to keep the bilge dry, water will still exist between the planking layers. This type of bottom will experience expansion and contraction every season, elongating fastener holes and eventually cracking frames and planks. Compressive set at the edges of the planks will create successively larger gaps each year. This type of loose construction invites dirt, debris, and rot spore. The vehicle of the bedding compound

This section, taken from a two-year-old hard epoxy bottom construction, shows the inability of plywood to conform to the multiply curved shapes of early bottom designs.

(mineral spirits) eventually evaporates and the bottom must be re-done.

Some restorers favor "epoxy encapsulation," in which the plank layers are glued together with a hard epoxy resin mixed with thickening agents. All surfaces of wood components are encapsulated in a hard epoxy resin coating meant to stop any moisture movement at all. In my opinion, this material should only be used in new construction with much thinner planking material. Professionals with temperature and humidity-controlled shops can re-design and build long term vessels with this technology using methodical procedures.

No moisture at all can be introduced to any part of the structure or enough wood expansion will simply tear surface fibers off, leaving one face of the joint bare and un-bedded. All surfaces, inside and out, must be encapsulated and maintained against trailer scratches or minute surface cracks caused by expansion and contraction due to temperature differences or an inflexible hard ride. And, as discussed previously, encapsulation of wood does not allow it to dry out if moisture does get in. This can incubate rot spore, causing it to grow at vastly increased rates. Plank replacement requires routing the damaged plank out.

A third option might be called "enhanced traditional" bedding, in which all wood is sealed with a flexible penetrating sealer that significantly slows the movement of moisture but does not completely stop it. All wood-to-wood joints are bedded with a flexible marine adhesive sealant that flexes with the movement of the components to maintain the seal. The bottom is coated with an underwater barrier coat primer to keep moisture out of the planks, thus diminishing expansion and contraction. With this method, plank replacement does require routing the damaged plank out. To achieve long-term results, the encapsulations, albeit flexible, should be repaired if damaged by component movement or trailer scratches.

Installing Inner Bottom Planking

The first step is to mark the keel and chines on the outside surface of the plank rabbet at the center of each frame. That way, you will know where these frames are after you apply the inner planking or sub-bottom and can no longer see them. Once the plywood is installed you can use a yardstick to connect the keel and chine marks and draw on the outside of the plywood the exact center of each frame so that you know where to place the screws. Note how far out from the keel the first plank-to-frame screw must be placed to avoid placing a screw in the frame weep hole at the side of the keel. Always refer to original screw patterns from the original planks.

Look at the placement and size of the original

Intermediate frames can be steamed and bent on a simple bench-top jig to conform to the hull shape.

On forward sections of the hull, the plywood must be laid in strips to handle the compound curves.

intermediate frames, which are the small frames (usually 5/8 x 1–inch) that run athwartships from keel to chine. The intermediate frames allow attachment points for the edges of the planks between main and auxiliary frames. Precut these now, checking for fit and carefully numbering them on the inboard side. See how far these were gapped from the original keel (usually 1/2 to 3/4 inch) to allow bilge water to weep towards the deepest point of the hull.

If your boat is a Century, then these intermediate frames are fore-and-aft battens (usually 1/2 x 1–1/2 inches) set into notches in the frames, but they create a major problem, namely that water and dirt do not weep toward the keel, but are held in puddles between frames at each batten, waiting to get into that wood-to-wood joint.

In the areas where the bottom frames are concave, usually the forward two-thirds of the hull, these intermediate frames should be steam-bent to the correct curve prior to installation. Trying to bend them cold is time-consuming and frustrating and can cause them to pull fasteners or split. Have these prepared and numbered before you start planking. It is a simple matter to clamp these to temporary blocks, screwed to a bench top, when bending them. It is also very easy to bend them onto the bottom by running them under a board clamped across the frames. Do not worry about cutting them to length until after they are steam-bent. The ends can lie upon the keel rabbet and the chine; this gives them a little over-bend, which should make up for the spring-back when they are removed.

Have all butt blocks precut and sealed and ready to go as well. Remember that butt blocks should not fit tightly against the side of frames, but should allow at least 1/8-inch space for water to drain into the bilge. The grain of the butt block must run in the same direction as the plank stock.

The diagonal sections of the inner ply must be carefully shaped forward, where no frames exist to pull them into shape. Temporary battens can be used to confirm these shapes.

Forward plywood strips can be temporarily held in place with blocks backed by waxed paper until the rubber sets.

The next step is to fit and apply the inner planking layer. If you are going totally traditional, rip and surface the mahogany planks for the diagonal placement, duplicating the originals. I personally recommend using a BS-1088 certified marine plywood to avoid all of those end grains. On boats under 20 feet I generally use 1/8-inch; on boats over 20 feet I usually use 1/4-inch. Note the original inner ply thickness. Fir marine plywood is as good if not better than mahogany plywood. Always seal the plywood edges well.

Starting from the after end of the hull, I fit as large of a piece of plywood as possible, one side at a time. Fit one 8-foot edge into the keel plank rabbet (this should be a straight line) with the aft end flush with the aft end of the lower transom bow and temporarily tack it in place. If your boat has two-part chines, then you need only to trace the outboard edge of the inner chine. If your boat has a chine with a routed plank rab-

bet, you will first trace the outboard edge of the chine and then look at the chine and mark the additional material you will need to remove to get a tight fit.

If your bottom has a concave shape athwartships, you will need to clamp the plywood to this arch to obtain the correct width. The aft end of the sheet is marked directly from the lower transom bow and cut flush to it. The forward end of the sheet should be marked to fall in the center of the farthest forward frame it will reach. This piece and the next forward piece should butt on the center of the same frame. Cut this piece out and after testing the fit; flip it over on the other side of the boat to see how well you (and the factory) did on the framework. If a duplicate can be traced, do so.

I generally seal and paint the interior surfaces of the plywood before they are installed. Two applications of CPES and one of bilge paint will stop immediate absorption of water from rain or spray

Planks can be held in place for dry-fitting with the same jigs used to bend them after steaming.

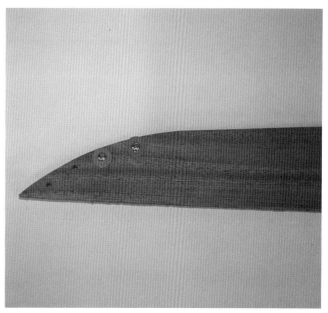

When steam-bending, the hood ends of the planks can be temporarily fastened with screws as long as washers are employed. With the wood in a softened state, screw heads can pull through.

while still allowing excess moisture to escape.

Apply 3M 5200 to the surfaces of all of the frames and pay it out evenly over the surfaces so that there will be no resulting voids to trap and hold water. Remember, when the boat is once again upright, this will be the low point of the bilge. It is a good idea to climb in there and clean up the resulting "spooge," which can be re-used if done immediately. Check all limber holes in the frames alongside the keel to verify they did not get plugged with bedding compound.

Once the plywood is laid and tacked in place, the frame locations can be drawn from the keel and chine marks. The plywood can be applied with bronze ring shank nails or stainless steel or Monel staples. It should be held tightly enough to be evenly bedded to the frames, but that is all that is necessary—you will soon be applying a few thousand screws to secure the planks. If you are working on a concave surface you will have to fasten the plywood from the center out in both directions, fastening at the keel and chines last, otherwise you can cause the plywood to bridge an area that the fasteners cannot pull down.

If you are able to, attach the next forward pieces of plywood so they will fit tightly onto the frames. The plywood can be formed to fit one curve, not two. At some point, determined by your boat's bottom shape, the plywood can be cut at an angle approximately 45 degrees or so back from the keel.

At the forward sections of the hull, where the bottom is concave and also turns up to meet the stem, the plywood will not bend in two directions and 6-inch-wide strips will be necessary. Make these strips from the cutoffs of the after pieces. The average 18-foot boat will only require three sheets of plywood. When placing the forward strips, seal the edges with rubber and wipe them clean on both sides.

To get these forward pieces to fit well, it is sometimes necessary to temporarily screw or staple the edges together with a small piece of wood backed with waxed paper until the rubber sets. This can be hastened by spraying the rubber, which is moisture-cured, with water.

After the rubber has set (three to seven days) you can remove the small blocks and lightly dress any unfair plywood joints with a grinder and seal the outer surface with a penetrating sealer.

Installing Outer Bottom Planking

I do not recommend re-using the original bottom planks. They were not properly sealed at the factory and were not meant to last more than 10 years or so. If they have gone through more than 20 seasons of expansion and contraction, then there are probably no original oils left in the wood, leaving them brittle and weak. The surface fibers of the wood will fail long before any sealers or bedding compounds will.

The original planks should be temporarily laid on the boat in order to mark original butt joint locations and to determine if alterations from the original have been made with short section repairs. The original planks should be used as patterns only and new ones surfaced and cut to fit. When cutting the new planks remember to leave them slightly larger than the shrunken old planks. When cutting new planks, I always leave the aft ends of the plank sections longer than the originals by 3 inches. This will allow final fitting of the forward ends and if any mistakes are made, the plank can be slid forward and refit. Then the aft end can be trimmed at the correct butt location, usually within 3 to 4 inches of a frame and halfway between the frame edge and the edge of the future intermediate frame.

Remember that almost every boat has one or two

Bottom planks are hand-planed to fit and temporarily assembled with locator screws.

SCHOOL OF HARD KNOCKS

Using the Right Tool

Long ago, I worked at a restoration shop where a fellow boatwright had planked a curved transom bedded in 3M 5200 without noticing minute windbreaks in the plank stock.

On returning to work the following Monday he was shocked to see the top two planks split across their entire width. He removed the screws, picked up a large chisel and mallet, and began beating away at the offending planks. Cursing the tenacity of the rubber, and probably wishing it had never been invented, he began removing strips and chunks of the planks as well as pieces of the transom framing. I calmed him down and asked if I could have a go at it. I picked up my large router with a straight 3/4-inch plunge bit and set it for the plank thickness plus a bit more for the rubber. Following only the outline of the transom frames and letting the larger sections fall away, I had a clean flat surface ready to re-plank in about 15 minutes. The right tool makes all the difference.

To this day, when we chance to work together, we covertly draw tiny jagged pencil cracks on each other's fresh transom planks.

Make sure the bottom planks overhang the transom bow by at least the thickness of the intended transom planks.

After all bottom planks are dry-fit and pre-drilled with locator screws, they can be removed and well-sealed with CPES on the inboard side and edges. The outboard side will be sealed after installation and fairing.

If you do not have decent plank patterns you can spile them in place with a spiling batten and dividers.

forward bottom planks that will show above the waterline at the stem and should be selected with grain and color to match topsides planking. As always, quarter-sawn planking is far more stable and less apt to swell, shrink, or cup than plain-sawn planking. If, however, you have chosen an adhesive bedding compound, the bottom is one place where you can use plain-sawn lumber. Since it will be glued to the inner ply, cupping will be held in check.

The forward planks should be steam-bent to take the curve of the bottom at the stem. This will make them far easier to fit and will avoid replacements caused by cracking.

This can be most easily done before the application of the plywood, when frames are still available to clamp them to. If you have not done this prior to plywood installation, it is a simple matter to set up a simple jig for this purpose that hooks on to the

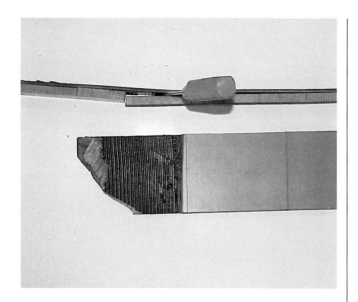

This application, from a failed bottom construction, shows that quick-setting compounds, in this case 3M 4200, will set long before the thousands of screws necessary can be drilled and set. This also shows an inadequate amount of rubber.

chine and is clamped to its partner on the other side. The planks are slid under these jigs and a simple wedge is all that is needed to hold them for overnight cooling.

At the hood ends, where clamping to the stem or gripe plank rabbet is difficult, you can use help to quickly drill and screw them in place. Washers should be used under the screw heads here to avoid splitting the plank or pulling the screw head through the temporarily softened wood.

The next step is what I call "dry fitting" the planks. One strake at a time, working outboard from the keel, the planks are fit and screwed to the frames with a minimal number of locator screws, not countersunk, applied to hold the plank snugly in place, usually two screws per frame. Follow the frame lines drawn on the outer surface of the inner ply. Start with the forward garboard planks (the plank strake that fits into the keel). It is helpful here to use washers under the screw heads to help prevent

splitting near sharp plank ends. Fitting is usually done with pencil marks and a hand plane or finger plane. I usually try for an even 1/16-inch gap between planks, which will end up filled with rubber as a hedge against swelling caused by temperature or moisture levels. Use the steaming jigs and clamps until you are ready for screws. No sealers or bedding compounds are applied until all planks are fit. I don't even cut out the farthest outboard plank until the first four or five strakes are fit.

It is possible to use the router technique to fit these plank edges. Please see the router technique described for use in topsides planking (Chapter 11). I find it easiest to clamp the plank as close as possible to its intended location and spile the correct line directly from the previous plank edge with dividers.

After fitting the forward garboards, trim their aft ends to the correct butt joint location and fit the aft garboards. Remember to leave the aft "follower" planks hanging well proud of the transom bow as these must cap, or overhang, the lower transom plank.

After the garboard strakes are temporarily fitted and attached fore and aft with locator screws, the second strake should follow in the same order. Remember to trim the butt joints before fitting the follower planks and keep them even from side to side.

When all planks on both sides of the boat have been fitted, the planks can be removed and the inside surface and edges sealed with a penetrating sealer. Using 6-inch yellow foam epoxy rollers and throwaway bristle brushes, I apply two applications of CPES, one immediately following the other. Seal the plywood, as well, and wait 24 to 48 hours for the product to set. Provide plenty of good ventilation.

To reinstall the planks, I get help and complete the job in one long exhausting day. This allows every screw to be placed before the rubber has a

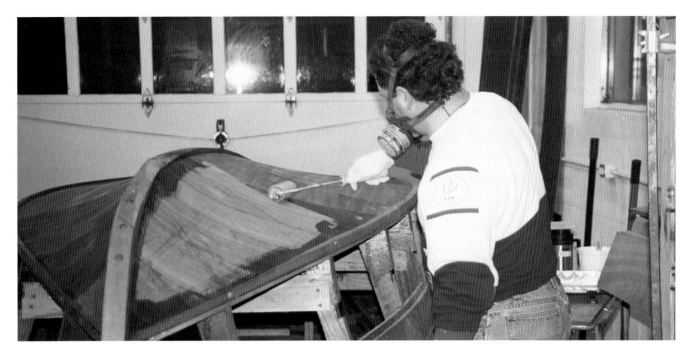

Plywood surfaces can be lightly ground at unfair seams and should be sealed as well. The Clear Penetrating Epoxy Sealer (CPES) glues the wood fibers together to make the surface stronger for bedding compound applications.

chance to set. Start early in the morning just in case you need another day to finish. 3M 5200 can set overnight in high summer humidity and in about seven days in dry winter conditions. I do not recommend quick-setting polyurethanes or polysulfides—I have replaced such bottoms because the rubber had set up before the thousands of screws could be installed to pull everything together.

The rubber is applied to the sub-bottom with a pneumatic caulk gun with the tube tip unscrewed. I use approximately two 10-ounce tubes per plank. If you have a 19-foot bottom with 20 planks, have 48 tubes on hand. Spread the rubber with a 3/16-inch toothed trowel so that a uniform layer is assured. I usually apply two plank strakes' worth at a time so that I don't have my elbows in it as I'm installing the planks. Remember to put a generous bead in the keel and chine plank rabbets as well as

3M 5200 is applied with a caulk gun and evenly spread with a 3/16-inch toothed trowel. At this point, note how well the bottom planks did or did not conform to the inner ply surface and ensure that an adequate amount of 3M 5200 is applied to eliminate voids.

Teamwork is required to get all fasteners and intermediate frames installed before the rubber can set.

along the side of each plank strake just installed. It is always best to clean up and re-use the excess than to leave a void. The 1/16-inch gap between planks should be completely filled with rubber, not air. Apply this edge bead before the next plank is installed so that any trapped air is forced up and out of the joint with the excess rubber. Remember to apply the compound to the plank butt joints.

The planks are installed using the pre-drilled locator holes so that they end up exactly where you had them during the dry fitting. Finding these holes can be tricky through a layer of rubber, so I use a few ice picks to verify placement before screws are set.

While one person is placing the planks with locator screws the others can be spreading the rubber on the other side. Work efficiently, as you still have a few thousand screws to install before the end of the workday.

Installing Screws

When one person is freed up from plank installing, he can begin drilling the plank-to-frame screw

holes with correct countersink. Use your yardstick and once again connect the keel and chine marks to locate frame centers. Remember to stay far enough from the keel to miss the frame weep holes. Bottom plank screws need not be counter-

Lines are drawn from keel and chine marks to indicate frame centers.

sunk as deeply as topside screws if you plan to use putty to fill them instead of bungs. This allows for a stronger fastener attachment if there is more wood under the screw head.

The next person follows, installing the screws. Make sure you are using an adjustable clutch screw gun with the correct torque setting to properly seat the fasteners without wringing off the heads. You should be able to see the plank being drawn down and note whether the screw head is properly seated in the bottom of the hole before continuing on.

Use one size of screw at a same time, so as not to confuse pre-drilled hole sizes. After all of the frame screws are in (usually #8 x 2-inch in boats under 22 feet and # 10 x 2-inch in boats over 22 feet), the keel and chines (usually #8 x 1-1/4-inch) and transom bow (usually #8 x 1-1/2-inch) can be done.

Following the original layout, the intermediate frames are predrilled next.

If your boat is a Century with the fore and aft battens already in place, you may fasten these as well. If there are three intermediate frames between main and auxiliary frames, it is a simple matter to measure between the centers of these frames and divide this by four (spaces) to determine and mark their locations. Do this in each frame bay near the keel and again near the chine and connect these lines with the yardstick. Use the millimeter side of the yardstick so you don't have to bother with fractions.

Lay your numbered, pre-cut, pre-bent, and pre-sealed intermediate frames on the correctly numbered lines and note where beginning and ending fasteners must be in order not to get too close to the ends and cause splitting.

After noting exactly where the screws should begin and end, I pre-drill and countersink all of these holes for the intermediate frames along the

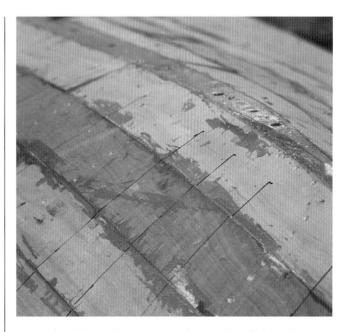

Intermediate frame placement is marked and pre-drilled. The screws in these should not be placed too close to the ends to avoid splitting the small intermediate frames that must be amply spaced from the keel to provide a weep hole.

drawn lines. In order to help keep from splitting the small frames, I stagger the holes from one side of the line to the other, no more than 1/8 inch or so. I drill these holes with an overlong bit so that the short (usually #8 x 1-inch) screw threads do not hang up on the plank stock but grip only the intermediate frame underneath. This also makes the screw line easier to see from inside the boat for placement of these frames.

Send your skinny helper inside the boat with some cushions and a light. Apply rubber to the correct side of the pre-cut, pre-bent, and numbered intermediate frames and carefully slide it in to him. As he is holding it in place over the line of predrilled holes, you must drill a couple of holes with the correctly sized bit and put in a couple of screws before he slides off of the line. Complete the re-drilling and install the screws while he is holding it tightly against the inner bottom and directing which screws to place.

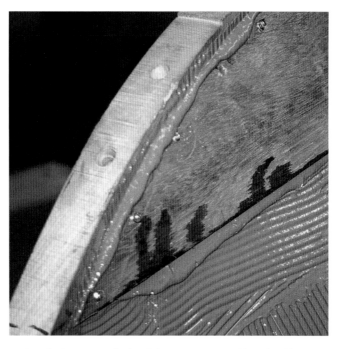

As planks are applied, a uniform application of 3M 5200 must be maintained—this shakes out to be about to two tubes per plank. The backside of the planks should also be rubbered, this time with a smaller-toothed (1/16-inch) trowel.

As the planks are installed with locator screws, rubber should squeeze out from all seams, leaving no voids.

Remember to apply a bead along the edge of each plank. It must be positioned at the bottom of the edge so that no air is trapped to create voids.

When dry-fitting and installing bottom planks, the plank or planks that will eventually be varnished (those above the waterline) should be fit first.

At the end of the workday, when all fasteners are set, hose down the bottom.

Very thin (.35-millimeter) plastic is applied and the air bubbles wiped out.

The bottom planking is ground fair with a variable speed grinder and soft foam pad.

Remember to watch the plank suck in as you are seating the screws. You do not want any voids left between the inner and outer plank layers. Continue with these until they are all installed. You will not want the rubber to set up before these are all installed.

After all the intermediate frames are in you must pre-drill and install the butt blocks in the same manner. Remember to place the grain direction of the butt blocks fore and aft, in the same direction as the plank stock.

It is possible to do this step prior to plank installation by temporarily fastening the intermediate frames through the plywood. When the bedding is set, remove these screws. Mark these intermediate frame locations on the keel and chine so you will be able to properly locate them after the planking is installed. If the intermediate frames are already installed it is not only possible for one person to apply the planking alone, but you need not get all the planks on in one day.

The forward area that will be stained and varnished above the waterline should be masked prior to two applications of CPES.

I know it is hard work at the end of a long day, but it really is wise to crawl around inside the boat and clean up the excess rubber. It makes for a clean bilge that is easier to keep clean. If you can stand the smell (evident despite the respirator which you, of course, are wearing), 3M 5200 wipes up easily (only when fresh) with terrycloth rags and xylol. Make sure the butt blocks can pass water down either side and all frame weep holes are clear.

Wetting the Bottom

The outside bottom of the hull can now be troweled free of the resultant spooge and hosed down with fresh water. This is a procedure I call "pre-soaking." After the bottom planks are thoroughly wetted out, I cover the entire bottom with a very thin plastic sheet (.35 millimeter) and rub out all of the air bubbles. The thinner the plastic, the better this works—99-cent painter's drop cloths work well. For the next two days, peel up edges of the plastic to wet it and again, rub out the air bubbles. This procedure changes the moisture content of the wood and causes it to swell forcing out all excess rubber, and hopefully, any trapped air.

As explained previously, the equilibrium moisture content of wood is dictated by the average relative humidity and temperature of the environment. In most states with lakes it is in the 18 percent range, as opposed to a state like, say, Arizona, where it is around 11 percent. Kiln-dried mahogany from my suppliers is in the 6 to 10 percent range.

Changes in overall moisture content of the wood can be retarded by protective coatings but not prevented. I know that if a boat is kept in Michigan, its wood will eventually learn to exist at roughly 15 to 18 percent moisture content. Personally, I feel it wise to set it to this level before sealing it.

The first time I used this procedure was in 1985 when I had my shop at the Herreshoff Marine Museum Complex in Bristol, Rhode Island. In the following 13 years, I used this method on every bottom I constructed. When properly sealed against seasonal variations in relative humidity, this type of construction exhibits little or no expansion or contraction that is great enough to crack the enamel paint at the plank seams. In order for this to work, of course, the exterior of the bottom must be well-sealed against excessive moisture absorption from extensive periods in the water.

After two days of wetting the bottom, allow it to set another two days until the moisture is noticeably absorbed and the surface appears dry. Remove the plastic and allow the surface to become completely dry. Now you must quickly cut off all of the excess rubber, fill in all of the screw holes, grind and fair the bottom, and get it sealed before it dries out too much. Remember to tape off the waterline forward and use bungs above that, where the planks will be varnished. Buy or borrow a moisture meter to test the moisture content of the wood.

If you are doing this job in the winter in a heated building, the relative humidity could be extremely low. Hosing the floor down every night can help maintain normal moisture levels in your shop.

Filling Screw Holes and Sealing

The product I use for filling the bottom plank screw holes is Famo-Wood. This putty, if properly applied, will last a long time. In order to drastically reduce the amount of time it takes to fill 3,000 or so holes, I thin this product slightly with Famo-Wood thinner and put it into an empty caulk tube available from Jamestown Distributors and many large paint stores. Insert the tube in a regular caulk gun and shoot it into the holes from the bottom up. When smoothing out the applied Farmo-Wood with a 1-inch flexible putty knife you must force it into the holes and burp out any trapped air bubbles. The putty knife should be stroked in at least three directions in order to assure contact, and thus adhesion, to all surfaces of the hole walls.

After this putty is dry, grind and sand the bottom fair and seal with two coats of Smith's CPES. Allow 24 to 48 hours for it to cure and apply three or four coats of Interlux Epoxy Barrier Coat Primer. This product is designed as an underwater moisture barrier that keeps the bottom planking from absorbing water and thus expanding and contracting which is harmful to the planks, fasteners, and frames. I currently use Interlux 2000E. Allow 48 hours for the last coat of this to cure and apply two coats of your bottom paint.

If you are not using an anti-fouling bottom paint, you should use an alkyd enamel such as Interlux Premium Yacht Enamel instead of a polyurethane, which can absorb moisture and cause blisters and peeling. I generally only seal and paint the bottom as far as the edge of the chines for now. The sealer, barrier coats, and bottom paint from the chine up to the waterline on the topsides are applied after the topsides are completely faired in.

If you installed a new keel and need to re-drill the rudder stuffing box hole or the propeller shaft hole, now is the time to do it. Actually, do it before applying the first barrier coat to ensure sealing these new holes as well. Using the original keel, transfer the locations for the rudder stuffing box hole and the propeller shaft-strut bolt holes. Take your measurements from the aft surface of the transom bow, not from the end of the keel, which is yet to be trimmed. If you did not replace the strut support block you may simply drill up from inside through the original bolt holes. Install the strut, making sure it is correctly aligned with the center of the keel by temporarily installing the propeller shaft

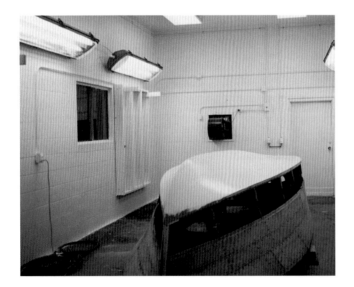

Four coats of barrier coat primer are followed by two coats of bottom paint. The application of CPES and barrier coat may cause the young rubber to expand slightly above the surface. This is carefully shaved off after the first barrier coat.

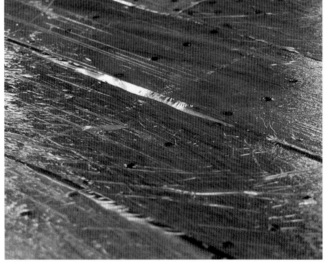

After two days wet, excess rubber and hopefully all air bubbles are expelled. Excess rubber must be trimmed with a knife or chisel.

A temporarily installed shaft strut can be used to bore a new shaft hole if the keel has been replaced. A line-bored piece of hardwood, or in this case bronze bushings, align the drill extension with the strut. An old propeller shaft that fit the cutlass bearing (the original most likely needs to be replaced anyway) can be milled at both ends as a drill extension.

or broom handle and tightening the strut bolts.

Lay the old keel alongside the strut and verify that the elongated shaft hole would be the correct distance from the strut. In replacing the keel and grinding in the new bottom you may have slightly changed the landing surface for the strut. Address this now with a grinder or chisel until correct placement is obtained when the strut is tightly bolted down.

I have had a 3/8-inch extension bit welded to a piece of 1/2-inch drill rod and line-bored piece of wood that fits tightly in the strut to correctly direct the extension. I use either a 1-1/4-inch or 1-1/2-inch Forstner bit to cut the hole. Scrap blocks of 4 x 4, diagonally cut, are temporarily screwed to the top and bottom of the keel to insure a clean entrance and exit to the hole. Keep steady and even pressure as you cut and back the bit and wood chips out often. Do not get impatient and push too hard, as this can force the bit off-center. Seal these openings plus any other through-hull holes that could admit copious amounts of water that would be easily absorbed into the end grains of the wood. This water could quickly build the moisture content of the wood to 30 percent or more, which would then awaken and nourish the ever-present rot spore.

Chapter 10

RETAINING ORIGINAL TOPSIDE PLANKING

With the bottomsides complete and painted, it is time to flip the hull upright and address the topsides, the area of the hull between the chine and the deck at the sheer. If you intend to strip the topsides varnish it is easiest to do this while the hull is still upside down. (Please refer to Chapter 3 for information on safely flipping a hull over and chemically stripping finishes.)

At this time I recommend removal of the deck. This is an opportunity to make your deck framework—and thus the boat—straight, tight, and secure from existing rot conditions. Address the deck beams before re-planking the hull topsides.

I recommend that you replace your topsides planks with sound, new wood. It will cost less in the long run and last longer than re-using the dried, brittle, cupped, and cracked wood that originally came on your boat.

If you're determined to preserve the brittle, cupped, and cracked original wood, use the following procedures. I rarely re-use the old wood unless the customer requires it after fully understanding that he is getting a product substantially inferior to new wood at a cost, due to labor, from removal to fairing, that is at least twice the cost of new wood. Remember, however, at the very least you must expect the original wood to react differently than it did when it was new; you must expect unsightly surfaces and occasional repairs.

Once the boat is upright it should again be thoroughly secured in a position that is plumb and level using a spirit level or laser level. Temporary bracing from the chine to the floor will hold the hull in position. Take diagonal measurements of the transom to insure it is square with the world. Half-breadth measurements, outboard from a taught centerline with plumb-bobs to the keel, should be taken at every frame station.

If the sheer is completely level and the half-breadth measurements are not all equal, this is an indication that there has been some spreading of the deck through broken or loose fasteners or frame end-splitting at the joint of deck beams to topsides frames. At any rate, the hull should be square, plumb, and level and all frames including deck beams should be properly sealed, bedded, and re-fastened before the topsides planks are either re-fastened or replaced. As with the bottom, once these planks are tightly secured, they will hold whatever shape the hull frames were in, straight or not.

Make sure that your work area allows for planking both sides of the hull at the same time. If you attempt to plank the hull one complete side at a time, the weight of the planks as well as the tension created by thousands of fasteners will pull the topsides out of shape. This will cause the boat to always want to pull to one side when underway and look noticeably crooked at the stem. It is best to install the planks one strake at a time, from one side to the other. A plank strake is any number of planks in a straight line from stem to stern (usually two planks, a forward and a follower, in hulls under 22 feet).

This hull planking was begun at another shop without care for leveling or bracing. Four starboard side planks were installed before any portside planks, causing the hull to twist to starboard under the lopsided weight.

The boat should be plumb, level, and square before planking. Temporary bracing to the floor can be screwed to the chines to hold this condition until the planking is done.

Count the planks in your topsides from the chine up to the sheer, if there are five planks you have a five-strake hull.

Surveying Existing Planks

Survey the existing topside planks carefully. Are there bungs standing proud of the surface or exhibiting surrounding discoloration? These indicate loose or broken fasteners. Does the overall topsides surface exhibit faceting—flat surfaces at individual planks rather than a smoothly fair hull? This indicates a great number of loose or broken fasteners. Does the varnish crack open at the plank seams visually displaying each plank? This tells you that the overall hull planking and/or framing is loose or shrunk with age. Do the plank edges show a dark discoloration at the seams? This tells you that the

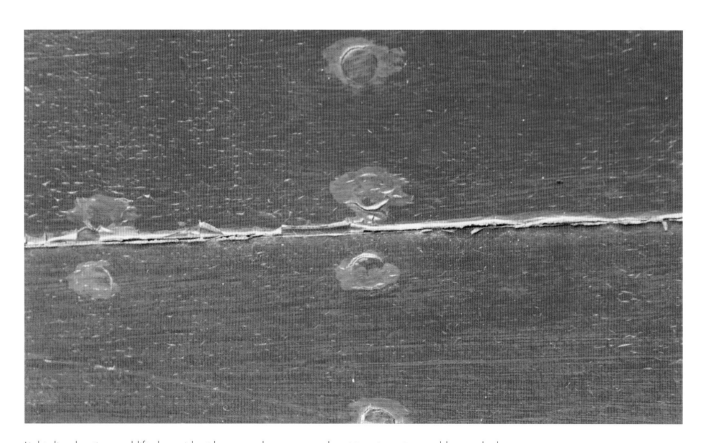

Light discoloration and lifted varnish at bungs and seams reveal moisture incursion and loose planks.

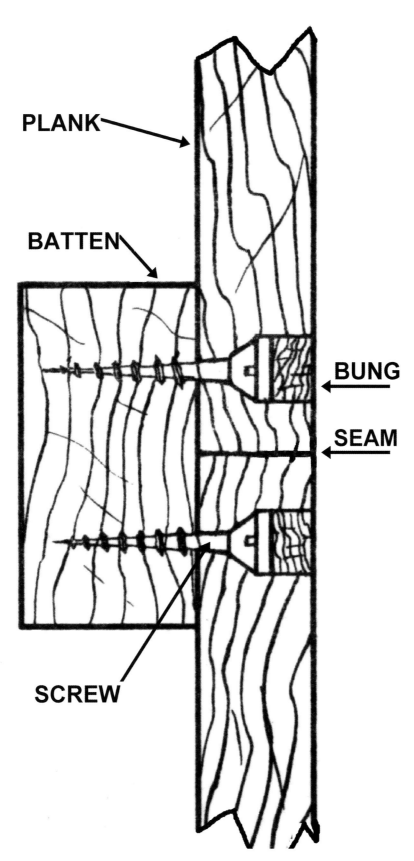

PLANK

BATTEN

BUNG

SEAM

SCREW

An illustration from a Chris-Craft owners' manual displays typical plank-and-plank-batten construction and fastener placement. *Courtesy of The Mariners' Museum, Newport News, Virginia*

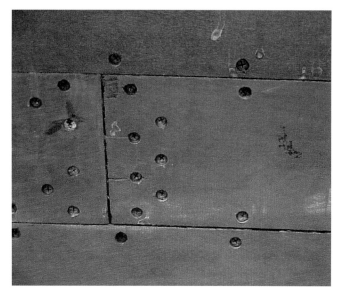

To avoid pulling chips of wood from around the screw holes, the varnish should be completely stripped from the hull before popping the bungs. Plank gaps display shrunken original planks due to loss of original oils.

Since wood expands and contracts about only 2 percent longitudinally, gaps at butt joints indicate that the entire hull has expanded outboard in its circumference. This condition is due mostly to loose and broken framework.

For bung removal, a thin, sharp ice pick is the best tool to avoid damaging the surrounding wood surface. The first approach (shown) is to crack the bung at the center. The second approach is to crack a section of the bung by prying against only the bung itself.

If a sliver or small chunk of wood breaks away from the edge of a fastener hole or plank edge, it should immediately be glued back in place using a quick-setting glue.

The chine strake and second strake are installed and the fourth strake removed so that the third strake can be installed.

Transom planks should be removed first, as they cap the topsides planks. Covering boards may have to be removed before the sheer strake can come off.

planks are loose enough to allow water and dirt to sit in these joints. I have seen hulls such as this refastened in place, bleached, stained, and varnished only to have the stains re-appear the next season.

Do the plank butt joints or transom ends or hood ends (at the stem) exhibit discoloration or cracks or softness? These originally unsealed and un-bedded joints invite rot spore once they are loose. No amount of surface treatment will prevent these problems from reoccurring. Have the planks been excessively thinned from many years of over-sanding? If this is so, expect your hull to be weaker than the factory expected it to be. Fastener heads set deeply enough to bung may be holding very little wood. Do the planks show cracks or cupping or brittleness due to many seasons of unsealed expansion and contraction?

If the wood has lost its original oils due to seasonal moisture cycling, expect all of the above problems to reoccur. Fairing a hull in this condition will

The inboard sides of the planks should be scraped clean to expose the cracks that have begun at the fastener holes. The plank edges are carefully cleaned of varnish debris and old caulking compounds.

also remove a great deal more wood. The vast majority of these hulls are "batten-seam" planked. The plank battens, usually 1-1/2 x 1/2-inch mahogany, run fore and aft and are notched into the frames. The horizontal top surfaces of these battens provide a perfect place for moisture and dirt to accumulate and drain into the plank to batten joint. Rot at plank edges begins here. You could very well have sound looking planks that are being rotted from the inside out at these joints. Your popped bungs and loose planks could be caused solely by rot-weakened plank battens.

Think carefully before you decide to ignore these possible internal problems, hoping they do not exist (highly unlikely, if your wooden boat is more than 20 years old) and refinishing an originally planked hull.

If you are buying what appears to be a restored boat, ask to see photos and records of the restoration in order to assure yourself that these internal problem areas were not glossed over and remain hidden

trouble for your future expense. Verify that the proper marine grade lumber was used (white oak, dense rot-resistant mahoganies) as well as proper marine-grade fasteners (silicon bronze), sealers, and bedding compounds.

When you are restoring your boat keep careful records, with material receipts, and take photos of every procedure to enhance the sales value of your boat. Serious, educated buyers will ask for them and insurance company surveyors and appraisers appreciate it greatly, to your benefit. If you are paying a restoration shop to do this work, ask for photos every stage that you receive a bill. Verify that you are getting what you are paying for.

If you are planning to re-use your old planks in spite of any of the aforementioned signs of looseness or aging, they should be removed from the hull, cleaned, properly sealed, and re-bedded in place. While these planks are off you can address the frames as well.

Stripping and Removing the Topsides Planking

The old planks must be removed carefully in order to reuse them. All of the varnish, paint, and stain should be stripped from the topsides before you attempt to pop bungs or planks. These coatings may still have good adhesion to the wood and can pull splinters or wedges from the surface or at the plank edges or bung edges.

If you are using the same procedure with the deck and are relatively sure you will be re-installing it before the planks dry and shrink excessively, you may strip the deck at the same time. Remember to mask off any areas that you do not want the stripping to harm, such as the new bottom paint. A 6-inch skirt of 6-millimeter plastic attached with duct tape to the chine should prevent this. Do not leave this on for very long or chemical strippers will get under it.

CPES is soaked into the inboard sides and edges of the weak and porous old wood. This helps to stabilize the wood so it is not as susceptible to the moisture-induced movement that caused the cracking at the fasteners in the first place.

Some common sense will be required to adapt this procedure to the deck and topsides, instead of the bottom. When the varnish is all removed and before neutralizing the surface with water, apply fresh stripper to approximately 1-square-yard areas using a stiff, natural bristle scrub brush. Scrub with the grain to remove as much of the old stain as possible. Be sure to vary the edges of these areas so as not to leave vertical shadows in your applications.

The bungs must now be very carefully removed to leave a crisp tight line when the new bungs are installed after refastening. Obtain a padded, height-adjustable shop stool on wheels. After removing and replacing thousands of bungs, drilling holes, and placing screws, as well as hundreds of hours of fairing, sanding, staining, varnishing, sanding, varnishing, etc., you will come to revere this stool as the best tool in your shop.

To remove bungs without damaging the surround-ing plank surface, you must approach the bung from the center. To this day, I have not found a better tool for this than a thin bladed, very sharp ice pick. I have tried all manner of manufactured and custom built drill bits, which work a hundred times faster in areas to be painted, but will not leave the crisp line necessary for a varnished surface. The secret is to pry only against the bung material itself and not the surrounding wood. Stab the ice pick into the center of the bung and tweak it slightly up or down, against the grain direction. Re-insert an eighth of an inch or so above or below this and prying against only bung material, remove pieces of the bung from the center out. Do not attempt to remove the full depth of the bung at first unless it is a very shallow bung. When there is nothing left of the outer surface of the bung to pry against, simply stab the ice pick into the lower corners of the hole and wedge these pieces away from the hole walls. Do not be too concerned with every minute speck of old glue or wood as you will be re-drilling this hole with the proper counter bore when the plank is re-installed.

While you are down in there, clean the remnants of wood or glue from the screw slots. If the screw head is Reed and Prince (Frearson) or Phillips, simply stab the ice pick straight down the center of the depression and pry in all four directions to remove the material. You will need to re-sharpen the ice pick occasionally. The surface of the screw head must be completely exposed or backing the screw out could catch on the surrounding material and break a wedge of plank surface material out. If this should happen, and it will, the wedge of plank surface material should be replaced immediately or it will be lost and you will have to replace it with putty. I keep on hand a gap-filling cyanoacrylate "super glue" for wood called Insta-Cure. This and

An adhesive bedding compound helps to stabilize the cracked plank edges against the plank batten. If you want to leave the planks "easy to repair," use a boatyard bedding compound here.

similar products are available from hobby shops for the construction of radio-controlled model boats and airplanes. It comes with a product called Insta-Set in a little spray bottle that, as the name implies, instantly sets the glue so you don't have to sit there and wait. Wear rubber gloves or use the ice pick to hold the wood in place—this product will glue your your gloves—or your fingers—to the boat. If immediately and properly set, these wood chips become invisible repairs. Practice and develop your bung removal technique in an inconspicuous area such as below the waterline, or below the lower rub rails aft. Practice your wood chip repairs on a scrap piece of wood, on the bench; this is what scrap wood is for.

Recognize and mark any planks you intend to replace and you will not have to be so careful with these. Save these replaced original planks to cut matching bungs for the original planks that stay.

The above procedures can all be applied to the deck and interior furniture as well. Some models will require

that the outboard deck covering board fasteners be removed before the topsides sheer strakes can come off.

After all of the bungs are removed and screw slots cleaned, you may begin removing the planks. All planks should be marked for placement on the hull as well as indications for "up" and "forward." Starting with the chine strake and continuing up, these planks should be marked: "S1F" (starboard 1 forward), "S1A" (starboard 1 aft), "S2F" (starboard 2 forward), etc. Use chalk or a soft lead pencil for this; do not use magic markers or inks that can bleed into the wood.

You should use an adjustable torque screw gun—not the Sheetrock type. With this tool you can set the torque on a light setting and gently ratchet the brittle old fasteners out rather than immediately wringing the head off. Reed and Prince (Frearson) screwdrivers and bits are available from Jamestown Distributors. These are different from Phillips both in depth and shoulder angle and will strip each other; make sure you have the right one. If the screw does not start unscrewing right away set the gun for forward and gently ratchet it forward for a moment to hopefully break free of any mineral salts leeched from the old fastener, adhering it to the hole. Sometimes it is helpful to place a screwdriver on the screw head and rap it a couple of times with a small hammer just to break this brittle bond. There will be some troublemakers, these should be marked for now and addressed all at one time when you are tooled for their specific problem. Use bright blue chalk for this, or a piece of color-coded tape, to help you easily find the problem fasteners later.

If the screw head is sound and the screw simply spins in the hole without backing out, I draw a circle around the hole, indicating a "spinner." This screw will simply pull or need to be pried out of the frame with the plank and then removed from the plank later.

Early repair wedges had been used here at the toe rail and sheer, possibly to make up for wood lost to rot. Original factory construction did not use bedding compounds, so moisture wicked into these joints, which fed the growth of rot.

If the screw head slots strip and the screw is still sound in the hole, I mark this with an X over the hole, or a different color tape. These you will have to return to later with a drill and bit sized slightly larger than the screw shank and drill the head off. The shank will have to be removed from the frame with Vise-Grips after the plank is removed. If there is a really unusual situation—such as a previous repair using a machine screw with a nut inside the hull or a strange screw head such as a square-drive or hex-head screw—mark them with an X and a circle for now rather than keeping all of those different tools in your lap.

Carefully remove the planks from the hull once they are completely unfastened. Watch especially the edges of the plank. If there is still adhesion from varnish or whatever at the plank seams, small wedges of wood can be torn away from the supposedly sharp plank edge. If this becomes a problem,

carefully and accurately cut down this line with a utility knife prior to plank removal to help alleviate it. Remember to use the Insta-Cure to immediately repair these. Using the old planks does not allow for much stock removal when re-fairing the hull.

Cleaning and Sealing the Old Planks

Once the planks have been removed from the hull, the interior and edge surfaces must be cleaned, repairs made and properly sealed. The edges of the planks must be handled very carefully if you want them to fit tightly once again. Hard chips and bits of varnish must be removed without damaging the wood. Very careful use of a sharp scraper may work here.

If the inboard surfaces of the planks exhibit stress or mechanical damage cracks, custom fit backing blocks after the plank has been re-installed and glue the crack in place. If the inboard surfaces of the planks show many open cracks along grain lines, due to many years of seasonal moisture variation, these cracks must be thoroughly filled with Famo-Wood or a similar product and well sealed to take away at least one direction of possible movement. Expect this now brittle and weakened wood to eventually show cracks on the outside surfaces along these very same grain lines. Note where accumulations of this condition are prevalent and make bets with your buddies on where, and when, these will first come through and crack the exterior varnish and discolor the wood. If you like to give away money, bet against this happening.

Frame and Batten Inspection and Repair

Now that the planks are off and the frames and battens are exposed, you may make repairs. Supposedly, when the bottom, topside chine strakes and chines were off, all really bad topside frames were replaced then. The deck and covering boards should also be off by now so that deck beam fasteners were replaced. If there is anything exposed now that you didn't see, or ignored before, fix it.

The old fastener holes evident in the original frames should be filled with round toothpicks or fitted dowels and marine glue and ground flush. The frames should be thoroughly cleaned and well sealed. This same procedure with the toothpicks can be applied to the fore and aft plank battens, if they are otherwise sound. It does, however, take far less time to replace them with sound, new wood to screw your planks into. Number and save the forward ends of the original battens and it is a simple matter to duplicate the compound angle on the new pieces. In the area of the forward hull flare (the top two or three battens forward) the originals should be saved to trace and cut curved battens for easier fit. The same is true for the after top two battens in a barrelback. The rest of the battens in the hull can be cut straight on a table saw from your plank stock scraps.

Most prewar boats had a sheer clamp, which is similar to a plank batten in application, applied at the sheer at the top of the frames, meeting the underside of the deck covering board. The sheer clamp, however, is usually thicker (5/8 inch) and made of white oak. Many postwar boats of this type employed a sheer shelf, mounted horizontally across the tops of the topsides frames, fore and aft, in place of a sheer clamp. This change had to do with a new production technique that allowed the deck to be built on a jig elsewhere in the plant and later attached to the hull.

In the real world, on wooden boats intended to last two decades, both a sheer clamp and sheer shelf are not only employed but fastened together to create a multidimensional, longitudinal beam structure.

Either one of these, or both should you find them, must be repaired, sealed, bedded, and refastened before the topsides planks can be installed.

Seal these new battens well and install them with proper bedding and only a single screw or nail in the center of the batten at the frame. You will soon have two plank screws going through this batten. Use a fairing batten vertically against the installed plank battens to insure that the planks will lie flat against them when they are installed, especially in flare and tumblehome areas. A 40-grit disk grinder will quickly reduce any protruding edges here. All surfaces of frames and plank battens as well as the interior and edge surfaces of the planks should be cleaned and sealed with Smith's CPES or similar product prior to bedding and installation. Do not seal the outboard surfaces of the planks at this time, as the entire hull will have to be faired after the planks are installed and the bungs are replaced.

Installing the Planking

On almost all aspects of wooden boat construction I usually recommend 3M 5200 as adhesive bedding for all wood-to-wood joints. In dealing with old wood, however, that has lost the bulk of its natural oils and is therefore brittle, much weaker, and more susceptible to movement, perhaps a less-tenacious adhesive bedding is called for. Perhaps it would be better to have a contracting plank open at the seam rather than split in the middle. For this application and in preparation for future repairs I might suggest the old standby; boatyard bedding compound, available from Interlux and Dolphinite. These linseed oil–based compounds may volatilize (dry out) in 10 to 20 years, but by then these original planks may very well need attention. For now, I still use

A step-jack made of scrap plank stock is used to pry the plank down into place to force the removal of excess bedding compound at installation. The wide footprint is less damaging to the soft old wood than a clamp would be.

mahogany 3M 5200 with the knowledge that a flexible adhesive/sealant is much better suited for this purpose than a hard glue or epoxy.

Original plank stock, due to age, loss of oils, etc., is likely to be slightly smaller than it originally was when installed new. The effect of this may be that when you have completely re-planked your hull with tightened seams, the top edge of the sheer plank could end up short of the bottom side of the covering board. If this happens and the distance is less than 1/2 inch, a thin piece can be applied to the top of the sheer strake that should remain hidden beneath the metal rub rail.

If your original planks were substantially shrunken, exhibiting gaps at every plank seam, you can also consider adding a 1/4-inch piece to the chine rabbet, which, except for a small area forward, will be mostly covered with bottom paint. Make sure you still have solid wood in the frames to screw into as you will be following the original holes in the planks, but be drilling new ones into the frames. This is why you filled in the original holes in the frames with dowels, so that new holes could be placed. If the after ends of the planks end up slightly short of the topsides frames at the transom, a small strip can also be added here to be hidden by the metal transom guard.

Dry-fit the planks using clamps, one strake at a time. In this manner, any final fitting to obtain tight seams can be addressed with a hand plane or finger plane. When you are satisfied with the fit of both forward and follower planks, drill upper and lower locator holes at each frame. Be very careful here, as you will want to align the drill counter-bore to follow exactly into the original bunghole, so the new bung fits tightly without an unsightly, oversized glue ring. If you hit a piece of old fastener that was broken too deep in the frame for removal, you will need to drill the new hole at just enough angle, up or down, to miss that old shank piece and still

not elongate the bung countersink. If there is too great a problem placing the new 3/8-inch counter-bore exactly into the original hole, or the original holes are ragged with damage from plank removal, you can upsize to a 7/16-inch counter-bore and larger bungs.

This strake of planks can now be removed and the proper bedding compound applied to the chine rabbet, frames, and lower half of the first plank batten. The correct amount of bedding compound will be somewhat difficult to determine at first as you do not want to leave any voids, yet not apply it so heavily that it oozes out of the existing original

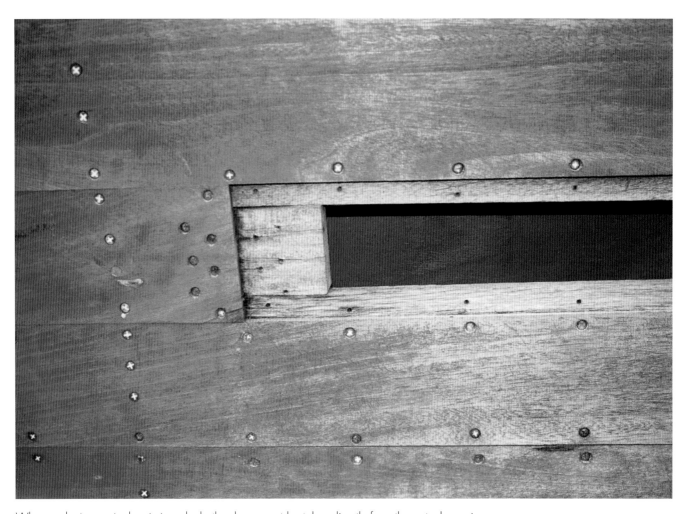

When replacing a single missing plank, the shape must be taken directly from the actual opening.

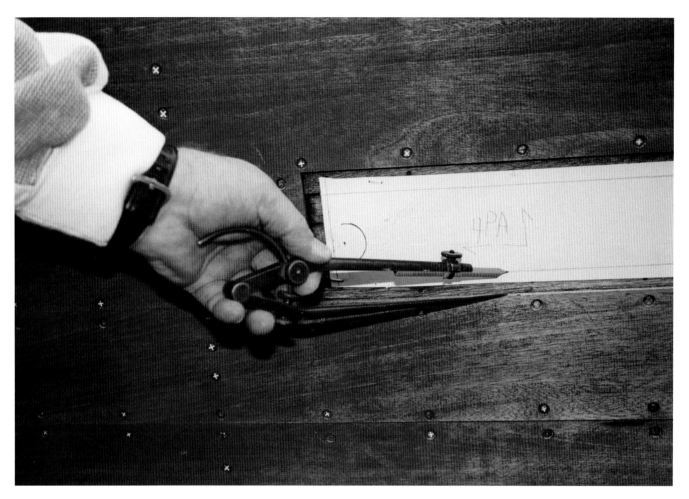

A spiling batten, or pattern piece, is cut to loosely fit the opening and then temporarily attached. A setting is determined for the dividers and scribed around the pattern at 90 degrees from the edge. If the dividers are not kept at 90 degrees to the edge being spiled, an incorrect dimension will result.

screw holes. This can be very messy and can only be completely cleaned out of the hole when re-drilling with the drill counter-bore. Keep a solvent rag handy to keep cleaning the drill and counter-bore. Any compound allowed to set up in the bung countersink will not allow the new bung to seat properly.

With the forward plank set in place and the locator screws positioned, yet not fully tightened, the excess bedding compound must be forced out as the plank is clamped down into the chine rabbet and forward into the stem rabbet. There are a number of ways of accomplishing this. Small 1 x 1 x 3-inch blocks can be temporarily screwed to the chine every foot or so to attach bar clamps. This will work for the entire hull if your bar clamps are long enough. After the first strake, the chine strake, is in you can use bar clamps on the inside of the hull from the bottom of the previous plank batten to the top of the next plank, providing you use a spacer to raise the clamp placement up from the top of the plank high enough to clear the next plank batten. Actually, since the planks have already been dry-fit, edge-setting pressure is not needed to any extent greater than is necessary to simply remove excess

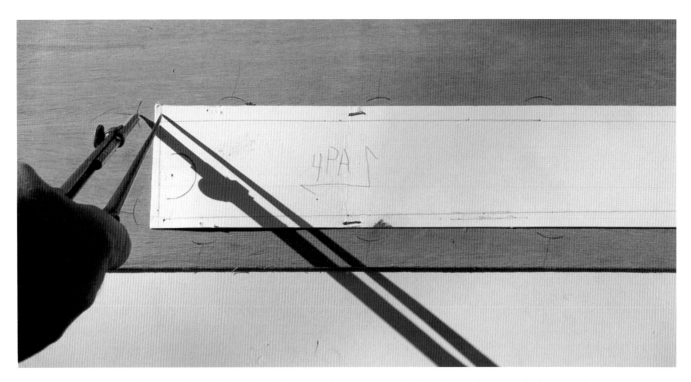

The spiling batten is transferred to the plank stock and the same distance is marked back onto the new plank stock. This must also be done at 90 degrees from the spiling batten line.

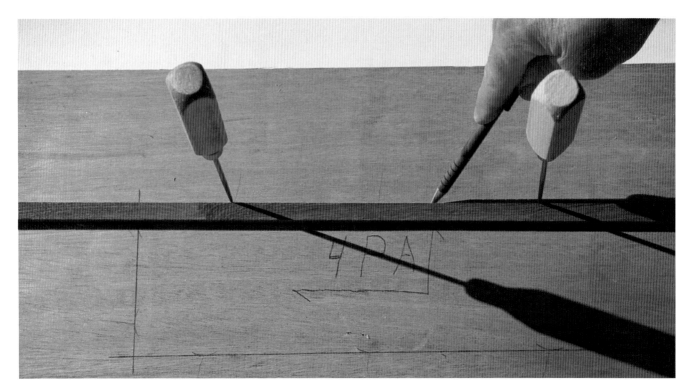

Using ice picks in these tick marks, a line is drawn with the aid of a limber batten. The correctly fitting plank can then be cut out outside the lines and repeatedly trimmed with a hand plane until a tight fit is accomplished.

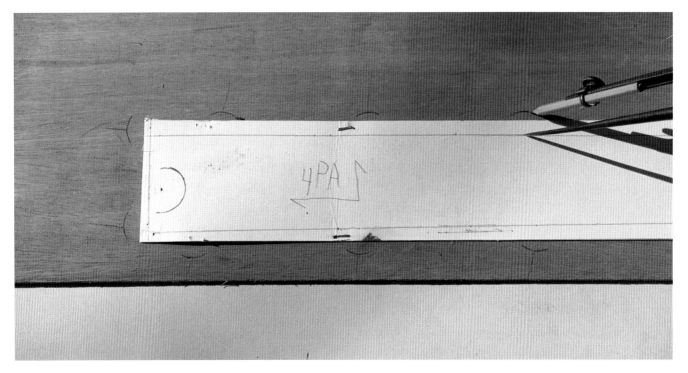

Without an edge to run the dividers against, tick marks are made with a short arc and a line indicating the point on it that is 90 degrees to the spiled line.

bedding compound. For this purpose I have developed a tool I call a "step-jack" that I usually make from scrap 1/2-inch plank stock. When it gets too dirty with compound, I throw it out and make another. It is basically a 6 x 6-inch piece of plank stock that I take to the band saw and cut a series of steps in 1-inch or so increments. The other piece of this tool is a prying arm about 18 inches long or so that is tapered in width. With the step-jack set on top of the plank being installed, it is a simple matter to locate the correct step that will fit under the next batten. With one hand on the pry, I can set and torque the screws. If I have to reach for screws with my left hand, you might find me holding the pry with my chin or elbow.

In order to set the planks forward to tighten them at the hood end and butt joints, I use a long bar clamp hooked from the next to last topsides frame to the aft edge of the follower plank. I remove this after the forward ends are tightly screwed in place as it has a tendency to lift the aft end.

After all of the locator screws are torqued home you may drill and screw all of the remaining screws. The step-jack will still be needed for areas between frames and especially at the hull flare forward. Make sure you are using the properly sized taper point drill bits and counter-bores. In 90 percent of these antique and classic runabouts the average screw sizes in the hull are: stem and chines, #8 x 1-1/4 inch; plank-to-frame, #8 x 2 inch; plank-to-batten and butt block, #8 x 3/4 inch; plank-to-sheer clamp, #8 x 1 inch. These are the usual sizes—note the originals when you are disassembling your boat.

If the screw holes in your original planks appear sloppy and worn from the boat being driven in a loose condition, it is a simple matter to slightly increase the screw size. For example: #10 screws have only a slightly larger shank size than #8 screws while the head size (3/8-inch) is significantly larger than #8s. This larger head will hold more wood. Be sure to order your drill bits accordingly.

Clean all of the bedding compound as each strake is installed, with a putty knife, spooge-board, and solvent-soaked rag (an old bath towel is best) before it has a chance to set, or you will teach yourself a lesson that you will not forget again.

After the first starboard (or portside) strake is installed take your stool, cord, and tools over to the port side and install that first strake. While your tools and everything are on that side, install the second strake. Now move everything back to the starboard side and install two strakes there. In this manner you are installing two strakes at a time per side without one side getting more than one strake ahead of the other; this cuts down on the set-up time of moving tools, cords, etc. Do not plank the hull one entire side at a time—the weight of the planks and the stress of a thousand screws will pull the hull out of shape.

With this method and everything prepared as described, a good, uninterrupted worker should be able to apply at least four to six planks per day, depending on the boat size. When all planks are installed, you may approach the deck in the same manner. When the deck is completed, you may take care of the transom.

Some makes, such as Century boats, may need the transom planked before the deck.

If all of your topsides and deck planks were re-installed without replacement, and you have none

of the original wood to make bungs of, I recommend replacing the lower transom plank with new wood (for many reasons, actually) in order to have original wood to cut the bungs from. Bungs are available new, precut in quantity, but I highly recommend against this as it is nearly impossible, even by hand with long-boards, to get this solid new wood to fair and sand at the same height as the softer old wood. Likewise, when you are installing bungs made of this original softer wood, tap them in gently so as not to crush them slightly, they might swell later after the boat is in the water, and protrude from the surface.

Spiling and Individual Plank Fitting

"Spiling" is a procedure using a temporary pattern piece in the space of a removed plank, along with an equidistant marking tool to mark extensions of that pattern piece, to produce an extended line to cut an exact-fitting new plank. The marking tool can be as simple as a block of wood with a pencil held against it or a set of dividers with adjustable pencil length.

Examine both sides of the boat prior to the removal and replacement of existing topside planks. Determine exactly where the original planks were butted. The end-to-end joint where the aft end of a forward plank meets the forward end of a follower plank is referred to as a butt joint, usually backed up by a butt block 5 to 6 inches long that the plank ends are fastened to. Butt blocks are usually made of the same material as the planks and must be cut with the grain running fore and aft in the same direction as that of the planks, perpendicular to the butt joint. This butt joint is usually within 4 inches, fore or aft, of a topside frame. Never attempt to butt the planks on a frame, there will not be enough surface to fasten them.

Individual planks can be fit into finished boats. Without the ability to grind the new plank's surface fair without damaging the surrounding varnish, the plank can be surfaced slightly thinner and its installation depth controlled from inside the boat with small wedges against the face of the frames.

Over the years planks could easily have been repaired or partially replaced causing short planks and uneven butt joints to become weak in the structure. If your boat has had various repairs to both sides of the hull and you cannot be certain exactly how long the original planks were, seek out similar make and model hulls and study those.

If the old planks are not badly cupped, cracked, or otherwise too warped to use as a pattern, then they can be directly traced to the plank stock. Before these are removed from the boat they are marked with the appropriate position and indications for up and forward. If the correct length planks are not available or are too badly warped through hogging, you may find it easier to spile the exact fit.

The spiling batten is made of any dimensionally stable stock such as 1/8- or 1/4-inch plywood or Masonite that can be written on with pencil and easily read. This batten is roughly cut to fit the space to be spiled within 1/2 inch or so without extending over an edge and is temporarily fastened with clamps, staples or screws. Great care must be taken when temporarily fastening the spiling batten to the curvature of the hull so that it lies flat without any edge-set; so that it is not forced into a curve on its flat plane. In the case of very long spiling battens the effects of gravity must be taken into account and carefully overcome. It is helpful to start clamping the spiling batten at the center and fasten outward towards both ends. If there is edge-set in your batten the resulting plank will have to be edge-set to fit.

Set the dividers to a distance that will read just far enough onto the spiling batten to be legible all the way around and at both ends. This distance is marked on the face of the batten along with the plank placement indication so it is not lost. The pencil in the dividers is set back in its holder the same distance from the point as the thickness of the spiling batten. This will maintain the correct arc distance. If there is an edge to run against, you may do so making sure the dividers remain perpendicular to the surface you are using. If the dividers are not at 90 degrees to the surface you are marking from, the distance will be wrong.

If you do not have a full edge you may tick off points from the position of the intended edge such as the centerline of the plank frame battens. I generally do this at each frame station and at two or three points between frames—the greater the curve, the closer the ticks. At a nearly straight section amidships 6 inches apart is OK, while the forward end of the garboard at the stem might require ticks every 1/2 inch or so. To maintain correct distance with these ticks I scribe a small arc of about 1 inch and then drag a short line up from the center of the arc at 90 degrees from the home surface.

To determine a line, such as the aft butt-end of a forward plank, you can use a slightly longer batten and simply mark the intended location with a straight edge and indicate "actual" on the batten. This should remind you not to tick off a greater distance.

If there are any plank edge bevels other than 90 degrees, such as the plank rabbets in the stem or chine, these should be taken off with a bevel gauge and noted at their positions on the spiling batten.

Set the pencil in the dividers even with the point and check the distance marked on the spiling batten to make sure your actions have not changed it. The spiling batten is carefully removed from the vessel and temporarily attached to the plank stock with clamps or tacks. Again, be mindful that the spiling batten is laid flat with no edge-set. Be mindful of the cracks in the plank stock ends and follow the grain with the plank shape.

This sheer plank could not be clamped in place because the finished deck left no place to clamp to. This strange rig was devised simply to provide clamping pressure. It is held in place with soft strap clamps around the hull. These surfaces were protected from the strap with cardboard and cushions.

Set the pencil in the dividers forward in its holder the same distance from the point as the thickness of the spiling batten. The procedure continues in reverse, ticking off from the spiling batten onto the plank stock. In the case of a butt end marked as "actual," simply overhang a straightedge and mark two short lines above and below the batten and remark that line after the batten is removed.

Now take out the spiling batten and transfer the plank position indications to the plank stock ("P2F," etc.). The ticks are connected by means of a long limber batten and clamps or spiling picks. It is usually helpful to place the batten at the center and working toward the ends.

The spiling picks are set just far enough into the plank stock to hold the batten's curve and, if possible, into the scrap sections of the plank stock. When securely held, the correct side of the batten is now traced with pencil or pen. I generally use a medium ballpoint pen, which is easier to see during cutting. The only time a pencil must be used in place of ink is on a plank you know will have to be steambent into place, as steaming tends to blend the ink into the wood. Use an appropriately sized batten to do the curves. In the case of the hood ends—where the forward ends fit into the stem, the topside gripe plank rabbet, or bottom chine strakes—when the curvature is too great to use wooden battens, I use adjustable plastic ship's curves, available at most art supply stores.

Strike off the butt ends with a straight edge. At this time, I leave the larger butt end slightly long to allow for any additional fitting at the smaller butt end.

If you are fitting the new plank into an existing opening it should be cut out outside the scribed lines and dressed with an appropriately sized, low-angle hand plane as you attempt to fit it. Almost all planks are wider at one end than the other. This will basically leave you with a wedge shaped piece you are fitting. You may use this to your advantage by leaving the wider end long by an inch or two until the last butt joint is marked and fit. If you have over-trimmed an edge in fitting, you may cut the smaller butt joint back a bit and slide the entire piece forward allowing wider stock to be trimmed more carefully this time. This will help to avoid replacing the entire piece.

Hang a loose loop of rope from the sheer of the boat 6 inches or so in from the aft end of the plank you are fitting. Adjust the height of this rope so that it holds the after end of the plank at the correct height while you mark and adjust the forward end. Use a relatively large size of rope so you can easily slip the after end of the plank in and out each time you trial-fit, mark, and adjust the forward end. As you fit and insert the forward end of the plank you may need to adjust this loop up or down minutely to allow the exact fitting of the plank.

As I sight the plank and its opening, I use a pencil to mark the areas to be addressed with the hand plane, starting with an aft-sloping line then a forward sloping line at the aft end of the area that I'm going to adjust. I often will add a vertical line between these to indicate where the greatest depth of the material will be removed. If multiple markings must be made in the same area, I will number them to avoid confusion.

Be careful not to back-bevel the edges of the plank as you are fitting them to the existing plank edges. At least two-thirds of the thickness of the new plank must bear tightly against surrounding planks or times of high wood moisture content will simply crush the outer plank edges. Fairing the hull will also open a successively larger gap in the plank seam. After the first foot or so of your new plank is fit in place you may address the forward butt end and hand plane it to a tight fit. When planing across the grain, such as a plank butt-end, do not cut all the way across the plank as you can easily chip off the trailing edge. Always approach end grain trimming from both directions to avoid this.

When the forward butt end is fit tightly and you are proceeding aft with the fitting process, you still need to hold the forward end in place as the plank wraps around the curve of the hull. Also, you want to minimize the number of times you pull this new plank out of place, otherwise you can easily damage the surrounding planks. Repair any damage immediately. I generally cut a U-shaped cleat from scrap 4/4 stock to span the new plank at the butt end with room to fit a wedge to hold the plank securely in place. This cleat must be cut to fit the hull and marked and drilled so that the fasteners that secure it fall into existing fastener holes in the surrounding planks. To do this, carefully remove the existing bungs and screws and mark and drill your cleat from the bottom edge so its fasteners will fall directly into the existing holes. The original screws and new bungs will be installed later.

With the forward end of the new plank secured in place with a wedge, you may continue aft, fitting the top and bottom edges as you go. When you reach the aft butt joint, you simply mark a straight line on the hull above and below the existing butt joint and transfer this with a straightedge to your new plank. If the existing topsides are varnished and you do not want to mar them, the lines may be drawn on temporarily applied tape. Remember, common sense is allowed.

Once you have achieved a good tight fit, you may seal the interior and edge surfaces of the plank and frames and, with proper bedding, install the new plank following the original screw patterns.

Chapter 11

NEW TOPSIDE PLANKING: THE ROUTER METHOD

The router method of fitting new planks is an ingenious blend of new technology with old material procedure. It is the one innovation that makes planking a hull with new wood easier and quicker than re-planking with original wood. In the end, you have a far more sound and usable hull.

I first read of the router method many years ago in both *Classic Boating* and *WoodenBoat* magazines and was immediately impressed by its speed and accuracy. One no longer needed years of experience tediously trial fitting planks with a hand plane.

The basic concept of the procedure is that a fence attaches to the router base and rides along the top edge of the chine or previously installed plank and trims the bottom of the next plank to an exact fit. An added benefit is that the base of the router follows the contour of the hull surface, automatically directing the router bit to cut the correct bevel edge for a dead-tight fit, plank to plank.

Before starting this procedure, complete all frame, plank batten, and deck beam repairs and have a thoroughly secured hull that is plumb and level. The hull should be blocked up high enough so that you will be operating the router in a comfortable position in front of you. Temporary bracing from the chine to floor will help hold the hull in shape while you are working on it. Take diagonal measurements of the transom to insure it is square. Half-breadth measurements, outboard from a taught centerline with plumb-bobs to the keel, should be taken at every frame station. The hull should be square, plumb, and level and all frames,

including deck beams and plank battens, should be properly sealed, bedded, and re-fastened before the topside planks are installed.

At the risk of sounding redundant—but I cannot stress this enough—once these planks are secured, they will hold whatever shape the hull frames were in, straight or not. Make sure that your work area allows for planking both sides of the hull at the same time. If you attempt to plank the hull one complete side at a time, the weight of the planks as well as the tension created by thousands of fasteners will pull the topsides out of shape. This will cause the boat to always want to pull to one side when underway and look noticeably crooked at the stem or stern. A serious buyer would consider such a hull no more valuable than a gray boat.

A typical laminate trimmer router with plank routing base and up-spiral bit.

154

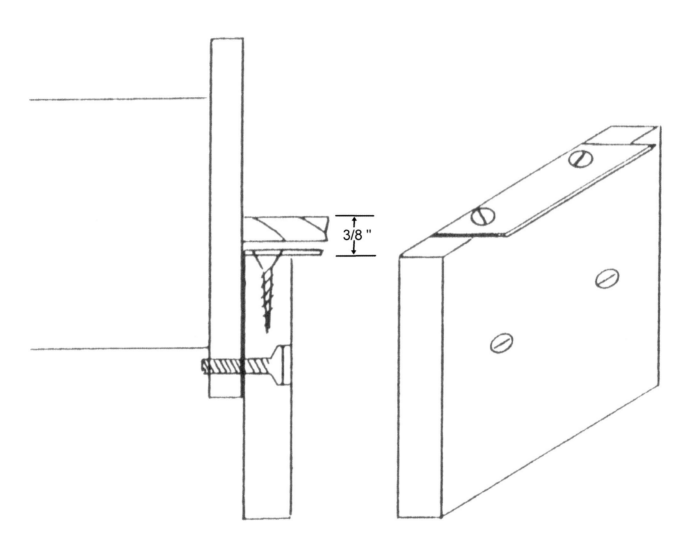

3/8 "

Diagram of router base

A simple router base attachment used to ride the top of an installed plank and cut the bottom edge of the next plank to an exact fit.

The hull may need to be blocked up or down to present the proper work height for each strake of planks.

Selecting a Router and Bit

The best router for this procedure is a small machine called a laminate trimmer that has adequate power for the job and will more easily fit around the many clamps needed for the job. The best router bit to use is a solid carbide 1/4 x 1-inch up-spiral bit. Straight bits may be cheaper, but are far more likely to splinter changing grain. The up-spiral design also removes the wood chips from the cutting area.

You will have to fabricate a new base for the router as shown in the photo and diagram (see page 155) and prepare a half-dozen or so 1 x 4 x 5/16-inch spacers. If the cutting distance mandates it, you may have to make these spacers after you make your router fence.

Selecting and Preparing Planks

I prepare the new plank stock with careful attention to grain configuration, color, etc. Hopefully, you will have obtained enough matching plank stock in adequate lengths to match the originals. The most cost effective means of obtaining 1/2-inch mahogany plank stock is to order 6/4 lumber and have it re-sawn and surface-planed to two book-matched 1/2-inch planks. I might plank as many as 10 boats a year and still find it less expensive to order wood from the supplier already re-sawn and surfaced than to waste my time on these procedures. To order wood for the total re-planking of a gray boat, determine how many board feet you will need for the project (for example, a 1950 Chris-Craft 17-foot Deluxe

The hull should be plumb and level with supports to the floor to keep the weight of many clamps from distorting it.

requires about 300 board feet of 6/4 re-sawn to 1/2-inch plank stock to completely replace bottom, topsides, deck, and ceiling planks).

When you receive your lumber, first select the most beautiful pairs of plank stock to complete the deck, transom and ceiling planks. This is 90 percent of the wood you will see at a boat show with the boat in the water. Mark this wood and set it aside for later. The next group of planks to be selected for color and grain, etc., will be for the topsides. The least beautiful and poorly matched planking can be used for the bottom, under paint.

If you are using original planks as your patterns, do not simply trace them onto the new plank stock until you have trial-fit them into their original positions. After you have straightened out years of

The entire hull must be blocked and braced level before the planks are installed.

The hull from the previous photo before blocking level. The starboard sheer dropped nearly a full inch.

sag or hog in the framework and have refastened this structure into a straight, plumb and level condition, you will most likely find that the original planks will still exhibit the hogged shape they have come to know. As you are planking the hull from the chine up, trial-fit each original plank in its original position to see if the shape is correct enough to trace. If the shape is no longer correct; use it as a spiling batten and spile the correct shape from it. After you have assured the correct shape you may spile or trace onto selected pairs of re-sawn plank stock. Make sure the book-matched pairs are properly aligned as to grain and keep them clamped together well and you can cut them out two at a time. Stay at least 6 inches or so away from the ends of your plank stock to avoid weaknesses and cracks created during the kiln drying process and inspect all surfaces along the full length for problem areas like reaction or compression wood or windbreaks, etc.

I have changed my router procedure in ways that I believe allow for quicker construction, more accurate plank lines, and built-in error control. One must, however, remain methodical when using a router. I cut out the pairs of plank blanks with a Bosch 1587

Plank butt joint location (butt schedule) must be determined from original planks. If short planks have been added from previous repairs, you may need to find a similar boat to determine what is correct.

Plankstock purchased at 6/4 is re-sawn and surfaced to 1/2-inch plank stock. I like to stack them on their edges in book-matched pairs so that I can leaf through them like the pages of a book to find just the grain and color I'm looking for.

jigsaw with hollow-ground blades. There are reasons this particular tool has won multiple industry awards—I have witnessed this jigsaw's ability to turn ham-fisted amateurs into proficient craftsmen. The only added direction I have had to give apprentices is to suggest steering from the back of the tool as opposed to steering it from the blade at the front.

Before you begin, experiment with the jigsaw on long straight or curving lines on scrap pieces of plank stock. Steering the tool 1/8-inch at the back of the tool means only about 1/64-inch change at the blade mounted 6 inches forward at the front end of the tool. Set its orbital action for "0" when cutting cross-grain so as not to tear-up the plank edge. Set its orbital action for "3" when ripping the length of the planks. The best blades, replaced often, will make the work proceed smoothly and accurately, and save time and money in the long

run. Changing the $2 blades every other strake of planks (four pairs) will not only cost about $6 overall on the average 20-footer, but will make you think you are some kind of expert. Believe me here, the blades will not look burnt or feel anything but sharp to the touch. There will, however be a decided difference in control.

The hand plane I use is a Stanley G12-060 (low-angle). Angle the blade's approach diagonally when cutting cross-grain, the shearing action makes end-grain easier to cut.

If nobody you know owns this quote; let's pretend it's mine: "The right tool makes all the difference."

Step-by-Step Procedure

When cutting out what I call the "plank blanks," I begin with the chine strake forward pair (Starboard 1 Forward and Port 1 Forward). Mark these indications on the proper surfaces with a pencil and include an arrow for up and for forward.

Starboard 1 Fore and Port 1 Fore (S1F and P1F)

1. Trim the hood end (the stem rabbet creates a protective "hood" for its forward end) or forward end and hand plane it to its exact intended line before you cut the top or bottom line. The excess wood at the top and bottom will help protect breaking short grain when hand planing across the grain. Remember to mark the plank stock cutoff so that it will be found later for bungs for that particular plank (S1F and P1F). In this manner you will have the best chance at perfectly matching bungs. Pile these inside the hull for now so they will not get lost.

2. Cut the aft butt end of the forward plank (again, remember to mark the bung-stock and put it away) and trim the butt joint with the hand plane so that you have a crisp, straight line without any back-bevel.

Once a boat's framework has been straightened, the old planks may still be too hogged out of shape to fit the hull correctly. Do not simply trace the old planks until you try the fit. They may be used as spiling battens.

Clamps or tacks can be used to hold the spiling batten in place. Care must be taken to lay the batten flat on a curve without edge-set.

3. Cut just outside the bottom line of the plank blanks leaving 1/16 inch of wood outside the line. This is the amount that you will hopefully be routing off during the procedure. DO NOT cut inside the line or that amount of wood will have to be routed off the entire length of the plank. If you have to, practice cutting lines on long lengths of scrap wood so as not to waste expensive plank stock.

4. Cut outside the top line by 1/2 inch. That's right, 1/2 inch of excess wood to be trimmed later will allow for one or two mistakes in the routing procedure without destroying expensive grain matched planks. Mark a line on the jigsaw shoe that indicates this extra 1/2 inch and just follow that when you are cutting.

5. Verify that the chine rabbet is clean and unobstructed and clamp these two blanks onto the boat with at least one clamp per frame. Set them up

from the chine rabbet with the 5/16-inch spacers. Do not set the hood end tightly into the stem rabbet at this height. Instead, do it in such a way that when dropped straight down, the hood end will be tight into the stem rabbet. The clamps may be placed directly onto the frames or placed between frames with the use of a scrap piece of wood that spaces the gap between the chine and the first plank battens, inside the hull. Figure out the clearance you need for the router to pass beneath the placement of the clamps. The best clamps I've found for this are 6-inch-long bar-clamps with 2-1/2-inch throat depth such as a Jorgensen #3701. Anything longer or deeper will get in the way of the router. When you get up into the area of the hull flare forward, on plank strakes four and five, you will need half-dozen deeper throated clamps, such as Jorgensen #4501s, to pull in the plank bottoms.

A heavy piece of 8/4 blocked up off your bench with 2 x 4s makes a handy plank bench to which you can clamp both sides of your plank stock.

A clamp is temporarily applied to avoid splintering under weight.

Larger routers would not clear the many clamps necessary to secure the plank.

The router fence guide rides along the bottom plank or chine to trim the bottom of the next plank to exact fit and bevel. The outer bit is set back just far enough to avoid nails or screws in plank batten, and to avoid cutting into the plank batten.

Starboard 1 Aft and Port 1 Aft
(S1A and P1A, first strake followers)

6. Cut off the forward butt end of the plank blanks but don't bother to hand plane it at this time. It will have to be fit to the forward plank's aft butt end on the boat (remember to mark and save the cutoffs for bung-stock).

7. Cut off the aft end of the follower plank pair, but this time leave 3 inches extra length. This will allow plenty of stock for final trimming of hood and butt ends for the entire strake. (Mark and save bung-stock—I should no longer be reminding you, but you will forget somewhere along the line. I admit I still do. It's exasperating to think you could end up with one plank in a perfect hull whose bungs don't match).

8. Cut off the excess of the bottom line leaving 1/16 inch wood outside the line. Do it right this time. Pay

attention. Change the blade, if necessary. Lock your wrist and steer from as far back as your elbow.

9. Cut outside the top line by 1/2 inch. This is another one that can be hard to remember. I've had to teach employees to write "+1/2" at the beginning and end of this line when spiling or tracing so they are reminded before they cut.

10. Make sure the chine rabbet is clean and unobstructed and clamp these followers onto the boat with the 5/16-inch spacers and the butt joint relatively tight. Final fitting of this butt joint must be done after the planks are routed and fit into their final position.

Check the full length of the strake to verify that the clamps are tight and that the planks will not move while you are working on them. Slide a "no-go" 3/8-inch spacer down the length of the opening to make sure you have no gaps larger than 5/16 inch. If the planks need to be adjusted in place, do so with a hammer and a block of wood to disperse the blow. Never hit the plank directly with a hammer, it could compress the wood, which could expand later after the

You can use a piece of tape on the jigsaw shoe to help you follow the line when cutting oversize stock.

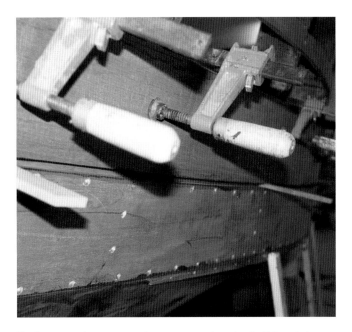

Planks are set for routing with spacers made to be 1/16 inch less than cutting height of the router.

Clamps can be placed at frames or between them with the use of blocking across battens. This leaves the frame area open to drill into when placing the locator screws.

boat is in the water. Never hit the end grain directly with a hammer, even if it is the extra 3-inch part at the end. I've seen this send a foot-long crack up the plank.

It is entirely possible that an ill-fitting plank edge, or poorly cut edge, will require that you route this edge more than once to get a final tight fit.

11. Route! The entire area should be prepared first; I use air pressure to blow the chine rabbet clean of debris. Sweep the floor clean of debris that might foul the stool wheels. Make sure the router cord and/or extension cord is laid out such that it will not catch on something. Watch that you do not step on the cord. Any of these surprises could yank this running tool out of your control and into your lap. This is a potentially dangerous and tiring operation, so take all safety precautions necessary. Wear eye and ear protection. A lightweight full-face shield works well. I keep a 2-foot wad of waxed paper in my pocket to occasionally dress the router base with to keep things running smoothly.

Make sure that the router bit is set to a depth that will not contact the back face of the rabbet or hit any fasteners. The cut should leave about 1/16-inch of stock at the back of the plank edge to be trimmed later.

Start at the aft end of the starboard side and work forward (Almost all router bits are designed to cut from left to right). Keep two hands on the machine at all times and maintain pressure down in order to keep the bit from cutting its way up into the plank—it will constantly try to do this. If the bit does cut up into the wood reset the plank and route it again (one reason for the extra 1/2 inch at the top of the plank).

As you proceed, listen for a high-pitched whine. Mahogany owes much of its beauty to a constantly changing grain direction that can make working with it difficult and exasperating. When you hear this high-pitched whine turn off the router and allow it to come to a complete stop before attempting to remove it from the work. The whine is generally caused by the vibration of a sliver of wood breaking against rising grain. Cut off this sliver and proceed with the router. If the sliver has broken off above the router's cut line, you may have to reset the plank down and route the entire plank edge again. This is another reason for the extra 1/2 inch at the top of the plank. If this happens too often, replace the router bit or slow your cutting progress. It is possible to run the router right-to-left, to back into an area that constantly splinters, but this must be done very carefully as the router will try to pull itself in that direction.

When you come to the stem plank rabbet, the guide fence of the router will prevent you from routing the last few inches. Turn the machine off, wait for complete stop and remove the bit from the work. Set your dividers for 3/8 inch (whatever your router cuts) and mark the last few inches to be trimmed with a hand plane after the plank is off of the boat.

On the port side of the boat you will still have to route left-to-right. This will mean having to insert the bit at the stem into the space while the machine is running. Hook one lip of the guide fence onto its running surface and make sure the base pad is flat against its running surface. With the machine running, slowly rotate the bit into the work. The beginning few inches at the stem will need to be marked with the dividers and hand planed later. This is one procedure you should practice well on scraps. If you goof it up, tap the entire plank down and do it again.

12. Remove the planks from one side of the hull and note the 1/16-inch lip left on the inner edge of the plank. If any of this excess remains, it will keep the plank from seating tightly into the rabbet at its face. It is better to trim this excess off with a hand plane than ruin the router bit on a screw or nail. Hold the hand plane at a 45-degree angle so as not to effect the angle of the routed surface. I usually leave a 1/16-inch chamfer at this inside edge. It's

A high-pitched whine from the router can indicate a sliver of wood has formed on rising grain. Using a utility knife, cut this back to solid wood and proceed.

The fairing batten is first set at half batten depth (usually 3/4 inch) mark.

Setting the fairing batten by eye is difficult but possible. Remember to sight down this battened line for unfair spots before you cut it.

Continue the fairing line onto the stem so both sides match.

okay; it will be filled with bedding compound. Remember to address the first few inches where the router could not cut near the stem.

13. Clamp the forward plank back onto the boat after using air pressure to blow the rabbet clean. Use the hand plane to make any final adjustments to the hood end of the plank so that it fits snugly into the stem rabbet. When clamping the plank on, adjust the clamps so that a 3/4 x 3/4-inch batten will slide beneath them. Use a hammer with a wooden block to tap the plank down or forward.

Clamp the follower plank in place and mark and adjust the forward butt end until no light can be seen through the joint. Try not to back-bevel the planks at the butt joint. They should seat tightly together. The aft edge of the follower plank should be protruding past the transom frame; ignore this for now.

14. When you are satisfied with the fit of the lower plank edge and the hood and butt joints, you may proceed with fairing and shaping the planks top edge. Set your dividers at 3/4-inch (half the width of the plank batten) and set the pencil 5/8-inch or so back in its holder. Riding the divider point along the top of the plank batten, mark the center point of the plank batten on the face of the plank at each frame station. This is ostensibly where the plank's top edge should be. I have, however, seen the factory installations of these battens terribly unfair. The fairing batten gives one an opportunity to clean this line up somewhat, as long as you stay somewhere near the center of the plank batten for fastening purposes.

Slide a 3/4 x 3/4-inch x 20-foot fairing batten through the clamps that are firmly holding the planks in place. Using another set of clamps, attach the fairing batten along the set of lines that you marked. Make sure the batten extends past the point of the stem so that the final position can be marked at the point of the stem to

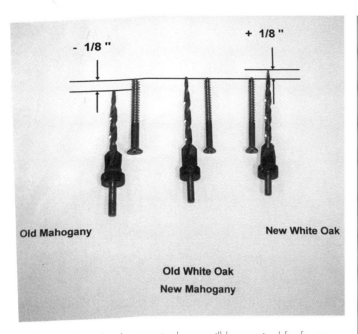

- 1/8 "

+ 1/8 "

Old Mahogany

New White Oak

Old White Oak

New Mahogany

Different settings for the counter bores will be required for frame and batten screws.

verify the same plank height on the other side of the hull. This line should also be measured at the transom so that it matches the same plank on the other side of the hull. It will be difficult to fair this batten with 30 or so clamps in your view, but not impossible. Walk up and down this batten loosening every other clamp a quarter turn and re-tightening it just to see if the batten wants to spring up or down to fair itself. Look at the batten from near and far and from different angles. Squint at it until the clamps disappear and keep telling yourself how good you are at this. Is it a sweet line? Is it in keeping with the shape of the hull? Look for humps or hollows in the line. Is the line still close enough to the center of the batten for effective fastener placement?

When you have decided on the final placement of the batten, mark the line well with a pencil or pen. If your hull is longer than your batten, simply move it aft and complete the procedure. When the line is fully marked, remove the batten clamps and fairing

batten only, leave the planks clamped tightly in place.

15. Verify once more that the planks are tightly in place by gentle tapping with a hammer and softwood block, and proceed to drill locator holes. Once the slippery bedding compound is applied it is impossible for clamps to hold things in place, whereas the predrilled locator holes will do just that. A slight angle down on these screws will help pull the plank down to expel excess bedding compound.

I use Fuller tapered point drill bits and counter-bores with matched plug cutters. In the vast majority of these antique and classic runabouts the average screw sizes in the hull are as follows: stem and chines, #8 x 1-1/4 inches; plank to frame, #8 x 2 inches; plank to batten and butt-block, #8 x 3/4 inches; plank to sheer-clamp, #8 x 1 inches. These are the usual sizes, but note the originals when you are disassembling

A power plane can be used for quick, accurate trimming of plank top edges. Practice on scrap stock first.

Pre-drilling locator holes allow exact placement after the slippery bedding compound is applied.

your boat. Never re-use the brittle old brass fasteners—replace them with silicon bronze.

The locator holes are drilled as follows:

Drill all four holes in the stem. In all topsides planks, use two plank-to-frame screws centered 3/8 inch from the top and bottom of the plank (the top of the plank will be indicated by the line you have just faired in and marked). (Note: for the chine strake only, use one plank-to-frame screw at the top edge and one plank-to-chine screw that is not in line with the frame as it would hit the chine/frame carriage bolt. Set this chine screw at least an inch before or after the frame or frame knee. The butt joint will require four plank-to-batten screws.)

16. After all the locator holes are drilled you may remove these planks to your plank bench. Before

Planks can be clamped down to internal plank battens, as long as the covering board is off.

The step-jack forces out excess bedding and sets the plank dead tight.

doing any cutting on the top edge, sight carefully down the line you have marked with the fairing batten. Look for humps or hollows you may have overlooked because of the clamps. You should observe a smoothly curving, or sweet, line. If there are minor adjustments to be made, use clamps and the fairing batten to mark them.

Trim this top edge with the jigsaw outside the line and finish it off with a power plane leaving just the line. Practice this procedure on scrap wood until you are proficient. This is the surface the router will ride against to cut the bottom edge of the next plank so make it smooth and fair. Take care that this edge remains at exactly 90 degrees to the plank surface. This is very important; the router's fence is set at 90 degrees and will automatically cut the necessary bevel in the following plank edge to fit the curvature of your hull. When you are finished shaping the planks, set the dividers at 3/8 inch and mark a line down the full length of the planks, top and bottom. This line will direct where to center your screw holes when you drill the remainder of the top and bottom plank fasteners. You will be surprised

how many times you forget this step.

I seal the inboard side and all edges of these planks with two applications of Smith's CPES, one immediately after the other. Set these aside to cure. 17. While the starboard first strake is curing, return to the port side and repeat steps 12 through 16. Make sure you continue the fairing batten all the way to the forward point of the stem so that the planks are visually balanced from a front-on view. Take measurements up from the chine bottom at the transom to insure the same plank heights there. It would not hurt to check this measurement at amidships point as well. Set the port side planks aside to cure and return to the starboard side for plank installation.

18. Apply your chosen bedding compound to the first-strake chine, plank battens, and frames. Trowel this application out so that there will be no voids left to hold moisture or dirt once the planks are permanently in. It is best to have a small amount of bedding compound ooze out from each joint to

SCHOOL OF HARD KNOCKS

Planing by Hand

In the late 1980s I completely planked a 55-foot William Hand schooner with about 4,000 board feet of 8/4 Honduras mahogany. Even though I had become very proficient with a power plane, I still had to have a helper to carry these 50- to 80-pound planks up and down the scaffolding a couple times each to clamp and mark and adjust and eventually edge-set into place. There sat my 3-1/2-horsepower router on the shelf collecting dust, a tool that would have produced the perfect fit, including the perfect bevel, in one pass. Had I the presence of mind to see this extrapolation, it would have saved this boat owner tens of thousands of dollars. I am reminded by this lesson every day that there is so much more to learn.

A bar clamp is used to force planks forward during fastening and set the butt joints tight.

The serpentine-shaped plank at left will look straight when installed on the varying shape hull of a 19-foot Chris-Craft barrelback.

prove the absence of voids. You are the one who will be cleaning up the excess compound so learn early how much to apply.

Use clamps to install the forward plank first, using locator screws partially installed to get it in position. With the forward plank set in place and the locator screws positioned but not fully tightened, the excess bedding compound must be forced out as the plank is clamped down into the chine rabbet and forward into the stem rabbet. There are a number of ways of accomplishing this. Small 1 x 1 x 3-inch blocks can be temporarily screwed to the chine every foot or so to attach bar clamps to. This will work for the entire hull if your bar clamps are long enough. After the

first strake, the chine strake, is in you can use bar clamps on the inside of the hull, from the bottom of the previous plank batten to the top of the next plank, providing you use a spacer to raise the clamp placement up from the top of the plank high enough to clear the next plank batten.

Actually, since the planks have already been dry-fit and the router makes for such a perfect fit, edge-setting pressure is not needed to any extent greater than is necessary to simply remove excess bedding compound. For this purpose I use the aforementioned step-jack that I make from scrap plank stock. With the step-jack set on top of the plank being installed, it is a simple matter to locate the correct step that

The router, riding on the previously installed plank edge, cuts the exact bevel necessary to fit the plank edges tight.

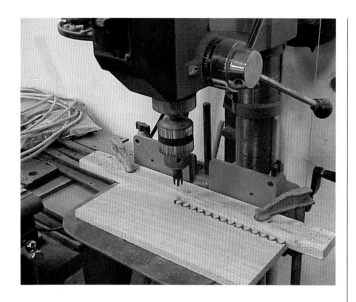

My favorite method of cutting bungs. With a temporary fence clamped to the drill press table, the saved plank scraps are cut in a straight line with the grain.

will fit under the next plank batten. With one hand on the pry, I can set and torque the screws. If I have to reach for screws with one hand, you might find me holding the pry with my chin or elbow.

In order to set the planks forward to tighten them at the hood end and butt joints, use a long bar clamp hooked from the after edge of the plank to the next frame forward. Remove this bar clamp as soon as the forward end is securely fastened, as it will have a tendency to lift the after end of the plank. Keep a spooge board and putty knife handy to clean up excess bedding compound. Any compound allowed to set up in a bung countersink will not allow the bung to seat properly.

After all of the locator screws are torqued home you may install the follower plank in the same manner as

The strips of bungs are kept in a freezer bag that is marked for that particular plank and saved until after the hull is faired, just in case some shallow screws need to be reset. The bung is lightly swirled in glue and the excess wiped from its bottom.

the forward plank. Do not forget to apply bedding compound to the butt joint. After all of these locator screws are torqued home you may drill and screw all of the remaining screws. The step-jack will still be needed for areas between frames and especially at the hull flare forward.

The screw pattern should follow the pattern in your original planks. Since the frames are never evenly spaced, the batten screws end up differently spaced in each frame bay. The easiest way I've found to make this look good is to take a measurement from one frame screw to the next with the millimeter side of a yardstick. Look at your original plank to see how many screw spaces the factory had in that plank and divide your measurement by that number. For example: if, in a given frame bay the frame screws measured 637 millimeters apart and there were six screws (seven spaces) in the original plank, you would divide 637 by 7 to obtain a 91-millimeter distance between batten screws. Set your divider for 91 millimeters and, starting at the center of one frame screw, tick off

these distances one to the next. Remember to save these measurements for the same plank strake, same frame bay on the other side of the boat. A millimeter yardstick and hand-held calculator are much easier to deal with than inches and fractions.

After all the screws are placed and this strake is in, use a putty knife and scrap board and remove all excess bedding compound, especially from the plank's top edge and batten and from the surface of the plank. It will definitely effect the operation of the router or the proper seating of the plank on the next pass. Use a respirator and rubber gloves and a xylol-soaked terrycloth rag to completely clean all surfaces. I recommend cleaning interior surfaces as well. While not totally necessary, this will make it much easier to keep the bilge clean. If this excess bedding compound has wood chips from the drilling operation, you may use it on the next strake for the upper batten surface or frame surface. Use only clean, new compound for the plank-to-plank edge so that a dead-tight fit is possible.

19. After you have completed and cleaned this side you may return to the port side and repeat Step 18.

20. Install the butt blocks. The grain must be running fore and aft the same as the plank. Butt blocks should have chamfered edges and be spaced at least 1/8 inch away from any frame member so that water can drain into the bilge. Check your original planks for the proper fastener pattern for this. Remember that if your boat is a pre-war Chris-Craft, the butt block was most likely fastened from the inside of the hull. They called this "blind-fastened."

Finishing the Job

Repeat the above steps for each strake of planks. For most hulls, the top one or two plank strakes (at least forward), should be steam-bent onto the hull. This

With the bungs still attached in a strip, it is easy to keep the grain direction in line with the grain of the plank.

should be done early so that the planks have time—at least a week—to shrink back down in size before they are fit. Leave them clamped to the hull as long as possible, until they are in the way of the planking operation. These sheer-strakes should be cut out with an extra 1 inch at the top edge and the battening procedure will not be necessary. When the planking is done, you can use a hand plane or power plane to trim the top edge of the sheer strakes even with the tops of the sheer clamp or sheer shelf.

These are the steps I follow when planking antique and classic hulls. It takes me longer to type out the explanation than it does to actually do it. If I am uninterrupted I can usually complete the fitting and installation of one full strake all the way around the boat (four planks) in a single eight-hour day.

The average 18-foot boat takes about 65 hours to plank, including the cutting of the plank "blanks" and the steam-bending of the top two forward strakes. The transom should take another 15 hours or so but is usually not done until the deck has been planked, unless the boat is a Century in which case the transom goes on before the deck. This is far faster than hand planing and fitting and results in a far superior, tighter plank job.

Cutting Bungs

The plank scraps that you set aside as bung stock can now be cut into bungs to fill the screw holes. This should be done very soon after planking as changes in humidity will often cause the unsealed planking to expand or contract, changing the counter-bores hole size enough to make the fit difficult. When you purchased your drill bits and counter-bores you should also have bought matching bung cutters from the same manufacturer. These will have been machined to exactly the same specifications and allow a tight, crisp fit.

A drill press is absolutely necessary for this operation. It is not possible to hold a hand drill steady enough to cut bungs. The drill press can also be set for the same, repeated depth of cut. This is necessary to form the slight round over to the bottom of the bung that will allow for easier installation into the tight hole.

Many just cut these bungs randomly on the board and pop them out later with a screwdriver, producing a bag full of individual bungs. These can prove difficult to hold when installing and grain direction can be difficult to determine. I prefer cutting the bungs in a straight line, inline with the grain, with a fence set up on the drill press. Cut these in a manner that removes the excess wood between each bung, without hitting the previous bung. This line of bungs is then trimmed off on the band saw, against a fence set for this purpose. The result is a strip of bungs that is much easier to align grain direction and hold while hammering them into the screw hole. If the depth of cut has been carefully

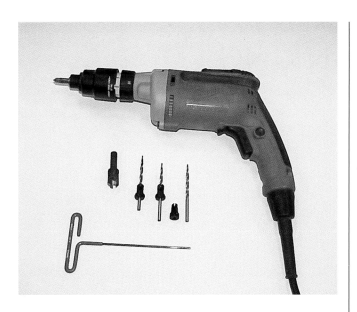

Drill and counter bore manufacturers also make a properly sized bung-cutter. The Fuller four-fluke cutter, with 3/8-inch shaft works best.

set, the strip should be very flexible and easy to tear free after the bung is set.

The bung hammer should be very light (2 to 4 ounces) with a plastic head. Multiple light taps should be used to set them. If the bungs are hammered too hard into the hole, some compression of the wood could result. After fairing flush with the surrounding wood, they may look perfect until the boat is placed in service in a much warmer and more humid environment. This could release that compression, swelling the bungs proud of the varnished surface. This would not only look unsightly but could damage varnish coatings as well.

An aggressive adhesive is not necessary for gluing the bungs. Some use varnish or shellac, even plain white carpenters' glue will suffice. I prefer Weldwood Plastic Resin glue. This is available from most any hardware store and comes as a brown powder that you mix with water. It leaves a brown ring around the bung when set, which is more likely to remain unseen against the mahogany. I mix this in a paper cup and then pour a small amount onto the inside surface of a plastic coffee can lid. It should spread into a shallow circle that you work with. Swirl the bung to get some glue to stick just slightly up the sides of the bung and then wipe the excess off of the bottom of the bung on an open area of the lid. The glue is not going to stick to the metal screw head anyway and could keep it from fully seating. The leftover glue can be allowed to set up on the plastic lid and the next day you just flex it until the remains crack away, leaving a clean surface to use again.

Chapter 12
DECK PLANKING

The deck of an antique or classic boat has two great enemies in the struggle for survival—the wind and the sun. Because of its exposure to the elements, the deck planking does not remain long at or above moisture saturation levels, which can host rot spore. Decks may rot, but they do it from the inside out where moisture can accumulate between joints of un-bedded planks and frames. The weather can make wood look good at the surface while it is devastated below.

Given that the value of these collectible craft has risen so greatly, so recently, the most visible part of this commodity, the deck, is easily recognized as the first place to invest cheaply, if one's personal values could allow this. "Mop & Glow" is one industry term for a "restoration" that involves varnish, chrome and little else. But as with the rest of the boat, the

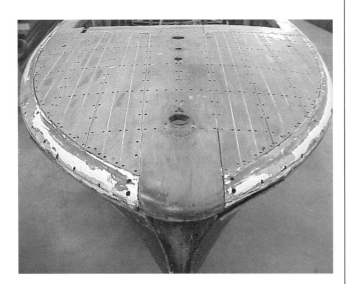

These deck planks may look as if they just need to be stripped, stained, and varnished to complete the restoration of the hull.

important parts that exist below need attention as well—I highly recommend at least the removal and replacement of all deck planking.

The outer covering boards are the place to start, especially with the larger, thicker postwar covering boards. These were normally mounted on a horizontal sheer shelf, very often made of pine, which was used in place of the earlier vertical sheer clamp. Water finds its way down the sides of the deck and underneath the metal rub rail at the sheer. This water then wicks its way sideways under the covering boards. Being protected from the wind and rain, these areas do not dry as exterior surfaces do. Since the factory did not seal or bed these interior surfaces prior to assembly, the aged bare wood surfaces draw in this moisture like a sponge. Even if rot has not gained a foothold here yet, this moisture is drawn up to the underside of the surface varnish coats by the heat of the sun. If the surface gets hot enough, the moisture vaporizes and expands, causing varnish coats to bubble from the surface.

The live seams between the individual deck planks also admit water that collects between the planks and plank battens below them, causing the same problems to occur. Likewise, hardware fastener holes and crash-pad upholstery edges will do the same. It is for these reasons that all deck planking, either new or old, should be well sealed and bedded to protect from moisture incursion. Ignoring such areas of known trouble spots will cause a great deal of future expense in money and time involved with maintenance and repair.

Removal of the above deck planks, however, exposes rotten deck beams, plank battens, sheer shelves, and inboard sides.

Using Original Deck Planking

If you are going to re-use the original deck planking, it should be understood that, after 30 to 70 years, the wood has lost most of its natural oils and it is very susceptible to expansion and contraction due to seasonal moisture changes. It now needs more than a sealer on its surface; it needs to be stabilized throughout. If left to expand and contract, varnish coats will crack open. The planks may themselves crack at the surface and moisture will once again be admitted.

It is possible to soak this planking with a penetrating sealer from the bottom up by laying them in shallow pans of a sealer such as Smith's CPES. Care must be taken not to totally or partially soak to the upper surface where sanding and staining would be effected, possibly leading to a blotchy stain job.

I must admit, I have never attempted this. Such a labor-intensive procedure, simply to save the old wood, would be prohibitively expensive for my customers. It would certainly be many times more expensive than re-planking with sound new wood. If you

intend to re-use the original deck planking, please refer to Chapter 10 for plank removal procedures.

Deck framing should be refastened, faired and sealed and all original screw holes in them plugged with glued dowels.

After proper cleaning of inboard surfaces and plank edges as well as proper sealing of these surfaces, one should be able to replace them into their exact original positions.

If you are going to try to tighten gaps in the live seams of the original planks, the easiest method would be to replace the original king planks with a new wider one to make up for the space created by gathering the deck planks outboard towards the covering boards. New screw holes would then be drilled for the plank installation.

Original wood, from somewhere in the boat, like the old lower transom plank or an original deck plank that has been replaced, or possibly from the seat frames, should be used to make the bungs. The softer old wood will fair the same as the original deck planks.

If new bungs are cut from sound, hard new wood, fairing will become very difficult. Electric sanders and even long-boards will tend to ride over this new harder wood and drop down, scooping more wood from the softer surface between them. A more or less dimpled surface can result. This effect may be alleviated, somewhat, by the use of a softwood sealer first.

New Deck Planking

Before deck planking can begin you must verify that the deck framing is secure and fair. The hull should still be secured in a plumb and level condition with proper supports and braces from the chine to the floor so that the weight of the clamps, the wood and you do not distort it.

SCHOOL OF HARD KNOCKS

Factory Heavyweights

Working at another shop some years ago, I was re-fastening and repairing the deck beams of a 17-foot Chris-Craft barrelback prior to fabricating new deck planks for it. This was a gray boat that clearly had not been previously restored. I was confused to find that the entire hull bulged out to the port side 3/4 inch, as if the boat had been stored on its side for a time. The inner king planks had been installed by the factory to follow this curved centerline, with modifications to the deck beams to allow it. I was more than confused. This was not age or misuse—the factory had built it this way.

I was standing there scratching my head and wondering where to go next when a frequent visitor and advisor to that shop, Chris Smith, walked in. I described my dilemma and he leaned over, looked at the hull number and recounted how these hulls were framed at the factory, upside down on a form, the pre-cut frames slapped together with finish nails in under an hour. He deduced, by the late hull number, that for some time that particular hull form had probably had a 100-pound worker on one side and a 200-pound worker on the other side. That well-used framing form itself was probably the cause.

He went on to remind me that these boats were not built one-off by master craftsmen but were mass-produced on an assembly line. The assembly line workers didn't have tape measures: all parts were pre-cut. If something was out of line more than the width of the workers thumb ("rule of thumb" = approximately 3/4 inch), a boatwright would be called in to make a quick repair and the assembly line could proceed.

First check for bilateral symmetry. The transom framing should be checked for squareness by taking diagonal measurements across its surface from chine to sheer. Temporary diagonal bracing can be installed to frames internally to hold the hull shape in place until it is planked. Measure your aft deck at the transom and mark the center; do not trust the

factory placement of the inner king plank, as they are rarely properly centered. Measure from sheer clamp to sheer clamp at every deck beam and temporarily mark a center there. Suspend a taught centerline from stem to transom and drop plumb bobs to the deck beams to verify the previous centerline marks. This procedure will tell you where you may have to brace the topsides framework, in or out, in order to build a straight deck. I have seen factory-built decks that were out as much as 3/4 inch from the centerline.

Put a nail in the center of the stem to hook your tape measure to so you can verify that cockpit frames and engine hatch beams are square with the centerline by measuring equal distances to their outboard ends.

When bracing topsides frames in or out remember that this will raise or lower the sheer line at that point which will have to be addressed later, with either a hand plane or a shim.

While you are adjusting deck beams up or down, it is wise to keep a couple of long limber battens (I use 3/4 x 3/4-inch x 18-foot red cedar or redwood) lying on the deck to insure fairness.

When you are satisfied with the centerline plumb bobs and half-breadth measurements, you can make sure your deck beams are properly sealed and bedded and refastened with new silicon Bronze fasteners.

Many of these factory deck beam installations involved fasteners from the sheer clamp into the end grain of the deck beams. If you want more than a six-year turn-around on your restoration it is advisable to add corner blocks (quarter-knees) here where the factory did not. Use 3M 5200 here (as in all joints) as adhesive bedding.

If it is not completely possible to bring all half-breadth measurements into line this can be accomplished later with the inner edge of the covering boards. I have seen factory-installed covering

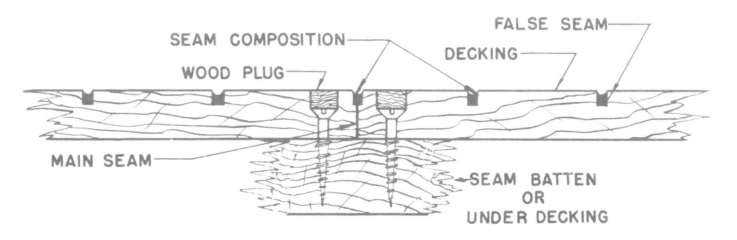

This illustration from a Chris-Craft owners' manual shows the anatomy of deck planks fastened to plank batten. *Courtesy of The Mariners' Museum, Newport News, Virginia*

boards that are an inch wider on one side of the boat to accomplish this.

If your boat is a runabout with engine hatches, you must verify that the deck beams, fore and aft of this opening, are square with the centerline, with outboard measurements to the stem. The fore-and-aft hatch carlins must be measured from your corrected center-

As in reconstruction that deals with framework, the hull must be carefully leveled and blocked.

line marks. Take diagonal measurements of this opening to insure squareness.

Using a water level or spirit level, measure and mark each frame station from side to side at the sheer to verify they are equal. On most mass-produced hulls the sheer is a straight line from transom to stem, when viewed from the side. If it is possible, obtain lines drawings with offsets from the Mariners' Museum. These will tell you exactly what your heights and half-breadth measurements should be. If they do not have lines for your make of boat, seek out others who have the same hull and ask if you can get measurements from them. The ACBS directory is very helpful here.

The sheer line, the top of the sheer clamp at the deck edge, must be faired in first. Many of the decks I work on have all new sheer clamps and deck beams and all new fastener placement so I can use my power plane and hand planes here for quick, set-depth material removal.

Many of the decks I work on include original hull components with pieces of original steel finish nails and broken fastener bits. This has taught me to use a

The installation of deck beams requires constant fairing with battens.

right angle grinder with an 8-inch disc. The tool I use is actually sold as the 7-inch variable speed Makita 9217FPC sander/polisher. I replace the hard rubber disc with an 8-inch diameter by 1-inch-thick foam disc. It is half the weight of normal grinders and far more controllable. I use 40-grit 3M Green Corps Stickit discs for major fairing such as this. This is also the tool I use for the initial fairing of the hull's bottom, topsides, and decks. When the sheer line is faired in to your satisfaction, you may fair in the deck beams.

Use long limber battens and keep them parallel to the centerline. Let them drop early to see if they hold up the same distance. Swap battens occasionally to make sure you do not have a crooked or stiff one on one side and not the other.

For the foredeck try very light, very limber battens, 1 x 1/8-inch plywood, six pieces laid at the same time. Watch how they lay on the surface. Mark low spots with an "L" and high spots with lines across the frame that indicate 1/16-inch increments that need to be

hand-planed or ground off. Two lines means 1/8 inch needs to be removed. Do not be too greedy with your initial fairing until you have determined any frames that are too low and have, at least temporarily, stapled shims to them. You must slide these battens in and

The inboard edges of deck hatches should follow the curves of the deck.

out parallel to the centerline (all of them) in order to determine the length (athwartships) of these material removal adjustments. Occasionally run the battens athwartships as well to insure uniform curves to the deck beam surface.

When you are happy with the shape of the deck beams you should set your larger router for the plank-batten depth, usually 1/2 inch, and make sure the batten notches are all the correct depth. If you have installed some new frames you may address these batten notches now by laying the battens in place, marking the notch placement, and routing out the notch. You may now install all deck plank battens, properly sealed and bedded.

If your engine hatch frames are shot and you do not have decent pieces to trace to fabricate new ones, it is possible to design them from the deck shape. The fore and aft crown of the inboard edges of the hatch frames is determined with a long batten that continues the

side view profile of the deck. If this line were flat, the deck profile would look faceted and not be a sweet line.

The outboard fore and aft hatch frames, however, must be flat or the piano hinge that is attached here would not work. This portion of the deck, outside the hatch, must also be flat if a piano hinge is used. This can be a very tricky job on hulls with extreme tumblehome like barrelbacks, but must still be addressed on all hulls with compound deck crowns. These hatch frames must be fit in place in the boat, as they will not lie flat on a bench. Once the hatch frames are assembled and fit to the deck's compound curves, I make sure they are properly centered with about 1/8-inch clearance around and between them. Run a couple of temporary screws up into these frames from the curved sill that supports them. This will hold them in place while you fair in their top surface with the deck.

If your old deck planks and covering boards are

Athwartships battening is necessary to remove high spots in that direction. When high spots are evident, they are marked and faired in.

Long limber battens are used to fair in the sheer.

Long battens must be used to insure "sweet lines" for the deck. The outboard edges of deck hatches, however, must remain a flat, straight line or piano hinges used on the hatches will not work.

Engine hatches must be faired in to the deck beams.

sound enough to re-use, install them at this point. If you are re-planking the deck with new wood, use the following procedure. Installing the covering boards first allows you to straighten up a misaligned deck by making the inboard edge of the covering boards follow exact half-breadth measurements from your true centerline where the sheer line may not. The covering boards form a visual frame for the fore and aft deck planks. If these inboard edge curves are not identical and equally spaced, the fore and aft kerfs of your deck planks will end up at noticeably different lengths. If these are painted white this will be even more obvious.

Whether you are using a spiling pattern or original covering board as your pattern piece, you must flip it upside-down from side to side and make adjustments until you are satisfied that this inboard edge meets the centerline distances of each frame. The placement of this inboard edge should follow the plank batten (sheer partner)

well enough to allow adequate fastener placement for the covering board and deck planks. Ignore the outboard edge of the covering board for now; in fact, when I cut out these pieces, I leave an extra 1/2 inch overhanging the hull sheer to be marked and trimmed later after I have final-fit them and drilled locator holes.

Once your final pattern pieces for the fore, mid, and aft covering boards are ready, you should spile or trace them onto matched pairs of plank stock and cut out each pair at the same time to insure that the inboard edge is identical. Leave the aft covering boards a few inches long to allow some stock removal when fitting the butt joints. Mark and save cutoffs for matching bung stock.

Before fitting these onto the deck, I clamp the pairs together and to the front of my workbench with the inboard edge up. I sand this pair of inboard edges together with an 18-inch flexible long-board beginning with 40-grit to remove any jigsaw marks. Be

The engine hatch's carling frames are flipped upside-down to mark the depth of its landing bevel.

Careful measurements for the covering boards should be taken at 90 degrees to the centerline for the full length of the boat.

very careful not to change the curve at the butt ends. I make sure I have a 90-degree edge that exhibits a sweet curve that is identical to both pieces. I use this procedure for all covering boards, from 1/2 inch to the ultra-fun 4-inch covering boards of barrelbacks.

Clamp and fit these covering boards to the deck beginning with the miter joint at the stem. If you have significant crown in your deck you may need to under-bevel this joint slightly. Make sure it is still a dead-tight joint or fairing the deck will expose the excessive under-bevel as a gap. Bear this in mind at the butt joints as well. Leave the inboard edges of the balance of the covering boards at 90 degrees.

Make sure you place the inboard edges at identical distances to your correct centerline. Do not worry about the outboard edges initially, they should be overhanging the sheer.

After you have determined exact placement of the forward pair of covering boards you can drill locator holes at the frames to assure replacement in this exact position after the slippery bedding compounds have been applied. Check your original planks to make sure you are following the factory screw placement pattern. At butt joints and the miter joint at the stem I will often angle the screw slightly towards the joint to help pull it tight.

After the forward pair are secured with locator screws you may address the middle or following pairs in the same manner, beginning with crisp tight butt joints. Always place the inboard edges with identical measurements to the centerline. Different lengths of white kerf lines will really show up at the aft deck.

When fitting covering board butt joints, especially with thick stock, I will often use the factory method of running a handsaw down the joint until I have a tight, crisp line. This may take several passes while you tap the following piece forward, but it works great.

After all covering boards have been positioned and

Inboard edges of pairs of covering boards should be faired in with a long board to assure that they are identical.

fit with locator screws, you may mark the overhang at the sheer all the way around the boat. Mark any overhang at the cockpit carlins at this time also. Remove the covering boards and trim to these lines. All pieces should receive a couple coats of sealer on the bottom, inboard, and butt edges and set aside to cure.

Proper bedding compound should be applied to the sheer shelf, short-beams, cockpit carlins, battens, etc., and troweled out so as not to leave voids. Never use a hard glue or epoxy with this type of construction.

Install your covering boards in the proper order, with bedding at the butt joints, and clean up excess bedding compounds. Some boats have two-part covering boards with very thick stock outboard and regular plank stock inboard. If your boat is one of these you may now repeat the previous procedures to install the inboard covering boards. Remember that the inboard edge is still the most important edge. In some boats you will also have to cut a kerf rabbet to the outboard edge of the board for seam compound. In others, you will want a tight edge

here. Research photos of the original construction for your boat; some seams that were tight when built may have spread open with age and previous restorations may have caulked and painted them.

If you are replacing thick covering boards and

Covering boards and king planks must be installed to the deck's true centerline, not just a centered mark on the inner king plank.

find, like me, that 16/4 (4-inch) is only available in Honduras mahogany, yet you will be using red Philippine for the deck planks, I recommend planking the inner covering boards and the king planks in Honduras as well. This is better, especially if you are going to have different colored covering boards and king planks anyway, either darker or bleached, than having to bleach or over-stain to get your inner and outer covering boards to match.

Fabricating New Oversized Covering Boards

Some boats used very thick stock for the covering boards to obtain rounded hull shapes made popular by the streamlined aircraft designs of the 1930s and 1940s. Apparently the lumber was cheaper than the labor to produce these shapes out of intricate framework and steam-bent plank stock. This is still true today.

Chris-Craft, for example, used 10/4 (ten-quarter or 2-1/2 inches thick) stock for the postwar covering boards of 17-foot Deluxes, 14/4 (3-1/2 inches) for the Holiday line, and 16/4 (4 inches) for most

of the barrelbacks. Look at some of their cruisers' forward toe-rails and you realize just how big those trees must have been.

Century used 8/4 and larger covering boards in some of their postwar models, as well. In utilities such as the Century Resorter, with no bridge-deck structures, these were very important structural members holding the topsides in shape.

The stock thickness may be somewhat greater than the normal 1/2-inch plank stock but the construction techniques are basically the same. The difficulty arises when it comes time to sculpt the proper outboard curving shapes.

The proper preparations for straightening, leveling, and fairing in the deck beams and sheer-shelves are even more important with thick stock that will not bend like 1/2-inch plank stock, to make up for errors in fairing the framework.

You are probably replacing the old covering boards due to excessive weather checking or because they are rotted at the butt joints or at their joint at the

Repeated passes of a handsaw produce a crisp, tight joint.

Deck planking must be well-sealed and bedded to avoid future moisture problems.

sheer clamp or sheer shelf. The important part to remember about covering boards is that the inboard edges must have identical curves and corresponding points must be equidistant to the centerline, otherwise the leading edges of the deck plank kerfs will end at different lengths and the deck will look noticeably crooked.

After you have restored the major hull framing, bottom, and topsides planking and have thoroughly straightened, squared, and plumbed the hull, you should place the old covering boards back in place to verify that they were not bent out of shape when the hull hogged.

Place the corresponding port and starboard covering board sections together, back-to-back, to verify that they are identical. Concentrate on the inboard edges. If one or both of these have been warped by time and weather you must come up with a pattern (1/4-inch plywood will do) that will work for both sides of the boat.

If large sections of the bottom edge of your originals are rotted away leaving you with nothing to trace, you can set a small square against the outboard profile of the piece at its widest point and mark the pattern at the bottom edge of the square. Don't worry too much about the outboard edges at this time; in fact I usually add at least a half-inch of outboard overhang at this point so that I have room to adjust the inboard edges when fairing. I also make the pattern at least 2 inches long at the aft end, in case it takes multiple attempts to tightly fit forward butt joints. When forward joints are fit tightly, trim the aft end to its correct length.

Covering boards are usually made of two, three, or more lengths, in order to complete the full length of the boat. Make each one of these sections' patterns 2 inches longer and 1/2 inch wider at this time.

A two-part covering board on a prewar 17-foot Chris-Craft barrelback requires 16/4 stock for the outer covering board, yet only 1/2-inch plank stock for the inner covering board. This model is meant to have a seam between the two.

A one part covering board on the 1939 19-foot Chris-Craft barrelback requires only 8/4 stock.

When you have verified that your patterns fit the hull correctly you can be confident you are not going to destroy that $500 mahogany log it took you so long to locate and ship.

Lay your patterns out on the bench to determine just how much stock you need to replace them. Your 2- to 4-inch-thick covering board may only be 4 inches wide at its widest point but require a 12-inch-wide board to get out its full curve. You will want to nest the patterns on the piece to keep down the amount of waste.

Most of the grain orientation of your hull's planks are quarter-sawn, which means that the edges of the annular growth rings are exposed. This is the most stable configuration for plank stock as it does not bow or cup with expansion and contraction. This also gives the traditional straight ribbon-grain look that is so prized with mahogany. Plain-sawn or flat-sawn lumber leaves the annular growth rings relatively flat to the surface of the plank and the intersected darker latewood grain layers give the wood a totally different look, much like rotary-sawn plywood.

You will want to lay out the patterns on your thick stock in such a way as to take advantage of the grain direction so your covering boards better match the hull's grain appearance. Once you have determined the minimum outside dimensions of the lumber you require, you can go to your lumber supplier and study the available pieces. I always try to get a single board large enough to get out all pieces. For example: outer covering boards for a 19-foot Chris-Craft barrelback require a piece 16 inches wide by 16 feet long and 4 inches thick to obtain the nested pairs.

Try to obtain the same species of wood that you are using to plank the hull. I have had trouble in the last five years or so finding Philippine any thicker than

This postwar Chris-Craft 17-foot Deluxe requires 10/4 stock for the outer covering board and 1/2-inch plank stock for the inner covering board. This design does not have a seam between the two pieces and must be fit as tightly as a topsides plank.

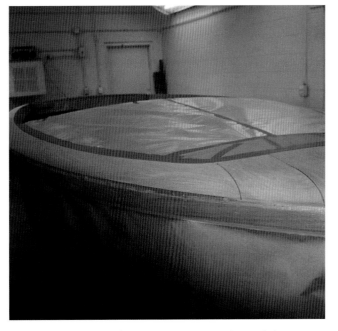

This postwar Chris-Craft Holiday requires 14/4 stock that tapers down to 10/4 at the after end of the boat. This model has three separate, shaped blocks mounted at the bow with caulked seams between them.

This prewar Chris-Craft 19-foot barrelback requires 16/4 stock for the outer covering boards, 1/2-inch plank stock for the inners, has a seam between them, and has three shaped blocks at the bow that are fit without seams.

senting a shape that would almost be triangular in cross-section. Note the sketches I have drawn to help you in deciding how to lay out the pieces.

I use a 6-inch blade in my jigsaw or Sawzall and separate the patterned pieces into chunks light enough for one or two people to pass through the band saw. Make sure you have several new band-saw blades on hand. I like one to three TPI (tooth per inch) by 1/2- or 3/4-inch, hook-toothed blades for this thick stuff. If your blades are too small, dull, or weakly tensioned you could mess up a lot of expensive wood very quickly. The initial cuts must be vertical and not be allowed to weave or wander.

While I have cut many of these pieces by myself, it is dangerous and stupid. These things are heavy; so get someone to help you feed them through the band saw and simply hold the excess weight while you direct the cut.

The inboard edge should be cut most carefully, exactly on the line, or you will not only have a great deal of work ahead of you to straighten this back out into a new sweet line but you will have to make the same alterations to the corresponding piece for the other side of the boat. Remember that these pieces must be bilaterally symmetrical, at least on their inboard edges, or the deck plank kerfs will be noticeably off. The outboard edge need not be so carefully cut at this time and should even be 1/2 inch oversized at this point. Your patterns should also have left each piece a couple of inches long at the aft end.

Make sure you transfer the piece designation and arrow for forward to the underside of each piece.

If your original covering boards taper in height from one end to the other, you can set them inside the newly cut replacement and carefully transfer the finished height of the piece. This excess can be

12/4, or 3 inches. For Honduras, 16/4, or 4 inches is still available but it's usually plain-sawn. This is not too great a problem as covering boards are very often stained a lighter or darker color anyway. Just make sure to match the inner covering boards and king planks of the same wood.

Look carefully at the end-grains of the stock you are going to use and consider how you are going to get the quartered grain to show on the outside of your finished covering boards. Remember that the finished outboard edges of the covering boards will be cut almost diagonally to the top or bottom surface pre-

Sheer lines must be faired in first to insure fairness of the deck beams.

After shaping the butt joints and bases, making certain the inboard edges are equidistant to the centerline, the excess height at the aft end may be removed with the band saw.

removed on the band saw, but I would still leave it full thickness for now, to be trimmed to the mark later. There may be residual tension in these thick logs and when cut, warping may occur. If this should happen, alter the base of the piece so that it seats properly on the sheer-shelf and framework. You may then trace the finished height from the original.

At this point I clamp, or screw, these pieces to the face of my bench, and, with a flexible long-board and 36-grit, dress the inboard curve to a sweet line removing any band-saw blade marks. Compare the port and starboard pieces to insure they are identical on this inboard edge. Set these pieces in place on the sheer shelf, or sheer-clamp and frames, and see to it that it will rest flat and sound when fastened. Alter the sheer-clamp or sheer-shelf or the bottom of the covering board until this is so.

Start at the bow with either the mitered ends of the

Some boats, such as this 19-foot barrelback, need their massive 16/4 outer covering boards installed and shaped first because the deck beams were hung from their inboard surface. A temporary jig should be installed before the old deck beams are removed to insure proper replacement.

Layout of the patterns must be done carefully to present the proper grain direction. Nesting of the pieces saves on waste.

forward pieces or the shaped, centered blocks that some models use. Do not try to shape the outboard profiles at this time. Concentrate on getting the most forward joints fit first, while maintaining exact centerline distances of the inboard edges.

On some models, such as the Chris-Craft Holiday line, there are three blocks forward that have caulked seams and must, in the end, line up with the caulked deck seams. Some careful future planning must be done here with the deck plank kerf dimensions in mind.

Study catalog photos of your model as well as the original pieces. It is entirely possible that your model started out in life with tight seams in the covering boards only to have shrunk open in the mid-1980s and

then gotten caulked. You do not want to faithfully duplicate a design change caused by a repair.

Performing the actual butt joinery of these large sculpted pieces is far easier than you might think. Note the sheer-shelf or the 6/4 butt block where the originals were joined. You will notice a cut line. At the factory, they simply set the covering boards carefully in place and ran a handsaw between the two pieces, repeatedly, until the butt joints were perfectly aligned. Start with the forward blocks or miter joint of the two forward pieces and clamp them in place, with careful measurements of the after ends, and with respect to the centerlines. I highly recommend a Ryoba, a Japanese backsaw that cuts on the pull-stroke and has one side of its blade cut with the teeth not set to the sides. Run this saw straight down the line, tap the pieces together (maintaining bilateral symmetry) and run the saw down again. Repeat this until your concept of perfection is achieved.

When bow joints are fit, clamp your forward pieces in place and, after studying the original pieces for fastener placement, drill and install a number of locator screws that will hold this piece firmly in place. Verify that your centerline distances are correct.

You will need to order oversized tapered drill bits and counter-bores for these pieces that require #14 x 4-inch screws. Jamestown Distributors and Clark Craft Fasteners both carry Fuller tapered point drills in the "L" (long length) sizes. Determine the actual after butt end and saw the extra 2, or so, inches off.

Sand the inboard surfaces of the next following set and verify the inboard edges are identical. Clamp your next following set of covering boards in place, mindful of the centerline, and do the handsaw trick again, tapping the pieces forward until that joint is perfect. Temporarily fasten, trim the after ends and continue. Install any further lengths in the same manner.

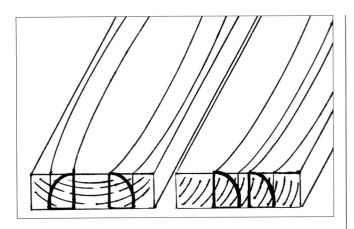

Pattern pieces may be rotated to expose quartered grain, based on the grain direction of the stock available.

When all pieces are fit with their locator screws, you can now trace a pencil line all the way around the perimeter of the hull, at the sheer-line, on the underside of these pieces to mark the exact outboard cut line. You may now remove the locator screws and trim the outboard edges of all pieces. Then seal their inboard surfaces, including butt joints and sheer shelves and frames.

Install these on the boat, from the bow aft, properly bedding all adjoining surfaces. Use a flexible adhesive/bedding here, as hard glues would quickly release from the movement of lumber this size. When all pieces are installed, following the screw patterns of the original pieces, use the long-board to dress the inboard edges of the butt joints if necessary.

Make sure the screw heads are set deep enough for the shaping operation. Often, it is necessary to re-set these screws after some sculpting has been done.

Your task now is to sculpt the outboard shapes of these pieces. I use a power plane to do the initial shaping. Do not work in short lengths—obvious high areas can be removed but, ideally, each cut should run from one end of the boat to the other. This will leave you with a facetted surface. The original pieces should be set upon the deck just inboard of pieces you are working on for quick visual reference. You should have huge scraps of wood to practice on until you develop the necessary confidence. When the greatest bulk of the wood that needs to be removed is gone and all screws re-set, cut your bungs from the scrap stock, glue them in place, and trim close with a chisel.

I use a pattern template to check the curves I'm cutting, every 12 inches or so. This tool is sold at woodworking supply stores (don't buy the cheap one) and is usually a line of sliding steel or plastic pins that, when pushed against a shape, slide back and conform to that shape. I like to take the shapes from the originals and trace these on cardboard so they can be cut out and marked, every 12 inches along the deck for quick reference.

Work the power plane to shape these curves until you have approximately 1/2-inch facets. At this point I use the variable speed grinder with an 8-inch diameter by 1-inch-thick soft foam 3M Stickit pad (available at auto supply stores) and adhesive-backed, 40-grit discs. This type of pad has

Band-sawing these heavy pieces without help is not recommended.

Fit entire blocks before removing excess height. In this case the portside covering board sprung up because of the release of tension when cut. Alter the bottom side to seat properly before any stock is removed from the top.

The large shaped blocks forward should be pinned together with glued dowels to avoid movement of the varnished seam.

no large center-locking nut, which would not work in this application. Roll this grinder pad up and over the surface to remove the facets and do 80 percent of the actual shaping. If you do not have a variable speed sander, be cautious. Be mindful of the height line you drew on the inboard edge of these pieces. That should be the deck height; you will not want to go past that.

If your shaping efforts expose screw heads, remove them, counter-bore them deeper, and reset and re-bung them. I do the balance of the shaping with the grinder and a pneumatic long-board, through the grits, after I have installed the deck planks and then I'm ready to fair in the entire hull.

These same procedures should help you to replicate toe rails, such as those on the Chris-Craft Sportsman, though the final fairing would be done before installation.

Installing King Planks

When all covering boards are installed you may install the king planks. If your model boat requires a king plank in the engine hatches, be sure to save some matching plank stock for that. I like to start out with a 16-foot or so board trimmed to the appropriate widths and cut lengths, keeping them in numbered order, with an arrow for forward, so that the grain runs true from stem to stern. Don't forget to mark and save bung stock for each piece.

If your foredeck has extreme athwartships and fore-and-aft crown to it, you may find that you will have to shape the forward king plank wider at the high points of the crown so that it properly fits the straight edges of the deck planks mounted on this curve. If your foredeck has extreme crown, leave the foredeck king 1/4 inch wide for now. Think of it like the staves of a wooden barrel; they are wider at the bulge. If you

Some very careful planning is required on some models where the designed seams of large, shaped blocks forward must be aligned with the deck plank seams. These will noticeably be white and will show any deviation .

Using a power plane and full-length cuts, shape the outboard profiles. Check often with the numbered profile patterns.

shape the inboard edges of the first deck planks, it will be too noticeable against the plank kerf lines.

After preparing the king planks from matching stock you can clamp the aft end of the foredeck king plank in place, leaving a 1-inch overhang at the cockpit edge to be marked and trimmed later. Make sure that it is properly centered with measurements to the inner edge of the covering boards on each side. Make these measurements at 90 degrees to the king plank edge. Follow a deck beam with your tape measure. The forward end of this plank should be overhanging past the installed covering boards.

Using a soft-lead pencil or bright chalk, run along the upper, inner edge of the covering board. leaving an adequate amount of lead or chalk on this sharp inner edge surface. Holding the forward edge of the king plank dead-centered down against the joint of the covering boards, rap the king plank on top with your fist or rubber hammer. This will transfer the lead or chalk to the underside of the king plank and show you exactly where to cut for a perfect fit. Trim this vee or curved shape with a low-angle hand plane until you have a perfect fit, tapping the plank forward until it's trimmed correctly. Install the foredeck king with only locator screws at this point. Then install any mid-deck, bridge-deck, engine hatch (split in the middle), or aft-deck king planks. Install and pre-drill them with overhangs and mark and trim the fore and aft ends from the underside. Remember that if the king plank and covering boards are not perfectly centered, your final plank kerfs will show it.

Completing the Deck Planking

It's time to bring forth those perfectly book-matched planks you have been jealously hiding since your lumber arrived. Those long quarter-sawn beauties with

Using simple measurements and a profile gauge, make numbered profile patterns every 18 inches or so from the originals.

the slight grain curve that follows the bulge of the mid-deck were the first chosen and are the last used.

You have paid your dues; the dirty framework you made sound to keep these treasures from cracking, the bottom job that absorbs the forces of wake and wave! The topsides that took forever! This is the fun stuff, building the deck of a mahogany boat. On the other hand, mess this up, and you will likely put the boat in storage and buy a sports car.

Lay your plank stock on the deck and mark with a pencil the starboard and port pieces, #1S and #1P, #2S and #2P, and so on. Mark an arrow for inboard and for forward on all pieces. Mark lengths for the foredeck first and then slide the plank back and mark lengths for mid-decks, bridge decks, engine hatches, and aft decks. Leave at least a 1/2-inch

overhang for each section, to be trimmed after locator screws are placed.

A single 16-foot plank might be marked #1S foredeck for 6 feet or so and then #1S bridge-deck for 6 inches or so and then #1S hatch for 3 feet or so and then #1S aft deck for another 3 feet or so. In this manner you could stand on the dock and see the grain of the wood follow from the stem to the stern with gaps caused only by cockpits. To accomplish this example, you will need only a 13-foot length to plank a 20-foot boat while keeping its grain true from stem to stern. Imagine how gorgeous this deck will be if you have book-matched planks and #1P is cut this same way.

If you ordered a large enough pile of wood in the first place, chances are good that the wood came

Leave surfaces high until deck planks are installed before final fairing. If your thick stock is a different species than your plank stock, make the 1/2-inch inner covering boards of the same species of wood as the covering boards.

After the covering boards are installed, fit and install the king planks to an exact centerline. Chalk or graphite can be applied to the sharp inner edge of the covering boards. When rapped with your fist or a rubber hammer, the lines are transferred to the underside, indicating where to cut for an exact fit.

from the same supplier, possibly even the same tree. This is, in fact, how it usually happens, even with orders as small as 200 board feet. The lumberyard has no particular reason to shuffle the pile.

Keep each of your plank pieces marked well, with soft-lead pencil, as to side (P or S), number (outboard from king plank), placement (foredeck, mid-deck, bridge-deck, hatch, aft-deck, etc.), and the always necessary arrow for forward and an arrow for inboard and you will be able to put this piece back in place, where it belongs, after the kerfing operation or the sealing phase or whatever. Get any one of these puzzle pieces wrong and you'll lose "Best of Class." You may even have to buy drinks for those who spot it to keep them quiet. Make sure you mark cutoffs for matching bung stock.

You must determine, from actual clues, how wide your plank stock needs to be milled. Measure your old shrunken and cupped planks. Measure centerlines from your deck plank battens. Is this a prewar Chris-Craft (7-1/8-inch, three-kerf, four-strake) or postwar? Is it a prewar Gar Wood (10-1/4-inch, five-kerf, six-strake)? There are many permutations here. The same factory changed their kerf settings from model to model, year to year. Your rebuilt hull could be 1/4 inch wider than it used to be, or narrower. Who can tell? Some Chris-Crafts, for example, use 7-1/8-inch, four-strake planks on the foredeck and 8-7/8-inch, five-strake planks on the aft deck.

Most important is deciding what looks best for your boat. I highly recommend using the millimeter side of all of your measuring tools from this point on.

The new deck plank blanks are passed over a low-set table saw blade to create the new kerfs. These must all be done at the same time to make sure the kerfs are perfectly aligned.

After you have determined how wide each of your plank sections should be and have milled them to these widths, making sure the grain patterns still match, you can kerf the outboard surfaces on a table saw. You should use a 1-foot-long scrap piece of one of the milled planks that you saved for bung stock and lay out even kerf lines.

First, attach a straight length of wood to the inside edge of your table saw fence. Your blade will be running very close to this and you don't want to hit the fence. This operation will require the removal of the blade guard and splitter. Be very careful here and take all safety precautions necessary.

I install a new, fine-kerf blade in the machine for this operation. Set the blade height at no more than one-third the thickness of your plank stock and, with the motor running; slide your new wooden fence into the blade until only one-half of the blade is exposed. This fence setting will cut one-half the nor-

mal kerf width on the inboard edge of the planks.

Use your prepared scrap piece and run it, face down, with the marked inboard edge against the fence. You should have a one-half blade kerf cut one-third the thickness of the wood. Adjust the fence in or out and the blade up or down until you have the setting you want.

The king plank will have no kerf in its edges, nor will the outboard edges of the individual deck planks. Rather, the inboard edge of each successively installed deck plank should be cut with one-half the chosen kerf width. The reason for cutting only one-half of a kerf here has to do with the crown of the deck. As each plank is installed on this curved surface, the crown forces open the top of this plank edge. If a full-width kerf were to be cut here, it would thus end up wider than the rest, looking unsightly. If these end up looking smaller than the cut kerfs upon installation, it is a simple matter to sand the gap wider when fairing the deck until they match the others. As in all matters of

King planks are pre-drilled and temporarily screwed in place before fitting the remainder of the deck planks.

The old plank stock is used to roughly shape the new deck planks and to verify correct factory screw placement patterns. They will be saved until the boat is completely varnished to determine correct hardware placement.

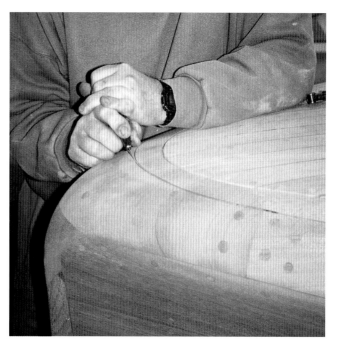

Some details, such as this continuation of a designed plank seam, must be hand-carved into the covering boards after fairing has been done.

woodworking, it is always easier to remove wood than to add it.

Pile all of your deck plank pieces on sawhorses to one side of the table saw, in order, face down, with the marked inboard edge facing the direction you will address the saw blade. Note that the arrows indicating 'forward' on your plank pieces will be pointing away from you for one side of the boat (starboard) and towards you for the other side of the boat (port). In this manner you will be kerfing only the inboard edges of each plank piece. As you pick up each piece, peek under it to make sure the inboard arrow is towards the blade. Slide the edge of the plank piece into the blade, tightly against the fence, and flat down against the table. Without flipping or rotating the piece, set it face down on sawhorses on the other side of the table saw. Pass every piece through the saw until completed.

Now, get out a millimeter ruler and determine, on your scrap piece, where you want the remaining kerfs to fall. Don't forget to mark widths for the blade kerf itself. For example, say you have a 7-1/4-inch (183mm) plank and you want to evenly space three kerfs to create a four-strake plank. Through a little trial and error on paper you will start after the 2mm partial kerf already cut and lay out 43mm for the first strake, 3mm for the kerf, 43mm for the second strake, 3mm for the kerf, etc., and you will end up with four 43mm strakes. Mark these kerf locations on the leading end of your scrap piece and adjust the fence and cut them. Using this scrap piece as a gauge reset the blade to cut the next kerf on your planks. When properly set, you should be able to slide the scrap piece back and forth against the fence without causing the blade to spin. Keeping all the plank pieces properly oriented, pass them back across

A wide-lead carpenter's pencil is used to transfer graphite to the inboard upper edge of the covering board. Bright chalk can be used here as well for better visibility.

The plank is clamped in place at one end and a rubber hammer or fist used to tamp along that surface above the edge. The graphite is transferred to the underside of the plank blank, indicating where to cut for an exact fit.

the saw until they are all stacked on the other side. You should no longer have to peek underneath at the arrow but simply feel the first kerf with your fingertip. Reset for the next kerf and go again. If you feel uncomfortable about risking your expensive matched plank stock, practice on plywood or other scrap.

You may now proceed to fit these planks to your deck, beginning with the foredeck. Start with plank #1P or S and clamp it to the cockpit opening just as you did the king plank. It should be overhanging the covering board, forward. Use the chalk trick here again and, with the plank clamped in place, rap it with the rubber hammer to transfer the line to the bottom side of the piece. This method can be used all the way down the deck to fit into the covering board.

After this piece has been trimmed to fit tightly with band saw and hand plane, clamp it in place to see if the king plank needs to be adjusted on its outboard edges for the effects of the deck crown. After

the king plank has been dealt with on both sides you may apply locator screws and proceed outboard with planks #2P and S, and so on. Working from the king plank out, fit and temporarily install the remaining deck planks with locator screws. Mark the undersides where planks overhang hatch or cockpit openings and trim these after removal.

After all planks have been fit and temporarily installed with locator screws, you may remove them from the boat.

A kerf where the deck planks meet the inner edge of the covering boards will usually have to be cut at this point on the outboard curving sides of each deck plank. Reset the table saw for the original one-half kerf you made to the inboard edges of the deck planks. Flip the planks face down and run these curved edges over the blade. You should not have to worry, as the fence will keep you from cutting too deeply. It helps to mark the position of the center of the

After all deck plank sections are fit with locator screws, mark the cockpit overhangs with a pencil and trim them when the planks are removed for sealing.

blade on the face of the fence so you will know where it is cutting its full depth even though you cannot see it.

After a couple of coats of sealer to both planks and frames you may permanently install these planks with proper bedding applied to the frame tops, plank battens and to the edges of the planks as well. Install all the of planks with two locator screws at each frame and when all are installed you should use a straightedge to mark clean lines for the balance of the screws. Follow the same screw pattern as exhibited by your original planks.

I use a couple of new drills and counter-bores for the deck to help insure crisp bung lines. Climb inside the hull and clean the excess bedding there as well. Clean all excess bedding compound right away, especially in the kerfs at the edges of the planks. I make a couple of small sticks with angled ends, cut to fit the kerfs tightly and go over the entire deck the same day they are installed. Make sure you clean the kerf along the covering boards as well.

Since deck beams, following topside frames, are almost never evenly spaced you should measure between deck beam screws, from frame to frame, to determine even distances for the plank batten screws at the plank edges.

Install new bungs, cut from the plank scraps that you saved and marked for the individual planks.

CHAPTER 13

FAIR AND SAND THE HULL AND DECK

Fairing the hull, deck, and transom of a mahogany boat can be tedious, seemingly unending work only if you are not paying attention to what you are doing. This one phase of a restoration will make all the difference in the final appearance of the boat.

If you have repaired and re-fastened the framework and bottom planking and re-planked or refastened the hull and deck, you should take this opportunity to do the job right and seal it well so that it will be trouble free for many years to come. If you have not re-fastened the entire structure from the keel out then you should probably not spend too much time on this phase as you will be removing stock from wood that is liable to move out of shape anyway.

At this point, the hull should be securely blocked high enough off the floor so that you can comfortably address it. Lower for the deck, higher for the topsides and transom. A height-adjustable shop stool on wheels will make things much easier at this stage as well.

Make sure you have recorded locations of the waterline, so that it is not lost. These should be marked with a sharp chisel at least at the stem and transom so they can be connected later with a water level or laser level.

The curved surface of the hull's frames, with the usual four plank-to-frame screws, pull the plank into

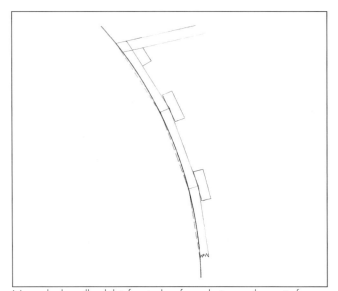

New planks will exhibit faceted surfaces between the main frames where they are only fastened to the plank battens at their edges. Fairing the hull shape forward at the flare of the topsides will remove more stock from the center of the plank than at its edges.

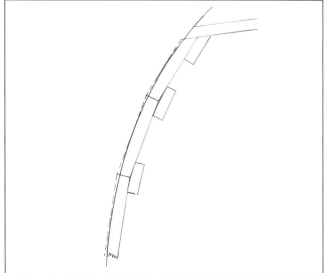

At the aft end of the hull, where tumblehome creates a convex surface, more stock is removed from the edges of the planks.

shape. The same will happen 2 feet away at the next frame. The area of the plank between these frames, however, is attached to the framework only at the edges of the plank to the plank battens. This area between the frames will exhibit the plank stock's original flat surface, leaving the hull surface faceted at this point. The hull's overall curved shape will be made of a series of flat planes. If we are discussing the topsides, forward, where the flare of the hull creates a concave surface between the sheer and chine, more stock must be removed from the center of the plank than at the edges of the plank to fair in this curve. If we are discussing the topsides, aft, where the tumble-home creates a convex surface between the sheer and chine, more stock will be removed from the edges of the planks than from the center in order to fair in this curve. The same will be true of the convex surface of a crowned deck. Cut cross-sections from your old plank stock to witness this effect.

These areas can be carefully prepared in the initial stages of fairing with the most aggressive grits and tools. Think of your approach at this stage as sculpture. You will be carefully removing a known (at least intended) amount of wood with a tool that you have practiced with and know the amount you are removing. One of the most important lessons in carving is knowing when to quit. You can always remove more material; you cannot put it back on.

Using a Sander/Polisher

I use the lightweight, variable-speed sander/polisher for this with the 8-inch diameter by 1-inch-thick soft foam sanding pad. This soft foam sanding pad is used in the auto-body industry for the initial sanding of fairing compounds on car bodies. Look at your car's hood, or clear down the side of the vehicle, assembled of three or more panels. It worked here, didn't it? Wood is far easier to fair than a combination of

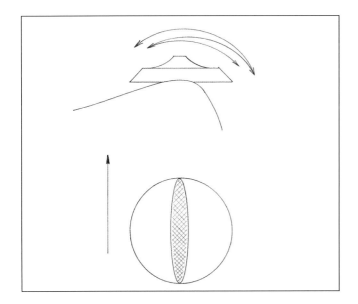

A soft foam pad forms over convex surfaces at the center where abrasive action is lessened due to a slower speed of rotation at that circumference.

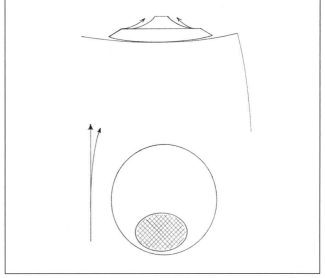

A soft foam pad should be used with the pressure applied in this general area to avoid gouging at the outer circumference, which is spinning faster and is thus the most aggressively abrasive.

When chiseling down the bungs that cover fastener holes, the first cut should be at least halfway up the bung to determine the slope of the grain.

Bondo and metal. Never use hard rubber backing discs on wood—it's too easy to get into trouble. I use 3M Green Corps Stickit discs, 40-grit for the initial controlled removal of stock and 80-grit for the removal of the 40-grit scratches. Practice on similar plank stock scraps until you are comfortable with the tool and the abrasives and the amount of wood you are removing. Learn to apply the tool in long smooth sweeping motions that do not create grooves at the beginning or end of each stroke. Practice on scrap pine or plywood first and then your leftover plank stock. Sacrificing a $20 piece of mahogany is far cheaper than wrecking a $20,000 hull.

Do not be cheap with the abrasives. They may be expensive but once they have lost their cutting edges, the disc may still look fine and feel abrasive to the fingertip, but you will begin to push harder than necessary and lose control of the depth you are cutting.

When you first learn to use this tool, start by float-ing it on a scrap piece of plywood, at least 3 x 4 feet. Hold it out, at arms length, with one hand on the long handle and starting with light grits and low speeds, learn to float the machine under its own weight. When you have mastered this, look at the sanding disc to see the area, still holding sawdust that your particular pad rides on. Under only the machine's weight, this surface should be a rather small, uniform circle. Applying pressure straight down with your other hand, centered on the head of the machine, should increase the size of this circle as well as increasing the amount of wood removed from your test piece. Note that tipping the long handle up transfers abrasive friction to the outboard (away from you) area of the pad and causes the machine to quickly scuttle off to the left. Tipping down on the long handle does just the opposite. With the other hand, on the side handle, tipping up causes the machine to pull away from you. Tipping the side handle down forces the machine towards you. You should quickly learn where you are comfortable cutting with this tool. For example; pushing down with your left hand on the side handle, while slightly raising the main handle with your right hand, will force the machine

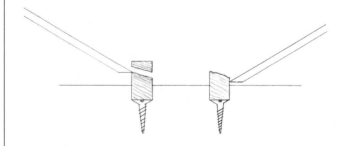

When the slope of the bung's grain is determined, the cutting action must be directed such that the bung does not break below the surface, which would require removal and replacement.

SCHOOL OF HARD KNOCKS

Adventures with Power Tools

While preparing dutchman repair areas for some large grounding damaged areas (20 x 8 x 3-inches deep) in the gripe of a 70-foot sailboat, one of my workers thought he would override my chisel-and-slick (a 2-inch-wide chisel with 2-foot handle) instructions and hurry things along with a grinder and 16-grit disc (that's 16 rocks per square inch).

The disc hit against one edge and instantly jammed into the corner of the other edge and, as the machine fled the scene at about 80 miles per hour, dislodging his grip from both hands, managed to spin itself around just as it passed his face. It disconnected itself from its extension cord long before it hit the ground, some 30 feet away. He stood up with a giant smile and hollered to me at the other end of the boat; "Hey! did you see that?" Before I could get much more than his name out of my mouth, his eyes began to well with tears as remaining pain sensors reported the lack of skin on the left side of his nose. At full rpm, with 16 grit, he's a very lucky boy—skin grows back, noses don't.

Treat this and all power tools with the utmost care and respect. Take all safety precautions possible. A light-weight, full-face shield is highly recommended here. A steel-studded leather apron is available for those who, one day, wish to have children. These are power tools and need to be treated as such, with respect for their power. They can get the job done, but used incorrectly, can send you to the emergency room in a hurry.

A non-flexible long board, or "flat board," sander is used on flat surfaces.

away from perpendicular surfaces, such as when fairing covering boards near raised coamings. The rotary pad can cut not only unsightly groves in a perpendicular surface, but it can quickly yank out of your control.

Removing Proud Bungs

The first approach to your hull will be the removal of all protruding, or "proud," bungs. You can remove the bulk of these with a chisel, or better yet, a slick. Start halfway up the length of the bung to make your first cut in order to determine the possibility of sloping grain. You do not want your cut to follow the grain below the plank surface, this would require digging the bung out and replacing it. Reverse the direction of your cut so that any sloping grain cuts rise away from the hull. Knock the bungs down to about 1/8 inch or so and finish the balance with the grinder. If you are uncomfortable with this, you can always tediously pare them down with the chisel.

I personally don't bother with the slick and just carefully go at the rows of bungs with the grinder set at a slight angle and simply mow them down. Get very used to your grinder's cutting action before you try this.

diagonally to your left side where you have the weight of your body to push back with both arms. The deepest cuts can be made this way. You can easily see why there are two handles on this dangerous machine. Directing the cutting action, however, is far more controllable than simply putting weight on the machine to increase its cut.

This type of rotary grinder should be used on single-plane surfaces, whether flat, concave, or convex. Stay

Diagonal strokes are used in fairing, one direction when moving forward on the hull and in the other direction when moving aft on the hull. Keep track of how many passes are made with each grit so that both sides of the hull receive the same attention.

Blocking the boat up to the right height lets you use shoulder power instead of back muscles.

Fairing the Hull

Once your bungs are all flush, you should take some time and go over the entire hull with limber battens or adjustable ship's curves and a soft lead pencil. Use a large-lead carpenters pencil with a smooth round point. Do not apply enough pressure to cause a scratch in the surface but as light as necessary to transfer a mark.

If you are working on the topsides, you should run battens from the chine to the sheer and watch for daylight at the low points. Mark the high points with the pencil. Circle entire high areas. Go over the entire hull with these battens and marks until you are comfortable with your understanding of the surface and what needs to be removed and where.

Working in one direction, usually left to right, use the grinder and 40-grit disc to methodically remove the high area marks. Do not be too aggressive or attempt to achieve the final fairing with this tool.

The next tool to apply is a long-board. This is a two-handled board about 2-3/4 inches wide and 18 inches long. This is the tool the automotive industry uses to achieve fair surfaces. It will ride over low spots and abrade the high spots until there are none of either left. This is a time-consuming and tiring operation and is known in the business as "sandercising," a wordplay on exercising. I myself, have had two hands on a three-man, six-handle, 6-foot x 8-inch x 40-grit long-board on a 70-foot Dutch stainless-steel ketch removing tens of pounds of multicolored Bondo. I have heard tales of five-man, 10-foot boards on wooden vessels. Obviously, the larger the board, the sweeter the fair line and the quicker it's arrival.

You may optimize the effects of the long-board with long sweeps of your arms. Make sure these sweeping lines follow the grain lines and not an arc. You do not want to apply grain-scratch "smiles."

Flexible long boards are necessary for curved surfaces.

The pneumatic air file, with its inline strokes, flattens surfaces quickly.

Both long-boards and long-board papers are available from auto body supply stores. Unfortunately, even the inexpensive plastic long-boards available here are too stiff for the usual un-flat surfaces of a boat. You could buy the cheap plastic long-boards and alter them with a 4-inch grinder by removing the cast-in stiffness supports.

You can make your own long-boards from scrap plywood with handles glued and screwed to them. Differing grades of plywood, and the application of grain directions, will allow many options in flexibility. Experiment with metals and plastics as well if you intend to do this again.

Approach your hull with this abrasive board at a 45-degree angle to the waterline. Do not press overly hard. Let it wear the weight of itself and your arms. Wash this board up and down, such that it is angled 10 degrees off of its long axis in travel. The 10-degree overlap assures the lack of a sharp cut edge. As your biceps improve, change this angle to 20 degrees. Extreme curves in hull shape, such as

at the flare, will require you to hold the sanding board at differing angles so it remains flat against the surface being sanded.

Use a uniform diagonal stroke, from sheer to chine, all the way down the hull. When you get to the other end of the boat, change the angle of your stroke such that it crisscrosses the previous strokes. Again, make sure you keep the board as flat as possible to the changing curves of the wood. Be careful that you do not cut lines with the hard edge of

The long board must be slightly skewed to avoid cutting a groove at the edges.

You can make your own long boards from varying thicknesses of plywood for stiffness or flexibility.

Very flexible boards must be made for extremely curved surfaces.

the board, and keep track of how many abrasive passes you make from bow to stern and duplicate that number on the other side of the hull. I recommend 60-grit 3M Green Corps or Imperial Purple paper for this first step. There are cheaper brands of abrasives that don't work as well or clog up quicker and end up costing much more in the long run—both in money and elbow grease. I have gone as heavy as 40-grit for the initial stages, but the resulting diagonal scratches are much more difficult to remove later.

Do not be stingy with the sandpaper, even the good stuff wears out and you are wasting your labors. You should soon recognize the correct pull against your stroke and the amount of sawdust falling to the floor.

After a couple of passes, up and down the hull, you should be able to see the areas abraded by this procedure and the unscratched low areas. One trick to help you see low spots is to use a soft lead pencil and draw zebra stripes about an inch apart on the entire hull. The pencil marks will quickly disappear from the high spots and will remain in the low spots until they are no longer low spots. Once this is achieved, you must occasionally run your hand, palm down, lightly across the surface. Very lightly slide your dust-encrusted hand up and down from chine to sheer, from one end of the boat to the other. Do this with your eyes closed so that you are not confused with visible plank lines. When you detect variations in the surface, mark them with a soft lead pencil.

This procedure can take a surprisingly long time and take a lot of physical work, but will produce the most fair hull in the long run. If you do the entire hull and deck with this method, through all the grits, you may well have over a hundred hours of backbreaking labor invested.

If you are doing this for a living, you can cut this time 60 percent by investing in a pneumatic long-board or air-file. You still have to apply the machine to the hull but the pneumatic inline strokes remove far more material. You will need a 5-horsepower air compressor and the more expensive brand of air-file used by the automotive industry. Cheaper air-files are available but they not only don't work as well and can spit lubricating oil onto the wood. Even if you decide to use the air-file, the initial long-strokes should still be applied by hand.

After the last set of pencil marks has disappeared and you are happy with the fairness and shape of both topsides of the hull, you should sight down the sheer line and chine line to make sure these remain sweet lines. If the edge of the sheer is undulating, the later application of a chrome rub rail will enhance the effect. Fix this with long passes of the long-board. You may also have to shape the correct flat surface here for the rub rail. Usually the topsides sheer planks are faired to a point where the covering boards are 90 degrees to the deck. Check your original planks to verify how the factory intended this edge. At this time, sight down the top of the sheer edge as well, at the outboard, top surface of the deck covering boards. This is another line that must be fair or will quickly show up against the rub rail. The flare or tumblehome of the transom edges must be addressed at this point as well.

DEBUNKING THE COARSE-GRIT MYTH

Many years ago I attended a seminar that included a talk by a finish expert. Before beginning his spiel, he handed out factory brochures for the types of varnish he sold. He talked about the various tools and procedures and then he came to the final finishing point, stating emphatically that one should never finish-sand above 80-grit! He claimed that to go past 80-grit would simply burnish or polish the wood and create a mottled or blotchy surface. As he stood there defending his claims, I was showing his factory varnish brochures to those on either side of me, pointing out the factory recommendations for their own products. All three said to prepare the wood to between 180- and 320-grit.

If the 80–grit claim were true, then 90 percent of the products in the abrasives industry are of no use. When it is worn out and its particles are no longer sharp, any sandpaper or grinder disc from 16-grit to 6,000-grit will burnish or polish rather than cut. This is why I recommend constantly maintaining fresh sandpaper. It's expensive, but it's also cheaper than elbow grease, and burnishing or polishing one area while abrading another area will cause blotchy work.

There is one good excuse for finishing a hull only to 80-grit. If you are refinishing an old hull and want to hide a lot of putty-filled dings and dents and mismatched planking repairs, you can create what is, in effect, a false grain with 80-grit scratches. Heavy use of a thick grain filling stain will fill these scratches and appear to be the straight grain of the hull. You will no longer be able to see the actual details of the real wood grain but that is what this finisher's trick is for, to hide bad work. I know of boat shops that use this trick simply so that they can construct their hulls of inexpensive, unmatched wood with carelessly fit, puttied or epoxy-filled seams.

This grit-scratch effect on filler stains can be used to your advantage at higher grits as well. If you have finish-sanded the hull to 220-grit and have a particular plank that is lighter in wood color than all the rest, temporarily tape off this plank at its edges with low-tack tape and re-sand it to 180 or 150. Experiment with scraps of these planks. The coarser grit scratch will hold more filler stain than the surrounding 220-grit scratches and this board will stain darker. The same is true in the other direction, if the entire surface is finished to 220-grit and a particular board stands out as darker than the rest, tape it off and sand it to 320-grit. It will take less filler stain than the rest of the wood and hopefully show as lighter. Experimentation on scraps will give you confidence with this trick and will also help you determine the stain color you want.

Hardware such as cutwaters, stem-head fairleads, and windshields should be test-fit during the fairing stage to insure their fit after the boat is varnished.

If you are working on the deck, now also is the time to grind in any plank overhangs at the cockpits or deck or engine room hatches. Dress these edges with the long-board as well.

'Sanding the Hull

When you are happy with the shape of the hull and deck and all of the adjoining surface edges, you can begin removing all of those diagonal scratch marks. This is where the in-line air-file excels; though the hand-held long-board will do the job, too.

If you began the shaping phase with 60-grit you must now sand the hull in-line (with the grain) with 60-grit until all non-aligned scratches are gone. You must proceed "through the grits," that is, thoroughly sand with the grain with one grit uniformly and methodically until you are ready to proceed to the next higher grit. In this manner, you will remove the deeper scratches of the previous grits You should not

jump more than 20 grit sizes at a time at first. For example: 80 grit will remove 60-grit scratches while 100-grit or more will not. After sanding in-line with 60-grit until all 60-grit diagonal scratches are gone, sand in-line with 80-grit, then 100-grit, and then 120-grit. At this point I begin jumping the finer sandpapers by 30-grit increments: 150-grit is followed by 180-grit, and then finally 220-grit.

The grit sizes that define sandpapers are merely a count of the number of abrasive particles per square inch; 40-grit paper has 40 little, sharp stones per square inch of surface area; 220-grit has 220 tiny little sharp stones per square inch, and so on. The grit size marked on the back of the paper is usually followed by a letter (A through F) that indicates the weight of the paper backing material—the heavier the better. Other codes indicate "closed-coat" (uniform grit application) or "open-coat" (open areas in

Complicated new interior furniture should be fabricated and fit to the boat before final fairing or finishes are done.

The furniture is then removed to finish separately from the hull.

A careful record of all sanding, staining, and finish coats must be kept to insure that this furniture will match the finish of the hull.

the grit application that allow for collection and removal of sanding "swarf"). Open-coat sandpapers are best for wood sanding, as they don't load up as fast and cut longer and cooler than closed-coat papers that can quickly build up "corns" of loaded material.

Sandpapers are available with many different materials for the abrasive:

- The least expensive use *uncoated flint*. These wear out quickly and cost more in the long run. Also, easily loosened grit stones can build up and cause much larger localized scratches to occur.
- *Aluminum oxide* sandpapers are the industry standard. These are what I use, usually 3M Green Corps for the heavy grits and 3M Gold Fre-Cut for the finer grits. This type of sandpaper is easy to recognize because, no matter the manufacturer, they come in a variety of colors.
- *Silicon carbide* abrasives are the most expensive but are not recommended for use on boats. This material is a metal that can leave tiny, orange rust spots visible in the varnish.

Read *The Wood Sanding Book* by Sandor Nagyszalanczy (The Taunton Press). This $20 investment will help you make sense of the fact that you can easily spend hundreds of dollars on sandpaper by the time you are completely done with a single boat restoration.

An alternative to the long-board is a half-sheet electric orbital sander, such as a Porter-Cable or Rockwell 505. This machine can leave swirl marks though, so I do not recommend its use with grits heavier than 120. Final sanding must always be done in-line with the grain following this machine to remove swirl marks.

You should go over the entire work surface with a very bright light between each grit change. Hold the light in front of you, pointed back towards you, at a low angle to the hull while you view that area at the same low angle. This low-angle lighting method should show shadows of even the tiniest of cross-grain scratches. Remove these now, before you go on to the next grit.

You can occasionally hose down the entire hull and get a fleeting glimpse of what a gloss surface would look like. Scratches reflect the light differently and

The finished furniture is installed in the hull and prepared, matching deck planking is installed and faired-in prior to finishing the deck.

show up darker. This is okay as long as you let it completely dry before you begin sanding again. This is especially useful in the winter when you are trying to keep the moisture levels up in a heated shop.

When you have sanded completely through the grits and have finished at 220 or so, it is a common practice in the woodworking industry to wet-sand the surface in order to raise remaining wood fibers that were not sheared off in sanding. This procedure is called de-whiskering and should be done with the finest grit you are using. I personally finish sand to 220-grit and de-whisker with 240-grit. The stain or sealer you are going to apply will cause the grain to rise so you might as well do it first so you don't have to over-sand the stain or sealer.

The surface you prepare will have an effect on the sanding procedures and tools you employ. If you have re-planked the hull with matched new wood and bungs cut from that wood, the resistance to the abrasives will be uniform for the most part. Watch areas such as plank butt joints where a particularly hard-grained plank meets an unusually soft grained plank. The resistance to stock removal will be greater for the harder grained wood and an even application of abrasive can ride over the hard grain and cut deeper into the soft grain. This is most likely to happen with electric orbital sanders but can even happen with sanding blocks and flat boards. When this happens you must simply alter your stroke so that the harder grained wood gets a little more abrasive attention than the softer grained wood.

If you are fairing the more dry, brittle, original hull planks and, after refastening, have replaced the bungs with wood cut from an original plank, then you are also likely to have a uniformly sanded, and stained, surface.

If you have a combination of original planks and some new planks fit into them you must be very careful with the fairing. The old wood that has lost most of its original oils will simply be much softer and abrade much quicker than sound, new wood next to it. You must be very careful here not to dish out the softer wood.

If you have refastened your original planking and did not keep a board or two from below the waterline for making matching bungs, you should cut new bungs from the lightest weight luan that you can find. I have seen a refastened hull bunged with by-the-bag new bungs. The sanders simply rode up over the sound new wood bungs and removed less from their surfaces than it did from the surrounding dry planks with each pass. This also left a cone of plank stock around each. After a few coats of varnish, the hull appeared to be pimpled. In this case, I would recommend experimentation with a softwood sanding sealer. This product is meant to seal surfaces such as pine plywood that have a combination of hard, highly resinous, non-porous grains combined with areas of porous, soft wood between them. This product is actually made to be used before staining so that the softwood areas do not suck up more stain than the resinous hard grains. Perhaps it can help the sanding procedure as well. A uniform coat of this product would have to be applied to the entire hull before staining.

When you are applying the grain-filling stain and come across the frustrating cross-grain scratches that you missed (admit it, you missed it; I still do), do not throw up your arms in despair and decide that it's too late to do anything about them. These are actually very easy to get rid of if you do it immediately. The minute you notice it, wipe off the newly applied stain and sand it out, with the grain, starting with whatever grit is necessary and following up through the grits, slightly overlapping each previous area. When the scratch is gone, immediately apply fresh stain to the area and continue with the rubbing-removal process. If you wait more than a few hours and the stain you are applying dries, you will have trouble with a halo of over-stain between the new and old stain applications. Good news, huh? You can get rid of scratches if you do it right away. Practice this procedure on scrap plank stock, sanded exactly like your hull was, before committing to the hull. Get someone to help you and teach them how to do this. Actually, I pay someone to do the tedious repetitive rubbing while I jump in for the last minute repairs.

A Final Warning

When you are in the process of fairing and sanding your hull you should prepare serious-looking signs that you set on the deck that implore, PLEASE, DO NOT TOUCH. The first thing you want to do is show off the fruits of your labors. The first thing a visitor wants to do is run their hands over the surface you are working on. Be nice but be firm.

The natural oils in their skin will transfer to the surface on the cellular level and you won't even know this oil is there until you are applying stain. You will be feverishly applying and rubbing out your grain filler stain, hurrying to get a uniform job after hundreds of hours of sanding when, seemingly inexplicably, a large, yellow palm-print will appear in an area already soaked with oil and will not accept stain. You have no choice but to sand this oil out of the surface with at least 180-grit, followed by whatever grits necessary to return the surface to how it was prepared. Do this immediately and you will not have a halo of stain framing it. While you are sanding the surface, the oils have been absorbed from the surface of your hands by the sanding residue, and it is okay for you to stroke and feel and take pride in the fruits of your labors. Remember to not do this when you are not sanding, or you will be the culprit. If you want to go in there and just feel it up to find and mark trouble spots or attempt to foresee the future, set your beer down and rub some sawdust on your hands before you caress it.

Chapter 14

SAND, STAIN, SEAL, AND VARNISH

After all the work you've done to get to the finishing stage, you want to make sure you spend the time and effort necessary to not only make your boat look as good as ever, but protect it from moisture and make it last. With the restoration so close to completion, it can be tempting to rush to the varnishing stage. Be patient. Surface preparation is critical to the quality of the job.

Repairing Dents and Filling Holes

If you have small dings, dents, or screw holes, you can use filler putty to repair them. I personally like Famo-Wood. It dries a bit lighter than others on the market and accepts stains well. I use their mahogany color and their ash color for areas that will be bleached for blond decks. While this product does accept stains well, it is unaffected by bleaches. When applying this or other fillers it is advisable to tape off the immediately surrounding surface area. Using a flexible blade putty knife to force the putty to the bottom of the hole can also fill the grain of the wood around the intended repair hole. This area of putty-filled grain will accept stain differently than open grain and it will end up as a halo blemish around the repaired spot. If I have a number of uniform small screw holes to fill, I like to use a leather punch, or paper punch, to make a quick hole in the center of the tape.

There are ways to help make these repairs disappear into the background. You can use a fine point pen or pencil to draw in grain lines matching those

When using wood putty to fill dents and holes, tape the surrounding area to avoid a stain halo of the material in the wood grain.

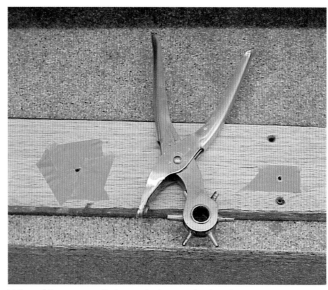

When filling screw holes, a hole punched in the tape is easier than many pieces of tape.

around the repair. You could mix up a brownish colored paint to match the darker colored grains in your wood and apply this with a very fine brush. A friend of mine, a sculptor and painter who specialized in *trompe l'oeil* (to fool the eye) taught me to use a pigeon feather for painting wood grains. Bend the feather until you have the correct tip spread distance and tape the ends to a popsicle stick. Again, practice this on wood scraps before you apply it to your hull.

If you have a depression such as a dock scrape where wood was not removed but merely crushed in or compressed, you might try swelling it back out by soaking it with water rather than filling it in with putty. Imagine what would happen to the putty if this area swelled back up once the boat was in the water.

If you have an area that you deem too large to hide with putty, you could use a veneer, or dutchman, to fill the hole. You must find a piece of wood that is the same grain and color as the surrounding wood you will be trying to hide it in. Shape this repair piece to help it hide as well. Do not simply use a geometric shape such as a square or circle but try to shape its perimeter to fit grain shape as well. If you are in dead straight grain try something like a pointed-end football shape. Try to fit the edges into dark grain lines to hide the edge glue line.

Make your dutchman slightly thicker than the intended depth of the repair so that it can be sanded flush with the surface. When you have finalized the shape of the repair piece, hold it directly against the surface and trace its shape with an Exacto-Knife with a #11 blade. It will help to hide the repair if you slightly bevel the edge outboard from the piece. Once this repair perimeter has been cut to the proper depth you may remove the internal portions with a small, very sharp, chisel. Once you have achieved the proper fit, you can glue the piece in place. I use a gap-filling cyanoacrylate glue for this. It is available from hobby supply stores for the construction of radio-controlled model boats. Use rubber gloves and waxed paper to hold the piece in place until the glue sets. Again, tape just around this area, especially below it, to avoid getting glue into the surface grain.

This type of repair, or course, should be done before the shaping phase of hull sanding so that it is faired in through the grits with the rest of the hull. Prior to staining, remember to return to such repairs to draw or paint in any fake grain lines.

Finish-Sanding

Final sanding should always be done by hand, in-line with the grain. When you have opposing grains at adjoining pieces of deck planking such as where fore and aft deck planking meets the curved covering boards, you can tape off one of the pieces to avoid noticeable cross grain scratches. Use low-tack tapes

A bright light aimed toward you and the wood surface, while you view back at the same angle, will shadow and help you locate cross-grain scratches before staining.

Areas of different stain colors should be masked off. In this particular case, low-tack tape was used on the bare wood to avoid pulling up tiny silvers of wood on removal.

here to avoid ripping grain slivers from the bare wood surface, such as Scotch #2070 Safe-Release, or similar. Do not leave this tape on the surface for long.

Tape off the covering boards and the edges of athwartships planking at cockpit bridge-decks as well as the top of the transom planking. You may now make sure the ends of the fore and aft deck planking are finish-sanded in-line and free of cross-grain scratches. Use a bright light at low angles aimed towards you to look for these.

When all of these planks are addressed you may now remove these tapes and apply new tape to protect these plank ends. You can now sand the curved covering boards, in-line with their grain, without hurting the previous plank ends.

When sanding, staining or varnishing boat hulls, you should separate them into doable sections. The standard edge between the hull and deck is the line

Project areas should be separated into doable sections defined by hardware installations such as rub rails and quarter-guards.

Good taping and masking procedures produce tight, crisp color lines.

When bleaching or staining, scrap boards of the wood used in the boat that have been sanded exactly as the boat has should be used for experimental purposes beforehand. This will help you to decide when you might go too far.

between the lower edge of the covering board and the upper edge of the sheer planks. This line very often delineates a color change between the hull and darker or lighter covering boards. This line is also, almost always, covered with the metal rub rail trim. Even if your boat is to be all the same color, it is wise to break it up into workable sections so that you can maintain a uniform wet edge with the materials you are applying. The forward edge of the transom planks is a good place to separate the hull from the transom. This edge is usually covered by the quarter guard trim. Since there is usually no trim from the deck to the transom I treat these areas as one unit unless, of course, there is a color change there.

When taping off these work areas, I use Scotch #2080 Long Mask Blue tape. It is designed for days (not in the sun) without adhesive transfer. I also protect edges with 6-inch general-purpose masking paper, available from auto body supply or paint supply stores.

When taping off areas that require a tight crisp edge, such as when bleaching, sealing, or painting, use Scotch #218 Fine-Line tape. Remember not to leave this on for long, it has an aggressive high-tack adhesive to keep liquids from seeping under the edge.

While I am grinding and sanding the hull through the grits I will apply the exact same sanding procedures to a few pieces of scrap plank stock from that boat. Whatever grit you are using on the hull, remember to hit the scrap boards, all the way from beginning to the final grits. In this manner, you will have plank stock to test your stains on that have been prepared exactly as your hull was. If you bleached the hull, bleach these boards at the same time, with the same number of applications.

If cross-grain scratches are found during staining, sand them out, working through the grits, and immediately re-stain and blend in.

Staining

The stains I generally use are known as grain-filling stains. They are packaged as a very thick paste that must be thinned with the proper vehicle before use. Even after thinning to the consistency of thick house paint, it is a very heavy-bodied mixture. This is usually applied with a stiff-bristle brush, in order to force it into the grain. In five to ten minutes, the vehicle that you thinned it with will evaporate, or flash. The surface will begin to lose its gloss. It must now be rubbed in a circular motion to further scrub it into the open grain. The material used to rub it in is usually soft burlap or cheesecloth. This rubbing motion will also be filling the cloth with excess material and removing it from the hull. You must constantly re-fold the cloth to find clean surfaces as it fills up with excess compound. It must be rubbed out before it dries hard—

A sample stain board using scrap wood from the hull construction, sanded exactly like the boat. Remember to note results and record stain formulas so you can reproduce the amounts needed.

have plenty of these cloths at hand before you begin.

After all of the excess is removed from the surface, simply polish it uniformly smooth, finishing lightly in-line with the grain with a clean cloth. This procedure is best accomplished with at least two people, with one person applying while one or more do the rubbing. This is the best way to maintain a wet edge and a uniform application. Remember that if you discover cross-grain scratches, sand them out now while the stain is still wet (see Chapter 13).

If you are doing this by yourself do not apply more than a few square feet at a time before rubbing it out. Do not apply the stain with straight edges that may show a shadow of overlap. Always apply it in such a way that non-uniform edges result.

I favor stains made by Interlux. I personally make mixtures of these for each boat, sometimes mixing other oil-based stains in as well, until I, or the customer, are pleased with the sample tests. My personal favorite is two parts #573 and one part #42. It creates a deep, rich, warm color that is neither too dark nor too red.

Using small paper hot-drink cups (cold-drink paper cups are coated with wax which could affect the oil-based mixtures) and plastic mixing spoons, experiment with mixtures. Use your scrap plank stock and play with different mixtures until you get a spectrum from too dark to too light, or too brown to too red. Make sure you record the formulas for each of the marked stains so that you can then duplicate your final choice in quantity. Make sure you put a couple of coats of sealer and varnish over these test pieces so you know how this will affect the color.

Pick a clean window in your shop and varnish a strip of the glass with at least six coats of your chosen varnish (you can scrape it off later). Some var-

Darker stains should be tested on scraps with coats of varnish on them before making such a difficult-to-alter decision. You can always make stain darker—making it lighter is impossible without removal.

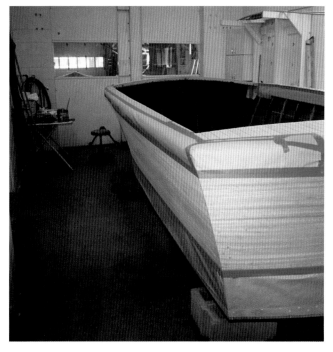

Areas to be stained or bleached differently should be carefully taped and masked. Unbleached areas should be stained and sealed before bleaching begins in case some bleach wicks under the tape.

Any area that is not going to get bleached should be carefully and completely masked. Hull masking should fall away from the hull, thus directing drips away as well.

Some woods bleach differently than others. These can be masked off and sealed while bleaching continues elsewhere.

nishes have a yellow tint, others reddish. My favorite varnish, Interlux Schooner #96, has a rich golden hue that deepens with each coat. Get to know how your varnish will affect the stain.

Dark covering boards can be a real challenge. I have seen far too many that appear green! What has happened here is that the stain was too close to black. I have seen some boats on which the covering boards actually were painted black. I have seen others on which black paint was thinned to a wash or stain so the covering boards would show black and still let the grain show through. The problem comes when successive coats of yellow tinted varnish, over the black, create a greenish hue.

Many want their covering boards dark. This is fine as long as the color is closer to brown so that its color is enhanced by the tinting effect of the var-

nish. You may have to stain these much darker than you would like, at first, as the build-up of clear coats tends to lighten darker stains. Remember, also, that while ultraviolet light darkens wood, it lightens or bleaches out stains. This is why Aniline dyes should not be used; they are not lightfast, and their colors fade quickly in the sun.

I have had the best luck with dark walnut jelled stains with multiple applications. I am still experimenting with these but so far I get deep rich browns this way. Time will tell just how lightfast they are.

Don't worry about getting everything perfect the first time. There are repair methods available at every stage of finish work. Only you will know what could have been. If, after six coats of varnish, you realize that your covering boards are not as dark as you intended, you can still darken them. Sand the

These ceiling planks, being bunged, had to be sanded and varnished in place. In most models, the ceiling planks can be sanded and varnished at the bench and installed with oval-head screws at the surface.

varnish to 220 grit and apply stain to this grit scratch. Apply it and rub it out with cheesecloth and let it set for 24 hours. Brush a very quick coat of varnish over it, so as not to disturb it and it can only be darker. In theory, this can be done with each coat of varnish, though it will weaken that coat's bond. This can also give the entire varnish coat a more cloudy or muddied appearance but what the heck, what you're looking for here is darker, right?

Another method of darkening or deepening a stain color involves mixing stain into the varnish, thus applying a darker tinted varnish. This would leave you with a stronger coating bond but is much harder to apply uniformly. The oil-based stain must be well mixed into the varnish and must be constantly stirred during application to maintain uniform application amount. The problem that arises with this applica-

tion procedure involves your flow-brushing capabilities. Where brush strokes overlap, two dark tintings will be evident. If you chose this approach, which I have seen work very well in multiple award winning boats, you simply must practice. Experiment with this technique on large sheets of glass—you will soon develop the required brushstrokes.

Bleaching Wood

If you intend to bleach parts of the hull or deck in order to achieve better color matching of the plank stock or in preparation for blond areas, it is wise to get other areas stained and sealed to protect them from damage by the bleach. Mask everything well that is not going to be bleached, let the masking paper hang straight down so that drips are led away from the hull. Do not allow the bleach to run across

Sanding between coats should be followed by a wash with a brushing thinner to remove excess sanding swarf. This is done with a lightly soaked piece of cheesecloth that is constantly refolded to present a clean surface to collect the swarf.

As in all surface applications, from sanding to varnishing, vertical application edges should be avoided. This is especially important when staining to avoid a noticeable edge of overlap.

After 10 build coats, this hull was diagonally wet-sanded with a long board at 240-grit.

your bottom paint, as it will discolor it.

I use a very strong, two-part bleach that is mixed just before use. It is applied with a natural bristle brush. I use 2- or 3-inch chip or throwaway brushes.

When you are applying bleach to a vertical or crowned surface, always start from the bottom and work your way up. Drips or runs will fall on previously coated surfaces. If you start from the top the early drips could cause unsightly streaks. You may need to apply this product more than once to achieve the uniformity of plank color you are looking for. Let it dry between applications to determine this. When you have achieved the results you seek, make sure you neutralize it per the instructions and rinse everything well. Remove tapes and

masking papers as soon as possible to insure it didn't bleed under them. If it did and affected unsealed wood, you will simply have to sand the bleached wood surface off.

Once the hull is dry you will need to de-whisker the surface before staining or sealing because this wet operation will raise the grain. Use your lightest -grit sandpapers and be careful, as it is possible to sand through the bleached surface.

When preparing blond areas I find that each boat and the wood it is made of can create a different color almost every time. I prefer a gold tint to it while some I have seen look almost greenish.

If your boat is a Century, its blond areas were likely planked with a naturally white mahogany look-alike called avodire. This wood should not need bleaching.

The type of wood you are working with can make a big difference here, even when bleached. A light red Philippine mahogany can look weak and washed out after bleaching. A dark red Philippine may still have enough depth of color to look good with just sealer and varnish. Rich brown African or deep salmon Honduras mahoganies may work the same after bleaching. What generally works best for me is a blond stain made of eight parts "Natural" grain filler and one part "Golden Oak." This works great on natural white oak decks as well. Experiment with these on your scrap bleached plank stock and throw a half dozen coats of varnish on it. Take these tests out in the sun to see them. Leave these pieces out in direct sunlight for a week to see the effect.

If your shop has only fluorescent lighting (no red spectrum) the color will be completely different outside. Where do you want your boat to look its best, in storage or at the show?

Sealing

Once you have stained everything and allowed it at least 24 hours to set, you must seal it. Varnish could be used as a sealer except for one thing; like the grain filling stains, varnish is oil-based. If you attempt to seal the stains with a sealer with the same base vehicle you will be re-introducing the vehicle to the stain and it will liquefy and get pushed around the surface while you are brushing on the sealer. Some areas will have less stain than others and you will have a blotchy stain job. The stain will dissolve into the sealer and you will have a muddy seal coat. Sealers are generally made with a different base vehicle, Naphtha for instance, so that it doesn't wake up the stain and move it around.

I personally use a wood resin-based sealer, Smith's CPES. Do not randomly attempt to use hard epoxy glues for this—they will not last. I apply two coats of CPES with a 3-inch natural bristle (ex-varnish) brush, with one coat immediately following the other. Allow this sealer 24 hours to cure and lightly sand with 220-grit before the first coat of varnish.

Varnishing

Prepare your varnish room so that there is no air movement—staple 3-millimeter plastic over the ceiling and walls if you have to. Hose down the floor before you begin so that you will not be kicking up dust as you work around the boat. For final coats, take a shower and work only in shorts. You would be surprised how much dust and lint comes off a clean T-shirt.

If you are working in the winter and have to heat your shop, remember that you cannot just heat the air around the hull. The hull itself must be up to temperature. This could mean leaving the heat on for days at a time, if not continuously. Open flame heaters should not be used as the exhaust gasses

Like a mirror, your varnish surface should reflect clean, crisp images.

could affect the varnish. Overhead gas blowers may be most common but they are the absolute worst for finishing boats. They not only kick around the most dust but they dehydrate the hull causing the planking to shrink and the varnish to crack. They also provide open flame in a room full of explosive fumes. Instead, look for few oil-filled, electric radiators—they are often available at discounted prices during the summer. These units provide clean heat without open flames or fans. They are, unfortunately, quite expensive to operate.

Varnish, for the most part, is made of natural wood resins. Formulas for its manufacture go as far back as the Egyptians, and the basic formula is little changed. Modern science has come up with some additives that extend its life, however, especially for marine use. The most important are ultraviolet light filters. Ultraviolet is a particularly aggressive wavelength in the non-visible spectrum of light. Even though invisible to us, it can cause a great deal of harm. A few hours exposure to unprotected human skin can cause blistering and second degree burns as well as cancers. A few minutes of unprotected exposure to the human eye can cause permanent blindness. You want the varnish to shield your boat from that same harmful radiation. The UV radiation in sunlight breaks down or photo-degrades the lignin that binds the woods cells together. This condition would continue with UV-transparent varnish. If the wood surface continues to break down on the cellular level, the varnish will quickly bubble and peel. The heat of the sun causes moisture in the wood to migrate to the warm surface and, if warm enough, causes the moisture to vaporize; building enough gas pressure to bubble the varnish coat away from the degraded surface.

Modern marine varnishes are formulated with UV filters to protect the wood surface. These platelets apparently are designed to float up to the top surface of each layer of varnish applied. The more coats of varnish, the better the protection, as long as this upper layer is not completely sanded off when you prepare the surface for the next coat.

According to Interlux, another additive in the varnish sets up above this UV platelet layer that forms a hardness layer at the surface. This layer is meant to provide scratch resistance and gloss retention.

There are high-build varnishes on the market specifically designed to form thick coats for a quick build-up of total film thickness. There are jet-speed varnishes that set at normal (thousandths of an inch) thickness, yet dry so fast that you can apply two coats a day. Both of these varnishes are available with UV filters, but the thick-set or quick-set formulations apparently don't allow for the addition of a hardness layer because both of these products

state, on their respective labels, that they should not be used as the final coat.

Interlux recommends against the common recent practice of wet sanding and polishing the surface with fine abrasive buffing compounds in order to remove excessive dust. Apparently, this process removes the hardness and UV layers and leaves a soft surface that would dull and scratch much easier. Look near the bottom of the label of your varnish can for an 800 number and ask for a technical representative to answer your questions. Talk to the chemists who make and test the stuff, and you will get real answers.

Too much has been said of providing the proper tooth for the adhesion of paints and varnishes. This so-called tooth refers to the grit-scratch of the abrasive used to prepare the surface of a material prior to the successful adhesion of the next layer of material, as if mechanical teeth must bite into or hold onto the previous surface.

The real tooth or grit scratch necessary for the successful adhesion of these high-tech coatings exists on a molecular level, not a mechanical level. Properly preparing the surface involves much more than sanding.

Sanding the surface, providing grit scratch, increases the surface area by changing a flat plane into a multi-faceted plane. One simply increases surface area, which could help adhesion simply because there is more surface to attach to. If this convoluted surface were not prepared on a molecular level to enhance surface tension of the film being applied, the newly applied film would attach only to the high points of this surface and thus, have less actual surface adhesion. After sanding one should always tack down the surface with a clean cloth lightly soaked in the thinner required by the product you are using.

Read your varnish can label, it will tell you what thinner to use. I use bulk cheesecloth and constantly re-fold it to present a clean surface to collect the sanding swarf. It is best to work in one direction only, constantly collecting any residue as you wash the surface. You do not want to just push this residue around but collect and remove it. This wash not only cleans the surface but, because it is generally the vehicle of the varnish, chemically prepares the previous coat on the molecular level for the proper surface tension and adhesion of the next coat. Do not soak your cloth to a point where liquid is left standing on the surface. It should be just enough to leave the surface temporarily glossy, completely evaporating within a few minutes.

The standard commercially available tack rag should be used on small areas, 1 square yard or so, immediately in front of your varnish brush. You must be extremely careful with this product. It is basically a piece of cheesecloth impregnated with a wax to collect and hold fine, light dust. If you press too hard on the surface you stand the chance of transferring wax to the surface. Varnish will not adhere to this; the surface tension is so different that the varnish will creep away from it, creating fisheyes."

A commercial tack rag comes out of the package flat and tightly folded. To use it this way would be like tacking the surface with a bar of wax. Completely unfold it and refold it softly. Apply this very gently across the surface, in one direction only, merely to collect any standing dust directly in front of your new varnish. When you set the tack rag down between uses do not set it directly on your varnish deck, as the wax could transfer. Set it on a clean piece of plastic wrap or its own plastic wrapper. If you accidentally drop the tack rag on the floor, get a new one, as it loves to pick up grit and

sand that could then scratch the varnish. Do not worry too much about dust in your build coats, as it sands out before the next coat. Just learn from each successive coat what you may be doing to cause it and take measures to reduce this before you get to your finish coats.

There are many different opinions on how to apply varnish. I am used to using 3-inch Red Tree badger-hair brushes because of the volume of varnish they hold and apply. Some use only foam throwaway brushes but these apply much less varnish so twice as many coats are necessary. Some swear by the roll-and-tip method, where small, yellow foam rollers are used to uniformly apply the varnish, followed by tipping-off with a foam brush to remove roller edge marks. Practice with each on your build coats and you'll decide what works best for you when its time to do the final coat, the second final coat, etc.

After the varnishing is completed to your satisfaction, you need to locate and cut all of the hardware holes for vents and such. Taking good measurement notes and photos prior to disassembly will aid in correctly locating these items. If you have saved all original planking, these locations can be confirmed. After the holes are cut, the exposed bare wood should be sealed. I usually do this with varnish, as sealers can be too aggressive should you spill some on the young varnish.

The mating surfaces of metal hardware should be coated with a light application of a bond breaker such as an automotive paste wax. This will prevent the varnish from becoming stuck to the hardware after years in the hot sun. When the time comes to refresh the varnish, however, this wax must be thoroughly washed off before sanding.

Wood items, such as quarter rails and splash rails,

that hopefully protect your hull from dock pilings, should be easily removable for replacement. These should be bedded to the hull with a non-adhesive boatyard bedding compound.

There are many varied procedures that must be researched and practiced in the cosmetic completion of the boat. Proper research will help you locate the professionals for this, and practice will help you gain the confidence necessary to do it yourself. Re-upholstery, hardware re-plating, and engine rebuilding are professions unto themselves and require far more tooling than is cost effective for one boat. Each one of these areas would require

an entire book each.

Memberships in the ACBS and other clubs mentioned in the appendix will prove invaluable in networking the proper resources for these items. It will also lead you to far more, possibly local, services than I have included in my appendix.

The focus of this book has been the woodwork—that which makes a boat truly a boat. It is much more important to bring the family back to shore, safe and sound, than it is to win an award at a boat show. The reality here is that once the hull is completed, you will be about halfway there in terms of time and monetary expense. At the very least, you will be con-

GLOSSARY

A

abaft — *aft* of, toward the *stern*

abeam — to the side of the vessel, *amidship*, at a right angle to the length of the boat.

aboard — within or on board a boat

ACBS — Antique and Classic Boat Society

afore — forward of, toward the *bow*

aft, after — near or toward the *stern*

ahead — in the direction of the *bow*

amidship — in the center of the vessel, either with reference to length or to breadth

anode — a positively charged electrode, toward which current flows. Opposite of *cathode*

antifouling — poisonous paint used on the bottom of the boat to prevent marine organisms from growing on the boat's bottom

astern — in the direction of the *stern*, the opposite of ahead

athwartships — lying along the boat's width, at right angles to *fore* and *aft*. Across the boat from side to side, perpendicular to the *keel*

auxiliary frame — transverse bottom frames that attach, at the outboard end, to the *chine* without a corresponding *topsides* frame

B

barrelback — a rounded *transom* design wherein the extreme *tumblehome* of the *topsides* flow into the *crown* of the deck shape to produce a continuous, rounded curve, as in the shape of a barrel

batten (seam) — a longitudinal *ribband*, usually let into *hull* frames for fastening *plank* edges, providing framework to back up the seam for water tightness

beam — the widest part of a boat. Sturdy wooden timber running across the width of a boat, used to support the deck of a wooden boat (deck beam)

bearding line — when forming a plank *rabbet*, a line formed by the intersection of the inside of the planking with the face or side of the *stem*, *gripe*, or *keel*

bedding compound — a material used to join two objects completely. Usually used to create a water tight or very secure joint

bell crank — an L-shaped piece of hardware, mounted on a pivot, to change the direction of thrust of throttle or choke linkage

bevel gauge — a tool consisting of a rule with a movable arm, used in measuring or marking angles and in fixing surfaces at an angle

bilge — the lowest part of the interior of the boat where water collects

bilge pump — a mechanically, electrically, or manually operated pump used to remove water from the *bilge*

bilge stringer — fore-and-aft framing attached to the transverse *hull* frames to stiffen the hull longitudinally. Most often located on either side of the keel, running as far forward as possible

blind fastener — plank fasteners, screws, applied from inside the hull so as not to be seen on the outboard surface

board foot — a lumber measurement equal to 144 cubic inches. One board foot = 1 x 12 x 12 inches. A piece of lumber 2 x 12 x 12 inches = 2 board feet

bookmatch — plankstock that has been re-sawn from a single, thicker, piece. Pieces are mirror-imaged when laying open next to one another, as the pages of a book

boot top — painted band at the *waterline*

bottomsides — sides of the hull below the waterline.

bound water — moisture caught up in the cell walls of the cell structures of wood

bow — the forward part of the *hull*, specifically, from the point where the sides curve inward to the *stem*

breasthook — a horizontal *knee* that mounts to the *stem*, to which the *sheer clamp*, *sheer shelf*, or *chines* attach

bulkhead — a vertical, *athwartship* partition, most often serving as a set-up member or frame partitioning the hull into separate compartments

bung — a circular plug of wood used to cover and hide the *fasteners* in wood

butt block — a section of wood used to back up the butt ends of plankstock, allowing two lengths to be fastened together as one

butt joint — joint formed by placing the butt-ends of two planks together

C

capillary action — a force that is the result of adhesion, cohesion, and surface tension in liquids which are in contact with solids, as in a capillary tube. The force that causes water to soak into and between wood joints

carling — structural pieces running *fore* and *aft* between the *beams*. A longitudinal structural member at the cockpit perimeter supporting the *inboard* side of the side deck

carvel — a planking method where the longitudinal plank edges abut at the sides, forming a smooth exterior surface

catalytic corrosion — when salt water or mineral-salt contaminated fresh water permits or accelerates metal corrosion, caused by the difference in the nobility of the metals

cathode — a negatively charged electrode, from which current flows

cellulose — the chief substance composing the cell walls or fibers of all plant tissue

centerline — the imaginary line running from *bow* to *stern* along the middle of the boat

chamfer — a beveled edge or corner, especially one cut at 45 degrees

cheeks — a Chris-Craft term for the *outboard*, *topsides*, *transom* frames

chine — longitudinal frame member running from the stem to the transom, delineating the junction of the side and bottom planking, the member backing this junction

chine strake — the lowest *strake* of *topsides* planks, mounted to the *chine*

coaming — a non-structural longitudinal member at the cockpit perimeter of some prewar boats; a decorative piece fastened to the carling, usually protruding above the side deck to prevent water from entering the cockpit

cold molding — a method of bending a material into an appropriate shape without heating or steaming to soften the material first. Multiple, thin laminations of wood, glued together to form curvilinear *hull* shapes. A modern, *monocoque* construction technique that is not recommended to mix with traditional construction covering board the outboard deck plank fitted over the *topside* frame heads, covering the top edge of the uppermost *topside* plank, the *sheer* plank

CPES (Clear Penetrating Epoxy Sealer) — a wood resin product of the paper industry

cross-spalls — temporarily installed transverse bracing, used to hold the framework in shape during *hull* reconstruction

crown — term referring to the convex curve of a deck beam, also called camber

cutlass bearing — *propeller shaft* bearing, mounted in the shaft strut

cutwater — the front edge of the boat, usually referring to the sharply pointed, metal trim piece covering the *stem* and *plank* hood ends

D

deck — the surface on the top of a boat on which people can stand

displacement — the quantity of water displaced by a vessel, which in weight is always equal to the weight of the boat

divider — an instrument consisting of two pointed legs connected at one end by a pivot, used for drawing arcs or circles, dividing lines, measuring or marking off distances

draft, draught, draw — the depth of a boat, measured from the deepest point to the *waterline*. The water must be at least this depth, or the boat will *run aground*. A vessel *draws* a certain amount of water

drift pin — a tool for driving bolts out of frame members

dutchman — a piece of wood, fitted into a like-sized hole prepared to fit it, as a repair to damaged or rotted wood. Also known as a *graving piece*

E

electrolysis — the decomposition of a metal caused by an electric current. Electrolytic corrosion

engine bedlogs — longitudinal frame members upon which the engine is mounted. Usually also the main *bilge stringers*

engine wedge — tapered piece of metal used under the engine mounts to align the engine

epoxy — a compound in which an oxygen atom is joined to each of two attached atoms, usually carbon. Any of various thermosetting resins, containing epoxy groups, that are blended with other chemicals to form strong, hard, chemically resistant adhesives, enamel coatings, etc.

F

fairing — the process of beveling the *stem, chine, sheers, keel*, and *frames* so that the *planking* will have flat surfaces to glue and fasten to, also the process applied to the planking. A *fair* hull is one with no dips or bumps in the longitudinal lines of the hull. *Fairness* is checked by sighting down the longitudinal lines, aided by *limber battens*

fastener, fastening — an item such as a nail, screw, rivet or other device used to fasten objects together

fay — to join one piece close and *fair* with another

fiberglass — a construction method using layers of woven glass mats that are bonded together with an *epoxy* glue

flare — to project outward, contrary to *tumblehome,* as a flaring *bow* where the *topside* hull shape gains width as it rises

flatsawn — the most simple method of cutting wood, a log is sliced from one side to the other

floors — the bottom timbers of a vessel attaching the transverse *hull* frames to the *keel*. Also called *frame tie*

fore, forward — toward the *bow* (front) of the vessel

fore-and-aft — running along the length of the boat, as from *bow* to *stern*

foredeck — the forward part of *the deck*

forefoot — the foremost pieces of the *keel* which cause it to rise to vertical for the attachment of the *planks forward, hood ends.* Usually including the gripe, stem, and sometimes the stem knee

forepeak — the most *forward* storage area of a vessel

frame — a transverse timber, or line or assembly of timbers, that describes the body shape of a vessel and to which the planking and ceiling are fastened. Frames are sometimes called "timbers" or, erroneously, "ribs"

frame tie — floor timber. The section of main or auxiliary frame that attaches two *bottomsides* frames together and to the *keel*

Frearson — a woodscrew drive design (Reed & Prince), similar to *Phillips* but with shoulder angles closer to 40 degrees and not rounded at the center

freeboard — the distance between the top of the *hull* at the *sheer* and the *waterline*

freewater — moisture in the center of a wood cell in the living tree, or in green, unseasoned lumber. This moisture is lost when the lumber dries

futtock — a frame timber, one of the individual pieces of a sistered frame. The timbers which join and butt called first, second, and third futtocks

G

galvanic corrosion — the deterioration of metals due to dissimilar qualities when there is an electrolyte present

garboard — the *strake* or bottom *plank*, next above the *keel*, into which it is *rabbeted* and fastened to the *keel*. The plank adjoining the keel. Also called *garboard strake*. Garboard drain plugs are installed at the lowest point along the garboard

gripe — the part that bolts to the *stem*, connecting the *stem* to the *keel*.

gunwale — pronounced "gunnel." The rail around the outboard edge of a boat at the sheer. Smaller versions are called *toe rails*. Name derived from the fact they were conceived to restrain deck cannons

H

half-breadth — measurement taken *outboard* from a central plane describing the width, or breadth, of a *hull*

hatch — a sliding or hinged opening in the deck, providing people with access to the cabin or space below

heartwood — the useful wood in a log, outside of the central pith and inside of the sapwood

hog — term used to describe a wooden *hull* that has been forced out of shape through displacement or gravity

hood-end — the forward ends of *topsides* planks that fit into the *stem rabbet*

hull — the main structural body of the boat, not including the *deck*. The part that keeps the water out of the boat. Comprises *topsides* from *sheer* to *chine* and *bottomsides* from *chine* to *keel*

hull number — many production wooden boats were stamped with hull numbers that can be used to determine the model style, original delivery destination and year built

I

inboard — towamrd the center of the boat

intermediate frames — smaller interior bottom or topside frames, providing a surface to attach the edges of planking to other than main or auxiliary frames

J

joint, joinery — the methods whereby wood components are cut and fit for strength in marine construction

K

keel — the main longitudinal timber of most *hulls*, upon which the *frames* and ends of the *hull* were mounted; the backbone of the hull. The junction of the bottom planking along the *centerline* of the boat or the inside member backing this junction *aft* of the *stem* and forward of the *transom post*

keelson — an internal longitudinal timber or line of timbers, mounted atop the frames along the *centerline* of the *keel*, that provides additional longitudinal strength to the bottom of the *hull*

kerf — a cut, made in a piece of wood, that does not go completely through the piece. The cut or channel made by a saw

king plank — the center plank on a wooden deck

knees — supporting braces used for strength when two parts are joined. A brace or reinforcement between two joining planes. On our boat designs, frame-knees are used to reinforce the junction between the transverse, bottom and *topsides* frames, the *transom bows* sometimes also use *standing knees* (mounted

vertically) or *quarter knees* (mounted horizontally)

L

laser level — an electronic tool that projects a level line for setting up framework or marking a *waterline*

lift rings — hardware, mounted *fore* and *aft* on the boat, attached to the main framework for the purpose of lifting the *hull*

lignin — an amorphous, cellulose-like, organic substance which acts as a binder for the cellulose fibers in wood and certain plants and adds strength and stiffness to the cell walls

limber battens — easily bent, flexible, pliant *battens* used in *fairing frames* and *hull* surfaces

limber hole — a hole in between compartments in the bottom of the boat to allow water to flow into the *bilge* where it is sent *overboard*. Also called *weep hole*, usually a small notch cut into the lower edge of the bottom frames alongside the *keel*

lines drawings — a plan of construction for a boat. An illustration that, along with a table of offsets, describes how to make a full-size *hull*

lofting — the process of drawing the hull lines to full size from the designer's scale drawings. The intersections of the contours of various horizontal and vertical sections are measured from an imaginary baseline using an architect's scale. These junctions are then laid out, point by point, in their full size. A listing of these points is called a *table of offsets*

long board — a double-handled board for holding sandpaper, when *fairing hull* surfaces

longitudinals — *hull framing* members that run the length of the boat (i.e. *chine, keel, sheer clamp, bilge stringers, battens*)

luan — the lowest grade of Phillipine wood

M

main — the most important timbers, or those having the greatest cross-sectional area

midship, midships — a contraction of *amidships* and consequently, in a general sense, it refers to the middle of the ship. A place on a boat where its *beam* is the widest

miter joint — a kind of joint formed by fitting together two pieces, beveled to a specific angle (usually 45 degrees) to form a corner

monkey rail — Chris-Craft term for an oversized, stylized *toe rail* on the *foredeck*

monocoque — a structure in which the outer covering (*planking*) carries all or a major part of the stresses

N

nobility table — chart designating metals in order of their ability to resist corrosion

O

offsets — measurements supplied by a designer for the builder in order to lay down the lines of the *hull*

outboard — on the side of the *hull* that the water is on. A direction away from the center

P

parallax error — error that can be introduced when not reading an instrument directly from its front, due to the separation of the indicator and the scale being read

pay — to apply to a surface, as in bedding compounds

Phillips — a screw drive design similar to *Frearson*, with two slots crossing at the center of the head, but with shoulder angles closer to 30-degrees slope and rounded at the center

phloem — the vascular tissue in vascular plants, that conducts and distributes sugars and other dissolved foods from the places where the food is produced to the places where it is needed or stored

planing hull — a boat rising slightly out of the water so that it is gliding over the water rather than plowing through it. A *hull* that lifts and skims the surface of the water causing the *stern* wake to break clean from the *transom*. In practical terms, a planing hull has a speed potential limited only by weight and power

planing surface — the exterior surface of the boat's bottom that a *planing hull* rides on when at speed. This surface shape should be flat longitudinally

plank, planking — shaped wood strips used to cover the *deck* or *hull* frames of a wooden vessel

port — the left side of the boat from the perspective of a person at the *stern* of the boat, looking toward the *bow*. The side of the boat traditionally tied to a dock so as to avoid damaging the *steering board* (Danish for *starboard*) when such, prior to the 17th century, was traditionally mounted for right-handed helmsmen. Also a place where boats go to dock

pounce — a fine powder sprinkled over a stencil to transfer a design to the surface below

pounce wheel — tool with a pointed wheel to cut holes in a pattern material through which pounce powder is dabbed to transfer a line

pound — action of a boat's *bow* repeatedly slamming into oncoming waves

propeller — device (in full screw-propeller) on a boat, consisting typically of two or more blades twisted to describe a helical path as they rotate with the hub in which they are mounted, and serving to propel the craft forward, by the backward thrust of water

propeller shaft — spinning shaft from the engine to which the *propeller* is attached

protractor — instrument in the form of a graduated semicircle, used for plotting and measuring angles

proud — refers to a boat part that protrudes above the surface to which it's attached, as in a bung before it's trimmed flush with the planking

Q

quadrant — device connected to the *rudder* that the steering cables attach to

quarter — side of a boat from *aft* of the *beam* to the *transom*. There both a *port* quarter and a *starboard* quarter,

quarter guards — metal trim, mounted to the after ends of the *topsides* at the *transom*, to protect the *after* corners of the *hull*

quarter knees — horizontally mounted frame knees (see *knees*)

quarter rails — rub rails, mounted to the *aft* quarters of the *topsides* of the *hull* at points where the hull protrudes, *outboard*, beyond the sheer mounted *rub rails*. To protect the aft quarters of the hull from dock pilings

quartersawn — method of cutting lumber wherein the log is first cut into quarters. Cutting lumber from these quartered sections produces stock with grain running perpendicular to the wide face of the piece

R

rabbet — groove or cut made in a piece of timber in such a way that the edges of another piece could be fit into it to make a tight joint

rabbet line — when forming a plank rabbet; a line formed by the intersection of the outside of the planking with the face or side of the *stem, gripe,* or *keel*

rib — curved members attached to the *keel* and forming framework of the *hull*

ribband — *fore* and *aft* longitudinal stiffeners, mounted *inboard*, or let into notches *outboard*, attached to the transverse frames of the *hull*

rub rail, rub strake, rub guard — rail on the outside of the *hull* of a boat to protect the hull from rubbing against piles, docks and other objects. Same as "fender rail"

rudder — device mounted underneath the *stern* at the *transom*, that steers the boat. A timber, or cast metal plane, that could be rotated about an axis to control the direction of a vessel underway

rudder post — post that the rudder is attached to. The wheel or tiller is connected to the rudder post

runabout — classic speedboat design, with separate cockpits and hatches in the deck over the engine compartment

S

scantlings — dimensions of framework and planking

scarf — overlapping joint used to connect two timbers or planks without increasing their dimensions. A "keyed" scarf has flat ends, rather than pointed, which prevents slipping past one another in compression

sea-kindly – refers to a boat that is comfortable in rough water

sheer — *fore* and *aft* curvature of the *deck*, as viewed in profile. The junction of the *hull's* topsides and the deck. A boat with a lot of sheer is higher at the *bow* and *stern* (or conversely, lower) than the center when viewed in profile; with little sheer, the sheer arc will be closer to a straight line

sheer clamp — longitudinal member backing the junction of the *hull's topsides* and the *deck*. Clamping together the tops of the *topsides* frames, the *outboard* ends of the deck beams, and the deck to the hull

sheer partner — *fore* and *aft* framing running *inboard* of the *sheer clamp* or *sheer shelf*, to provide a continuous surface to fasten the inboard edge of the covering boards to

sheer shelf — *sheer clamp*, horizontally mounted at the *topside* frame heads as a landing for deck beams and shaped, oversized covering boards

sheer strake — top plank on the side of a wooden boat that follows the *sheer* of the *deck*

shipwright — a master craftsman skilled in the construction and repair of ships. In many instances, the person in charge of a ship's construction, including the supervision of carpenters and other personnel, control of expenditures and schedules, and acquisition of materials. Similar to *boatwright,* referring to vessels under 200 meters in length

skeg — any flat protrusion on the outside of the *hull* that is used to support another object, such as the *propeller shaft* or *rudder*. Usually a vertically mounted extension of the *keel,* protruding *outboard*

sole — cabin or cockpit floor

spile, spiling — method of fitting pieces together, marking a set distance to determine a new cut line

spooge — used to describe the oozing action of bedding compound between planking

starboard — right side of a boat, from the perspective of a person at the *stern* of the boat and looking toward the *bow*. From the early Danish term for *steering board*, usually mounted on the right-hand side of the boat prior to the 17th century

station — one of a series of equally spaced transverse slices of the *hull*, as shown in the *lines drawings* of the plans. When building a boat, there may or may not be *frames* or *bulkheads* at all or any of the stations. Also referred to as section

stem — junction of the planking at the *forward* end of a typical *hull*. The member to which the planking attaches at this junction. The extreme forward component of the forefoot of the *keel*. The forward edge of the *bow*. On a wooden boat, the stem is usually a single timber

stern — *aft* part of a boat. The back of the boat at or near the *transom*

sternpost — vertical or upward curving timber or assembly of timbers stepped into the *after* end of the *keel* at the lower *transom bow*. Also referred to as *transom post*

strakes — A single line of planking extending from bow to stern. A row of wooden planks on the *hull* of a wooden boat

strut — exterior bracket that supports the *propeller shaft*

stuffing box — a fitting around the *propeller shaft*, also *rudder post*; to keep the bearing surface lubricated and to keep water out of the boat

survey — an inspection of a boat to determine its condition

surveyor — person who is qualified to inspect a boat in order to determine its condition

swarf — fine sawdust created by sanding

sweet lines — having a generally agreeable appearance, gratifying. Something, as an experience, that gives delight or satisfaction when a preferred shape has been achieved

T

table of offsets — see *offsets*

tack cloth — fine cheesecloth, saturated with a tacky, or sticky wax. Used to collect dust from a surface just prior to varnishing it

through-hull — fittings attached through the *hull* to which a sea cock and hose, a propeller or *rudder* stuffing box, or other device is attached. Through-hulls are used to expel waste water, such as from a sink; to let sea water in, such as for engine cooling; and to allow placement of sensors such as depth gauges

thwart — transverse plank in a boat used to seat rowers, support masts, or provide lateral stiffness

thwartships — also *athwartships*. Across the width of a boat

ticks — small marks made with a divider to mark a distance

toe rail — small *rail* around the *deck* of a boat. A larger wall is known as a *gunwale*. One can support their position on the deck of a boat underway by stubbing one's foot (or toe) against this to keep from slipping *overboard*

topsides — sides of the *hull* above the *waterline*, or *chine*, and below the *deck*

transom — the planked assembly forming the *aft* (*stern*) end of the boat. The *aft* side of the *hull*

transom bow — *athwartships* frame members, upper and lower, of the *transom*. The upper transom bow is attached to the top of the *topsides transom* frames or cheeks. The lower transom bow is attached to the bottoms of the cheeks as well as the *keel,* forming the framework for the bottom of the transom as well as the trailing edge of the bottom planing surface. Referred to as *bow* because most transoms dissect an arc in shape

transom post — see *sternpost*

tumblehome — the top is closer to the centerline than the bottom. Can be applied to the *hull* or cabin. When the sides of a vessel near the deck incline inward, the opposite to *flaring*

U

ultraviolet light — pertaining to a band of electromagnetic radiation having wavelengths from 5 to 400 nanometers in length. Just shorter than that of violet in the visible light spectrum. Beyond or out of the range of sight

utility — classic speedboat design, without separate cockpits but open except for a small foredeck and aft deck. With a motor-box over the engine

UV filter — component of modern varnish formulations that absorb or reflect ultraviolet wavelengths, protecting the wood surface from harmful photodegradation

V

vent — hardware, mounted on the deck to cover a hole or opening in the deck meant to permit passage or escape of fumes or moisture

volatilize — to make volatile; cause to pass off as a vapor, evaporate

W

waterline — the line where the water comes to on the *hull* of a boat. Design waterline is where the waterline was designed to be. Load waterline is the waterline when the boat is loaded. The *painted waterline* is where the waterline was painted. Actual waterline is where the waterline really is at any given time

wheel — one of two methods used to steer a boat, the other being an aft-mounted tiller. A wheel is turned in the direction that the *helmsman* wants the boat to go. Also slang for propeller.

X

xylem — the woody vascular tissue of a plant, characterized by the presence of vessels or tracheids or both, fibers, and parenchyma, that conducts water and mineral salts in the stems, roots, and leaves and gives support to the softer tissues

RESOURCES

The following resources include businesses that I have dealt with and can recommend. The information listings are clubs and societies that you can join or subscribe to.

Information

Classic Boating Magazine
280 Lac La Belle Dr.
Oconomowoc, WI 53066-1648
(262) 567-4800
www.classicboatingmagazine.com

WoodenBoat Magazine
P.O. Box 54766
Boulder, CO 80322-4766
(800) 877-5284
www.woodenboat.com

The Antique and Classic Boat
  Society, Inc. (ACBS)
422 James St.
Clayton, NY 13624-1202
(315) 686-2680
www.acbs.org

The Mariners' Museum
Chris-Craft Collection
100 Museum Dr.
Newport News, VA 23606
www.mariner.org

Chris-Craft Antique Boat Club
217 South Adams St.
Tallahassee, FL 32301-1708
(850) 224-2628
www.chris-craft.org

Century Boat Club, Inc.
P.O. Box 761
Manistee, MI 49660
www.centuryboatclub.com

The Gar Wood Society
P.O. Box 6003
Syracuse, NY 13217
asmollica@aol.com

Mahogany and White Oak

LL Johnson Lumber Mfg. Co.
563 N. Cochran Ave.
Charlotte, MI 48813
(800) 292-5937
  and
51315 N. U. S. Hwy. 31
South Bend, IN 46673
(219) 277-8350
www.theworkbench.com

RetroNautique
101 N. 700 W.
North Salt Lake, UT 84054
 (800) 936-1825
retronautique@aol.com

Certified Marine Plywood

Rare Earth Hardwoods
6778 East Traverse Hwy.
Traverse City, MI 49684
 (800) 968-0074
www.rare-earth-hardwoods.com

Instrument Restoration

Mark Clawson
Clawson Classic Instruments
2402 30th St.
Anacortes, WA 98221
(360) 299-8636
(360) 299-2836 fax

Pat Powell
2644 Willow St
Franklin Park, IL 60131
(847) 455-4918

Reproduction Parts and Vintage Marine Hardware

Maine Classics
P.O. Box 719
Waterboro, ME 04087
(207) 247-6862

California Classic Boats
Al Schinnerer
3267 Grant St.
Signal Hill, CA 90804
(562) 494-8482

Chrome Plating
Graves Plating
Box 1052-CB
Florence, AL 35631

Nu-Chrome
161 Graham Rd.
Fall River, MA 02720
(800) 576-6316
www.nu-chrome.com

Reproduction Fender and Quarter Rails
Buffalo Metal Works
J. D. Thorpe
3273 Grant St.
Signal Hill, CA 90804
(562) 498-0810

Cutwater, Transom Bands, and Stem Bead (Reproduction and Repair)
Mike Schreiber
(219) 662-9731
www.cutwaters.com

Fasteners (Silicon Bronze Screws and Bolts)
Clark Craft Fasteners
16 Aqua Ln.
Tonawanda, NY 14150
(800) 992-5151
www.ccfast.com

Jamestown Distributors
500 Wood St., Bldg. #15
Bristol, RI 02809
(800) 423-0030
www.jamestowndistributors.com

Jim Hastings
78 Meadow Hill Rd.
Barrington, IL 60010
(847) 381-5223

Leather Upholstery
Macatawa Bay Boatworks
297 S. Maple St.
Saugatuck, MI 49453
(616) 857-4556
www.mbbw.com

Keleen Leathers
(708) 409-9800

Chris-Craft Upholstery
The Upholsterer
P.O. Box 1067
Atwater, CA 95301
(800) 651-2628

Century Supplies and Support
A&A Marine
270 Third St.
Manistee, Michigan
(231) 723-8308
(231) 723-8309 fax

Battleship Linoleum
Tony Lauria
511 Church Hill Rd.
Landenberg, PA 19350
(610) 268-3441 evenings
Send SASE for samples and prices

Steering Wheel Restoration
Bill Peters
41 Vassar Pl.
Rockville Centre, NY 11570

Iva-Lite Spotlights
Grand Craft Corporation
430 W. 21st St.
Holland, MI 49423
(616) 396-5450
www.grandcraft.com

**Gray Marine Engines
(Carburetor and Fuel Pump
 Rebuild Kits)**
Van Ness Engineering
252 Lincoln Ave.
Ridgewood, NJ 07450
(201) 445-8685

**Chris-Craft and Scripps
Engine Parts**
Peter Henkel, Inc.
7650 South Channel Dr.
Harsens Island, MI 48028
(810) 748-3600

**Carburetor and Fuel Pump
Rebuilding**
Hal Houghton
P.O. Box 262
Sand Lake, NY 12153
(518) 674-2445

Wilson's Machine Shop
Mark Wilson
6504 State Route 8
Brant Lake, NY 12815
(518) 494-7952
mwilson@telnet.net

Drake Engines, Inc.
Bill Drake
2285 Ridgeway Ave.
Rochester, NY 14626
(716) 723-1333

**Cloth-Covered Wire and
Battery Cables**
YNZ Yesterday's Parts
333 East Stuart Ave.
Redlands, CA 92374
(909) 798-1498 Mon–Fri., 8–5 PST
www.ynzyesterdaysparts.com

Paints and Varnish
The Sandusky Paint Company
1401 Sycamore Ln.
Sandusky, OH 44870
(419) 626-2461
www.sanpaco.com

CPES
Smith & Company
5100 Channel Ave.
Richmond, CA 94804-4646
(510) 237-6842
(800) 234-0330

Vintage Boat Insurance
Hagerty Marine Insurance
(800) 762-2628
www.hagerty.com

Heritage Marine Insurance
P.O. Box 188
Bank Square
Mystic, CT 06355
(800) 959-3047

Ski-Safe
1 Hollow Ln.
Lake Success, NY 11042
(800) 225-6560

Vintage Boat Trailers
Liberty Trailer
8616 Grinnell
Detroit, MI 48213
(313) 923-6773

Jarvis Welding
Cadillac, MI 49601
(231) 775-7373`

INDEX

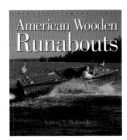
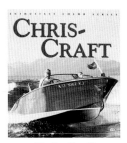

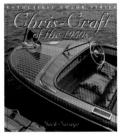

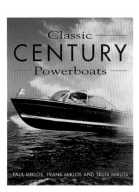
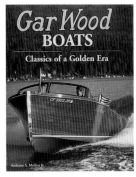
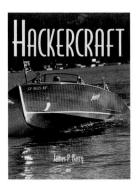
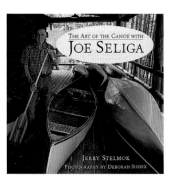